Acknowledgments

Contributing authors: David Alderton, Fiona Campbell, Charlotte Evans, Don Harper, Nigel Henbest, Tony Juniper, Mark Oakley, Dene Schofield

Contributing artists: Susanna Addario, Simone Boni, Lorenzo Cecchi, L R Galante, Paola Holguìn, Lorenzo Pieri, Ivan Stalio.

All Ladybird books are available at most bookshops, supermarkets and newsagents, or can be ordered direct from:
Ladybird Postal Sales PO Box 133 Paignton TQ3 2YP England
Telephone: (+44) 01803 554761   *Fax:* (+44) 01803 663394

A catalogue record for this book is available from the British Library

Published by Ladybird Books Ltd
A subsidiary of the Penguin Group
A Pearson Company
© LADYBIRD BOOKS LTD MCMXCVIII

THE LADYBIRD

DISCOVERY

ENCYCLOPEDIA

OF THE NATURAL WORLD

Ladybird

CONTENTS

BIRDS

CONTENTS

BIRDS PAST AND PRESENT

The first birds may have **evolved** from small, running dinosaurs. Birds were certainly not the first creatures to fly however, because the pterosaurs came before birds, gliding across the skies about 220 million years ago.

Archaeopteryx

This is the oldest known bird, which lived around 150 million years ago. Unlike modern birds, it had teeth in its mouth and had claws on the ends of its wings.

Bee hummingbird

The smallest bird in the world lives on the island of Jamaica off the coast of Central America. Here, a bee hummingbird is shown at full size—little bigger than a bumblebee!

Moa and ostrich

Moas are the tallest birds ever to have lived on Earth: up to four metres high. They lived in New Zealand and were hunted by the Maoris who settled there. They finally became **extinct** in the 1800s. The ostrich lives in Africa and is the largest bird alive today. When fully grown it is taller than an adult person.

THE FINCHES

A group of birds called finches feed mainly on the seeds of different plants, although they will also collect insects to feed to their chicks. They are quite small, and sometimes live together in **flocks**.

Seeds

Many seeds have tough coverings, which birds have to break open to reach the kernel inside. Finches have stout beaks for this purpose.

BEAK CHARACTERISTICS OF A SEED-EATER

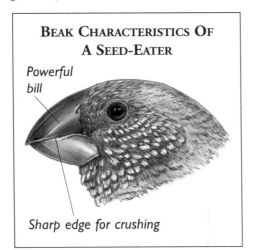

Powerful bill

Sharp edge for crushing

Tool-using Galapagos finch

These birds have learnt to break off twigs and use the ends to poke under the bark of trees to find insects which would otherwise be out of reach.

Large Galapagos finch

Separate types of finches live on the Galapagos Islands, off the coast of South America. By eating different foods, they avoid competing with one another for food.

Red-billed weaver

This is the most common bird on Earth today. There may be as many as ten billion red-billed weavers in Africa, where they live.

A FINCH'S FOOT

Leg *Claw*

Finches have four toes on each foot, with one toe pointing backwards.

Snow finch

These finches live and breed in the mountainous parts of Asia and Europe. It is very cold in the winter and snow finches are one of very few birds that can survive there.

Canary

Today's colourful canaries — white, yellow, orange-red — are descended from dull greenish finches which live on the Canary Islands, off the coast of Africa. The colourful canaries sing better than their wild relatives which are now quite scarce. These birds were first brought to Europe by the Portuguese in the 1400s.

THE FRUIT EATERS

Many birds eat fruits and berries, but some rely more heavily on these foods than others. Such birds are called **frugivores**, and most of them live in tropical parts of the world, where fruits are available throughout the year. Many frugivorous birds can swallow large fruits by opening their beaks very wide.

BEAK CHARACTERISTICS OF A FRUIT-EATER

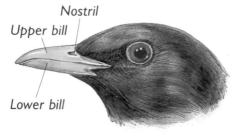

Nostril

Upper bill

Lower bill

Fruit-eating birds have stout beaks, and can pick berries and larger fruits easily.

Berries
Birds with short beaks peck at fruits and berries, rather than eating them whole.

Toucan
Toucans live in parts of Central and South America. Their colourful beaks have a honeycombed structure, so they are light. The length of the beak means that the toucan can reach fruits more easily.

Green broadbill
The green coloration of this bird helps it to remain hidden in its forest home. Its large eyes help it to see and find fruit in this dark environment.

Knysna touraco
Touracos live in Africa, where they feed on both fruit and leaves. They are often green in colour, with bright plumage on the sides of the head. They sometimes have a crest as well.

PERCHING
The touraco can change the position of one of its toes, to help it to perch.

Orange dove
Brightly-coloured fruit doves live on many tropical islands in the Pacific Ocean. The orange dove is found on Fiji, where it searches for fruit and berries.

White-cheeked cotinga
The home of this bird is the Andean mountains in South America. It feeds entirely on mistletoe berries which grow on the bark of trees.

TROPICAL NECTAR FEEDERS

Nectar is a sweet, sticky solution of sugars produced by flowers. Its purpose is to attract insects and other creatures to pollinate the plant so that it can produce seeds. Some birds feed on nectar, transferring pollen from one flower to another, either on their beaks or their feathers. All nectar-feeding birds are found in tropical parts of the world, where there are always flowers in bloom. They like red flowers best.

Yellow-backed chattering lory

The short-tailed lories, and the lorikeets, which have longer tail feathers, are parrots that feed on nectar and pollen. They live in Australia, Papua New Guinea and surrounding islands.

Upper beak

Rounded tip

Rough surface of tongue collects pollen

BEAK CHARACTERISTICS OF A NECTAR-FEEDER

Sunbirds

Sunbirds live in parts of Africa and Asia. Cock (male) birds are often brightly coloured, and sometimes have **iridescent** plumage, which looks shiny in sunlight.

Curved bill

Hummingbirds

Hummingbirds have curved or straight bills depending on the type of flower from which they obtain nectar. Hummingbirds live in North, Central and South America.

Straight bill

Blue-crowned hanging parrots

These small parrots can hang upside down to reach flowers. They may also sleep like this, which is why they are sometimes called 'bat parrots'.

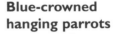

HONEYGUIDE AND RATEL

The honeyguide's call attracts the ratel to a bee's nest, which the ratel breaks open with its sharp claws. Both of them then take turns to eat the honey.

THE INSECT EATERS

Many birds eat insects and small creatures like snails and worms. In some parts of the world, birds help to control insect pests, such as locusts, which can destroy crops. When chemicals are used to kill such **invertebrates**, this can also harm the bird population.

Insects
Some insects are caught by birds in flight, others are dug out from underground.

BEAK CHARACTERISTICS OF AN INSECT-EATER

Slender bill for probing for insects

Pointed tip to the bill

Kiwi
Most birds have a very poor sense of smell. But the kiwi's nostrils, at the end of its upper bill, help it to find food. A kiwi feeds mainly on earthworms which it grabs quickly with the tip of its bill.

Blond-crested woodpecker
Woodpeckers use their feet and claws as they climb up trees to hunt for insects. Their tail feathers also have firm, pointed ends for extra support. The woodpecker's tongue is long, sticky and sharp so that it can pull out grubs easily.

Oxpecker
These African starlings take ticks off the backs of cattle and other large animals, using their strong beaks.

Carmine bee-eater
The bee-eater hits the bee against a branch to remove its sting, before swallowing the insect.

Flamingo
By filtering water through their bills, flamingos catch tiny shrimps and microscopic plants. Their pink coloration comes from the food they eat. Baby flamingos have straight beaks at first, which curve as they grow older.

BIRDS THAT GO FISHING

It is not just sea birds which feed on fish. A number of other birds prey on fish which live in lakes, rivers and ponds. Most birds prefer to catch fish that they can swallow whole. The fish is hit against a perch or rock to kill it, and is then swallowed head first so that it does not become stuck in the bird's throat. The bones and scales may later be spat out as a pellet.

Puffins

The colourful bill of the puffin is only seen during the nesting season. Afterwards, this outer part drops off. Puffins rear their chicks in underground burrows. Parents may fly as far as twenty kilometres out to sea to find fish for their young.

PENGUIN

The penguin's wings have changed into flippers, to help it to swim underwater. An emperor penguin can dive to a depth of over 265 metres, and can stay underwater for nearly twenty minutes. It catches squid and shrimps in the sea, as well as fish.

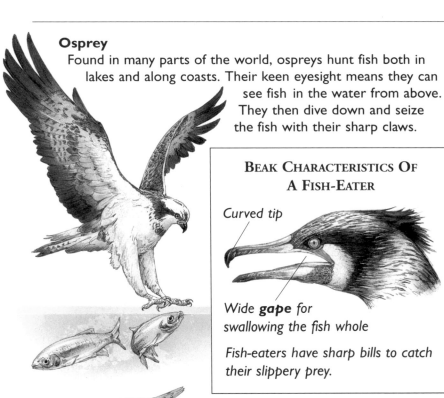

Osprey

Found in many parts of the world, ospreys hunt fish both in lakes and along coasts. Their keen eyesight means they can see fish in the water from above. They then dive down and seize the fish with their sharp claws.

BEAK CHARACTERISTICS OF A FISH-EATER

Curved tip

*Wide **gape** for swallowing the fish whole*

Fish-eaters have sharp bills to catch their slippery prey.

Kingfisher

In spite of the name, not all kingfishers feed on fish. Those that hunt insects have much flatter bills than their fish-eating relatives. Their plumage is covered with a special oil that makes it waterproof so it won't become heavy when the bird dives into the water.

Heron

To attract fish, herons will stand still and open their wings to cast a shadow on the water. They will then strike suddenly with their beak once a fish is within reach.

BIRDS OF PREY AND SCAVENGERS

Birds of prey are the most common meat-eating or **carnivorous** group of birds. Some, like hawks, hunt other birds and small animals that they can carry back to their nest easily. Others are **scavengers**, feeding on dead animals. Birds of prey have keen eyesight so they can spot their prey from a considerable distance.

BEAK CHARACTERISTICS OF A MEAT-EATER

Strong upper beak

Hooked tip

A broad, powerful bill to tear up an animal's carcass is common in this group of birds.

Kea
These parrots, which live in the mountains of New Zealand, used to be blamed for killing sheep and lambs. In fact, they are scavengers and only eat dead animals.

ROADRUNNER
Skilled at catching lizards and snakes, the roadrunner kills these reptiles with its powerful bill.

Vulture
These huge, scavenging birds of prey glide on hot air currents called thermals. Large numbers usually gather to eat where a big animal dies. Vultures have bald heads, because any feathers would soon become matted with blood as they fed.

TALONS
Powerful foot muscles.

Curved claws for improved grip.

Strong feet and sharp claws help these birds to hold prey.

Peregrine falcon
Diving through the air at a speed of 250 kilometres per hour, peregrines can kill their prey simply by hitting it from above.

Secretary bird
These strange, long-legged African hawks hunt on the ground, often tackling poisonous snakes. The snake is held down with one of the secretary bird's feet positioned just behind the victim's head, and may be battered to death with blows from the bird's wings.

BIRD BEHAVIOUR

Birds, like ourselves, control their body temperature, often keeping warmer than their surroundings. They need to eat frequently for this reason. Since finding food can be difficult, some birds establish **territories** for this purpose. A bird needs a light body in order to fly easily, so it cannot have a large store of body fat. Birds therefore depend mainly on their feathers to keep warm.

Giant hummingbird
This is the largest hummingbird in the world. It lives in Chile, South America, where the nights can be very cold. Giant hummingbirds become **torpid** at dusk, appearing dead until the warmth of the Sun revives them the next day.

Magpie
Bright, silvery objects ranging from bottle tops to coins may be picked up by magpies and hidden. No one knows why. Recently, in Britain, magpies have learnt to steal the shiny foil off milk bottles, and they will also drink the milk.

Tailorbird
These warblers stitch leaves together to make their nests. They pierce the leaves with their bills, then use the silk of spiders' webs or plant fibres as thread, knotting each stitch individually.

Birds singing
Bird song may sound attractive but it is really a sign of aggression. A bird sings to warn others that it has a territory. A male bird sings to attract a female and also to warn other males.

Poorwill
These unusual birds will spend several months in winter hidden in rock crevices, hibernating. They build up stores of body fat so that they can survive without feeding.

15

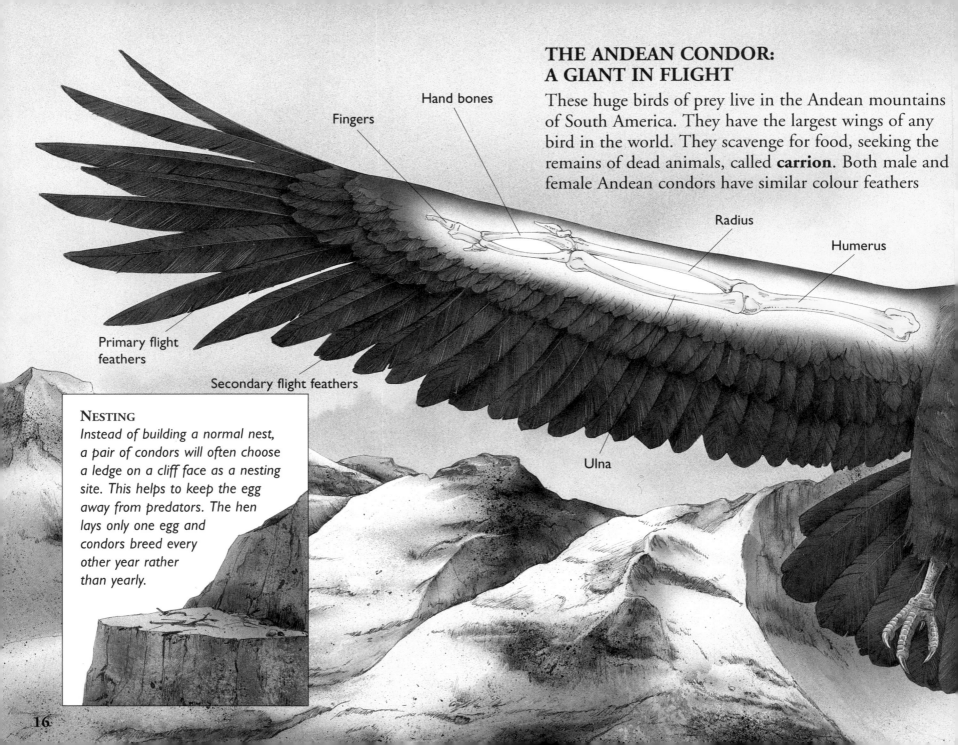

Fingers

Hand bones

THE ANDEAN CONDOR: A GIANT IN FLIGHT

These huge birds of prey live in the Andean mountains of South America. They have the largest wings of any bird in the world. They scavenge for food, seeking the remains of dead animals, called **carrion**. Both male and female Andean condors have similar colour feathers

Radius

Humerus

Primary flight feathers

Secondary flight feathers

Ulna

NESTING
Instead of building a normal nest, a pair of condors will often choose a ledge on a cliff face as a nesting site. This helps to keep the egg away from predators. The hen lays only one egg and condors breed every other year rather than yearly.

but males are bigger and have a large comb-like swelling on top of their heads. In spite of their size, condors are not fierce. In fact, their beaks are so weak that they sometimes have difficulty in eating an animal which has just died.

Bare head

Broad wings help these heavy birds to glide on warm air currents rather than having to keep flapping their wings to stay in the air.

SIZE
Andean condors are giant birds with a wingspan of over three metres. This is longer than a family car.

HOW BIRDS WORK

Flying birds have powerful chest muscles which they use to beat their wings during takeoff and flight. Not all birds flap their wings when flying. The albatross, for example, uses its long wings to glide on air currents and flies huge distances like this. Penguins cannot fly, but their wings have been adapted to become flippers, making these birds excellent swimmers.

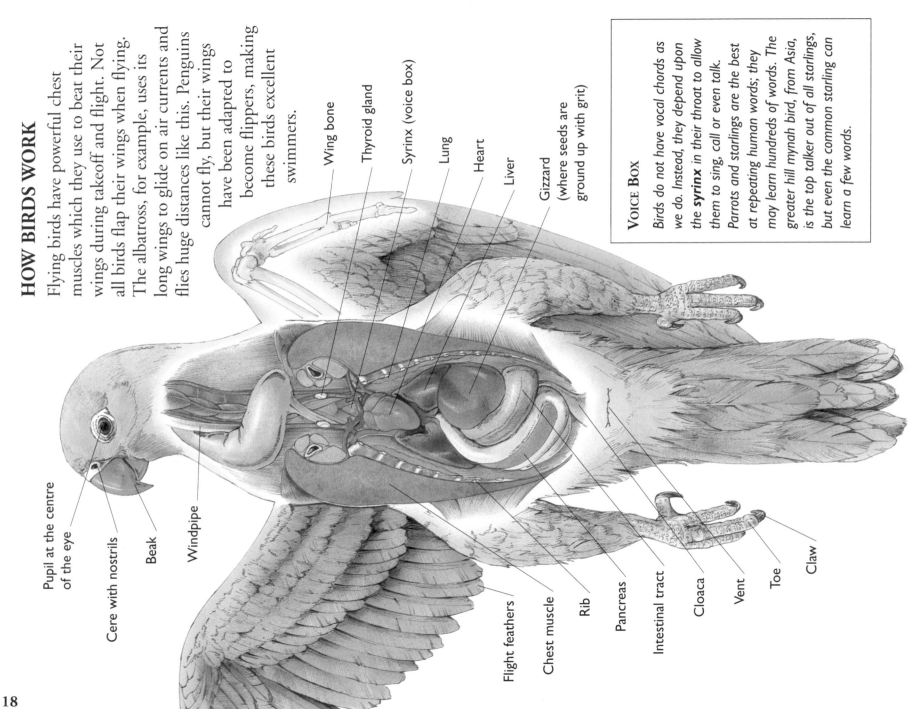

Wing bone

Thyroid gland

Syrinx (voice box)

Lung

Heart

Liver

Gizzard (where seeds are ground up with grit)

Pupil at the centre of the eye

Cere with nostrils

Beak

Windpipe

Flight feathers

Chest muscle

Rib

Pancreas

Intestinal tract

Cloaca

Vent

Toe

Claw

VOICE BOX

*Birds do not have vocal chords as we do. Instead, they depend upon the **syrinx** in their throat to allow them to sing, call or even talk. Parrots and starlings are the best at repeating human words; they may learn hundreds of words. The greater hill mynah bird, from Asia, is the top talker out of all starlings, but even the common starling can learn a few words.*

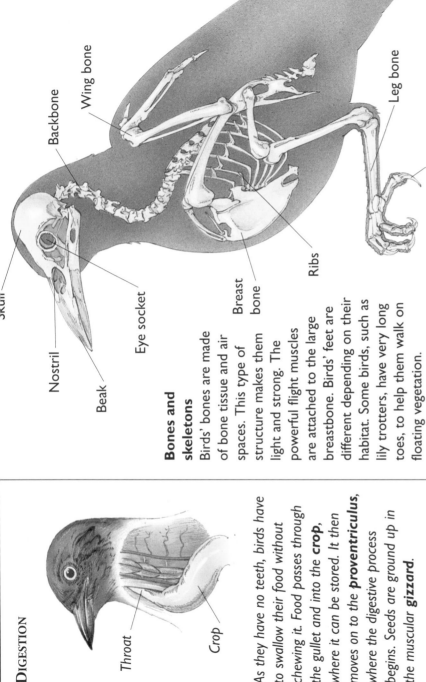

Wing bone

Backbone

Leg bone

Toes ending in claws

Ribs

Breast bone

Eye socket

Nostril

Beak

Bones and skeletons

Birds' bones are made of bone tissue and air spaces. This type of structure makes them light and strong. The powerful flight muscles are attached to the large breastbone. Birds' feet are different depending on their habitat. Some birds, such as lily trotters, have very long toes, to help them walk on floating vegetation.

DIGESTION

Throat

Crop

As they have no teeth, birds have to swallow their food without chewing it. Food passes through the gullet and into the **crop**, where it can be stored. It then moves on to the **proventriculus**, where the digestive process begins. Seeds are ground up in the muscular **gizzard**.

EGGS AND HATCHING

Although all birds lay eggs, the shape and colour varies significantly. Sea birds which nest on cliffs often lay pear-shaped eggs that won't roll over the edge of the cliff. Birds which breed in tree holes often have white eggs, whereas those with cup-shaped nests lay colourful eggs with markings. This helps to hide them.

Newly-laid egg
The yellow yoke at the centre provides food for the chick as it develops.

Hatching egg
The chick cuts its way out of the eggshell using its temporary 'egg tooth', near the tip of its beak.

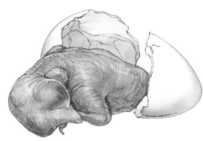

Born blind
Many chicks are blind and have no obvious feathers when they hatch. One or both parents have to protect them, feed them and keep them warm for two weeks or more, until they are ready to leave the nest.

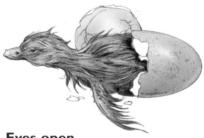

Eyes open
Chickens and waterfowl, such as ducks and swans, hatch with their eyes open. They have **down** feathers, and can move around almost immediately, but they stay with their mothers for some time after hatching.

19

BREEDING BEHAVIOUR

In the tropics, close to the Equator where there are no distinct seasons, birds may breed at any time of the year. Elsewhere, they will nest when conditions are most favourable, usually during the spring and summer. The weather is warmer, and food is more plentiful, increasing the chances of their chicks being reared successfully.

ORANGE WEAVER
Some birds change colour dramatically at the start of the breeding season. Cock orange weavers have stunning orange and black feathering at this time.

Breeding feathers

Normal feathers

Ruff
Certain birds have display areas, called leks, where males compete to gain females.
This cock ruff is showing its fine neck plumage to a hen at one of these sites.

Birds' nests

Ground nest
Ground nests need to be well hidden to avoid being seen by **predators**.

Bird's nest soup
In Asia, swiftlets' nests are collected and are used to make a special kind of soup.

Tree hole
Even here a nest may not be safe. Lizards and snakes may eat eggs and chicks.

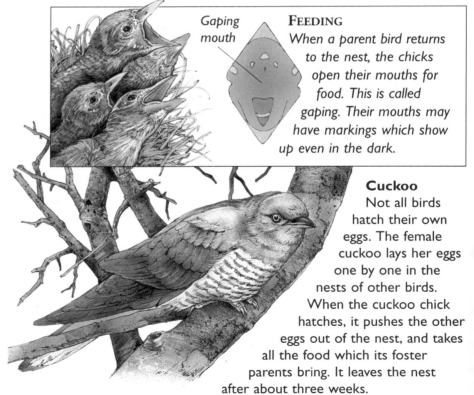

Gaping mouth

FEEDING
When a parent bird returns to the nest, the chicks open their mouths for food. This is called gaping. Their mouths may have markings which show up even in the dark.

Cuckoo
Not all birds hatch their own eggs. The female cuckoo lays her eggs one by one in the nests of other birds. When the cuckoo chick hatches, it pushes the other eggs out of the nest, and takes all the food which its foster parents bring. It leaves the nest after about three weeks.

BIRD MOVEMENTS

Some birds regularly fly long distances, to and from their breeding grounds, each year. This is known as migration. In other cases a shortage of food may cause birds to move to places where they are not often seen. These **irruptions** are only temporary, and once conditions are better, the birds return to their usual home. Sometimes, birds spread into new areas and start breeding, but this does not happen often.

Swallow

Before people knew that swallows migrated from Europe to Africa each autumn, it was thought that these birds hibernated at the bottom of ponds. This was because they were seen skimming over the water before they disappeared.

MIGRATION

Migrant birds probably use the Earth's magnetic field to find their way on journeys of thousands of kilometres. They fly back to the same area in the spring. Birds usually migrate due to cold winters in one area. Swallows cannot survive in Northern Europe over the winter, because there are not enough insects for them to eat.

RING-NECKED PARAKEET

There are thought to be about 1,000 of these parakeets living wild in Britain, descended from escaped pets. They live near towns, eating seeds and nuts left out on bird tables.

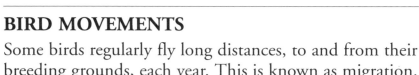

Pallas's sandgrouse

Although the home of this bird is in central Asia, large numbers have sometimes flown westwards. They have even been known to reach Britain and breed there.

Collared dove

This attractive dove has spread rapidly across Europe from Asia. It is not clear why it extended its range, but collared doves can now be seen in many European parks and gardens. Collared doves usually nest several times during the year in a loose nest of twigs.

THREATS TO BIRD LIFE

Birds face many dangers in the world today, and not just from their natural predators. Human activities have caused changes in the **environment**, and some of these have proved harmful to birds.

Pesticides

A **pesticide** called DDT was used in many parts of the world, before scientists realised that it built up in the **food chain**. Birds of prey started to lay soft-shelled eggs which did not hatch, due to DDT levels in their bodies, and some birds became endangered.

OIL SPILLS

When an oil tanker sinks, the cargo of oil floats on the surface of the sea, smothering the feathers of sea birds. When the birds try to clean their feathers they swallow the oil instead. Many thousands of birds can die as the result of a single oil spillage. Cleaning rescued birds can take a long time and is very expensive.

Deforestation

The magnificent bird of paradise is one of many birds who are in danger of becoming extinct because of **deforestation**. Every day, huge areas of forest are being cleared, threatening the lives of birds everywhere.

PASSENGER PIGEON

This was once the most common bird on Earth. Thousands of millions of passenger pigeons formed huge flocks which darkened the skies of North America. Shooting and trapping these pigeons for food resulted in their extinction in 1914.

Dodo

Although they are still quite famous, dodos are now extinct. By 1680 they had all died, from a combination of being hunted and having their eggs eaten by pigs. Dodos were as big as a turkey and were unable to fly. They lived on the island of Mauritius, off the east coast of Africa.

CONSERVATION PROJECTS

Many things are now being done to help endangered birds in countries around the world. In some cases, it is also possible to breed these birds in safety in **aviaries**, hatching their eggs in **incubators** and rearing the chicks by hand. The young birds can then eventually be released back to the wild, where they can be protected.

CARIBBEAN PARROT

On the island of St Lucia, a colourful bus which tours the island helps to make people aware of the rare Amazon parrots which live there, and the need to protect them.

Californian condor

This puppet, which looks like the head of an adult condor, makes the chicks think they are being fed by a real condor. It is important that young birds do not become **imprinted** on the people who are hand-rearing them.

Hawaiian goose

These geese had nearly become extinct in the wild when it was decided to try to save them with a **breeding programme**. It proved so successful that Hawaiian geese can now be seen in many wildfowl collections and have also been taken back to Hawaii, in the Pacific Ocean, to increase their numbers there.

Trumpeter swan

In 1936 there were only fifteen pairs of these swans left alive, but with regular feeding, their number grew to over 600 in just twenty years.

White-naped crane

Watching these cranes being fed in the wintertime has become a popular tourist sight in Japan. Extra food has also meant there are now more cranes than before.

BIRDS AND NUTS

You can help to increase the number of birds near your home by providing food. Peanuts are popular with many birds during the winter months, and can be bought in special bags. Hang the peanuts in a safe spot, where cats will not be able to catch the birds when they are feeding.

23

AMAZING BIRD FACTS

- **Seeing in the dark** Owls can spot a mouse from a distance of over 1,000 metres away when it is almost completely dark.

- **Fastest wing beats** The wings of hummingbirds can beat at a speed of up to 200 times in a single second. This is so fast that their wing movements appear blurred to our eyes.

- **A wealthy bird** In Guatemala, Central America, the quetzal has not only been adopted as the country's national symbol, but the coinage is also named after it.

- **Largest flying bird** This was a type of vulture called *Teratornis* which lived in Nevada, America about two million years ago. Its wingspan was thought to have been at least seven-and-a-half metres.

- **Fast spread** In barely 100 years, starlings have spread right across North America. Today's starlings are descended from a group of about 100, which were released in Central Park, New York, in the 1890s.

- **Short hatching period** The eggs of the North American brown-headed cowbird may hatch just ten days after being laid.

- **Natural incubators** In southern Australia, mallee fowl do not incubate their eggs like other birds. Instead, they bury them in mounds of soil and rotting vegetation. The heat generated inside the mound allows the chicks to develop, and they dig themselves out when they hatch.

- **Standing on an egg** Ostrich eggs are so strong that they can easily support the weight of a fully grown adult person.

GLOSSARY

Aviary A place where birds are kept.

Breeding programme A plan aimed at producing greater numbers of a bird.

Carnivore A bird that eats meat.

Carrion Dead and decaying flesh.

Crop The enlarged part of the throat where food is stored.

Deforestation Destroying trees and forests.

Down The soft feathers a bird has when it is born.

Environment Our natural surroundings.

Evolve To change gradually over many years.

Extinct An animal that has died out and no longer exists.

Flock A large group of birds.

Food chain Where one creature uses another creature as a food source, with grass and plants at the bottom of the chain.

Frugivore A bird that eats fruit.

Gape The width of a bird's open beak.

Gizzard A bird's second stomach where food is ground down so it can be digested.

Imprint The way in which a young animal becomes attached to its mother (or a substitute for her).

Incubator A place where eggs are hatched artificially.

Invertebrate An animal that has no backbone.

Iridescent Showing changing colours.

Irruption The appearance of birds in a new area.

Pesticide A chemical used to destroy insects or pests.

Predator An animal that lives by killing and eating other animals and birds.

Proventriculus The front part of a bird's stomach.

Scavenger A bird that eats dead or decaying flesh.

Syrinx A bird's vocal organs.

Territory An area belonging to one or more birds.

Torpid Being completely still.

SHARKS

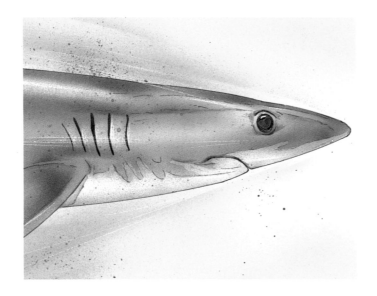

CONTENTS

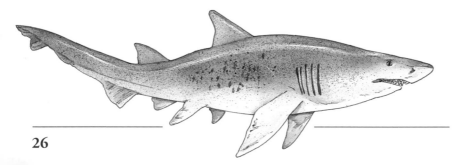

TERROR OF THE DEEP?

You may believe that sharks are quick, silent and deadly hunters. This is often the image of sharks in films. But, although sharks live in all the world's oceans, not all of them are large, or indeed even dangerous. As we learn more about sharks, their fascinating lives and abilities, so we must also learn to respect and admire these graceful creatures.

A sailor's nightmare
Since the days of the earliest seafarers, sharks have been dreaded as evil and dangerous.

OLDER THAN DINOSAURS

The first sharks patrolled our seas about 400 million years ago, 100 million years before dinosaurs appeared. Some shark species eventually died out. Most of those that survived have changed very little in the last 200 million years. Sharks are such expert hunters, with so few enemies, that they simply have not needed to change.

The biggest shark

A shark called megalodon lived in the world's oceans until about 12,000 years ago. You can imagine how big megalodon was, by comparing the size of ourselves to just its jaw bones.

Megalodon jaw

A megalodon tooth

A human tooth

Evidence

No one knows how big megalodon was, but most scientists agree that this gigantic shark would have probably grown to weigh as much as ten family cars.

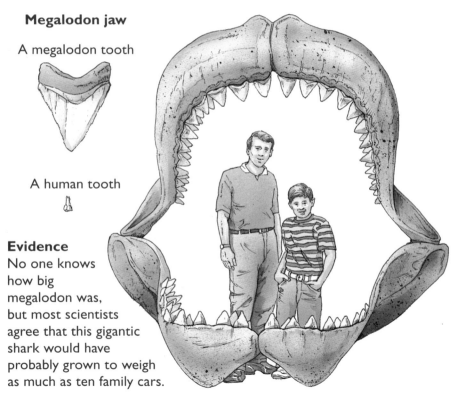

THE SHARK'S CLOSEST RELATIVES

Although they don't look like sharks, **rays** and **skates**, which swim with graceful, flapping 'wings', are closely related to sharks. So are the six species of sawfish and fifty species of guitarfish. Like all true sharks, the skeletons of all these fish are made not from bone, but **cartilage** – just like the bendy bits in your nose.

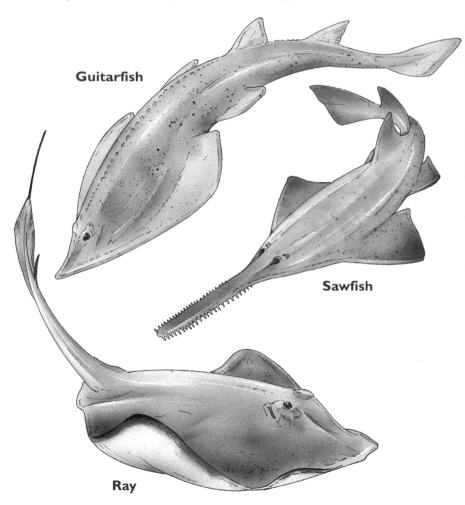

Guitarfish

Sawfish

Ray

STAYING AFLOAT

Sharks are heavier than seawater. This means that they could sink. But sharks' bodies have special adaptations. Sharks' livers contain oil, which is lighter than water, and so helps sharks to float. Also, some sharks gulp air into their stomachs, which provides extra buoyancy.

Most sharks are very **streamlined**. Their muscles are arranged in narrow zigzagging strips, which squeeze in and out as sharks swim. This gives sharks superb strength and speed in water and allows them to turn efficiently in tight circles.

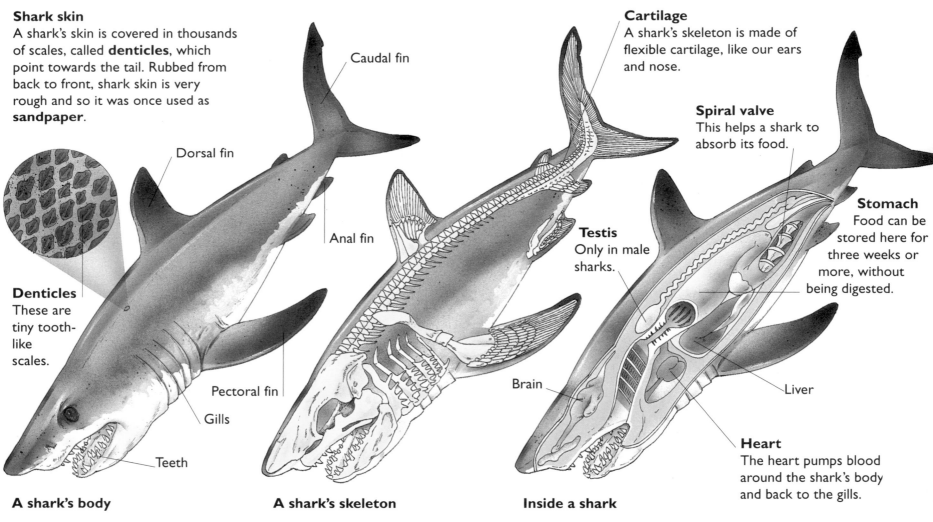

Shark skin
A shark's skin is covered in thousands of scales, called **denticles**, which point towards the tail. Rubbed from back to front, shark skin is very rough and so it was once used as **sandpaper**.

Caudal fin

Dorsal fin

Anal fin

Denticles
These are tiny tooth-like scales.

Pectoral fin

Gills

Teeth

A shark's body

A shark's skeleton

Cartilage
A shark's skeleton is made of flexible cartilage, like our ears and nose.

Spiral valve
This helps a shark to absorb its food.

Testis
Only in male sharks.

Stomach
Food can be stored here for three weeks or more, without being digested.

Brain

Liver

Inside a shark

Heart
The heart pumps blood around the shark's body and back to the gills.

WHAT FINE TEETH YOU HAVE!

Sharks' teeth come in different shapes and sizes, all designed for different jobs. What's more, there are several rows of teeth. When a tooth falls out, the tooth behind moves forward to take the previous tooth's place. This continues throughout a shark's life.

Slicing teeth
These are serrated to cut through flesh.

Spiked teeth
These are for gripping and tearing flesh.

Crushing teeth
These slab-shaped teeth are seen in sharks that feed on crustaceans on the sea floor.

Holding teeth
These long, sharp and pointed teeth help a shark to catch and hold on to slippery fish.

TAKING A BREATH

Like all fish, sharks have gills that draw **oxygen** from the water and pass it into the **bloodstream**. Shark gills are open slits – usually five of them – without the folding flap that other fish have. Most sharks need to keep swimming to ensure they receive a sufficient flow of water over their gills. Some, however, can breathe whilst remaining still.

Gill slits
As the shark swims, so water passes through the gill slits, which are like the arches in a bridge, through to the gills.

Slow sea floor swimmers
Not all sharks swim fast. Some, like the wobbegong, rest on the seabed. The spotted wobbegong moves from one rockpool to the next, searching for crabs and other crustaceans.

SHARK SENSES

A shark's senses are so acute that a shark can hear, smell and detect movements of **prey** from very far away. A shark's ears, for example, can pick up sounds more than one-and-a-half kilometres away. And if an injured fish starts to bleed, some sharks can smell the blood from 500 metres away – the length of five football pitches!

Shark ears
A shark's ears are inside its head, with tiny holes leading to the outside.

Sense of smell
A shark relies more on its sense of smell than its eyesight. A shark's nose and the front of its head are covered by tiny **pores** that can detect electrical impulses caused by the movements of other fish.

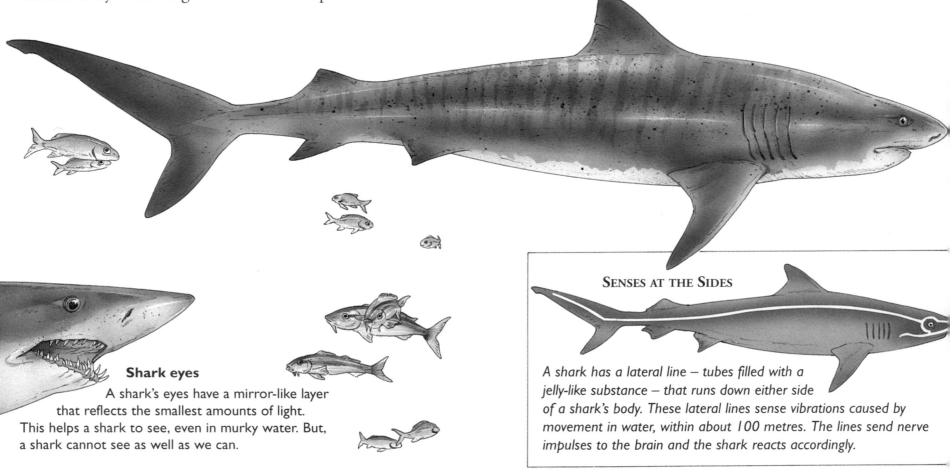

Shark eyes
A shark's eyes have a mirror-like layer that reflects the smallest amounts of light. This helps a shark to see, even in murky water. But, a shark cannot see as well as we can.

SENSES AT THE SIDES

A shark has a lateral line – tubes filled with a jelly-like substance – that runs down either side of a shark's body. These lateral lines sense vibrations caused by movement in water, within about 100 metres. The lines send nerve impulses to the brain and the shark reacts accordingly.

WHERE ARE THEY?

There are more than 370 species of shark in the world's seas. Sharks come in a wide variety of shapes, sizes and colours. Some sharks are wanderers, covering great distances, while others have their own small territories. Most sharks are found in warm seas – very few sharks live in cold water – although some are found off the coast of Britain.

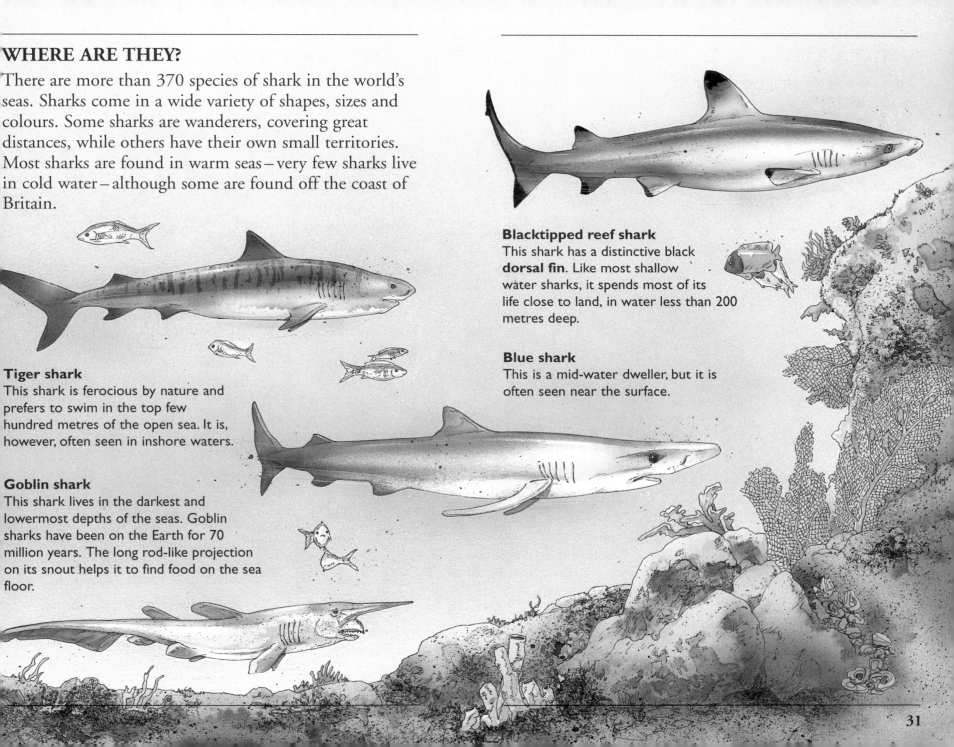

Blacktipped reef shark
This shark has a distinctive black **dorsal fin**. Like most shallow water sharks, it spends most of its life close to land, in water less than 200 metres deep.

Blue shark
This is a mid-water dweller, but it is often seen near the surface.

Tiger shark
This shark is ferocious by nature and prefers to swim in the top few hundred metres of the open sea. It is, however, often seen in inshore waters.

Goblin shark
This shark lives in the darkest and lowermost depths of the seas. Goblin sharks have been on the Earth for 70 million years. The long rod-like projection on its snout helps it to find food on the sea floor.

WHITE DEATH

The great white shark is the most dangerous of all sharks. It can be as much as six metres long. Great white sharks are found in cool to warm waters. Their favourite meal is seal. Usually, they launch a surprise attack and take one huge bite of their victim then wait nearby for it to weaken before returning to finish the meal. These are the sharks that may attack people in shallow water, and drag them out to sea.

Great white shark
This shark will eat almost anything that comes along—smaller sharks, fish, penguins or even people.

THREE THREATENING ONES

Several species of shark have been known to attack people. As well as great white sharks, tiger sharks and bull sharks are considered a danger. Bull sharks hunt in tropical seas and have even been known to swim up freshwater rivers and even into lakes. However, there is still more chance of being struck by lightning than being attacked by these sharks.

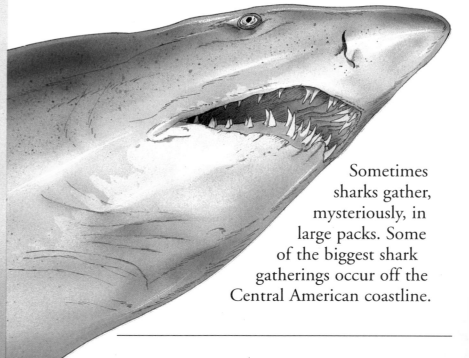

Sometimes sharks gather, mysteriously, in large packs. Some of the biggest shark gatherings occur off the Central American coastline.

WATER BABIES

When mating, a male shark grasps its partner with its teeth, sometimes causing cuts and gashes. These usually heal up very quickly. At birth, sharks are strong enough to look after themselves. Interestingly, sharks have three different methods of reproducing.

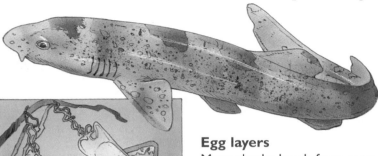

Egg layers
Many sharks hatch from eggs which are laid by the mother. The eggs are protected by a tough, leathery casing.

A shark develops inside each egg with its own food supply – the egg-sac. As the baby shark grows, the egg-sac shrinks. This takes about nine months.

Then, the baby shark searches for the weakest point in the egg case and forces its way out to freedom – a perfect miniature adult shark.

MOTHERLY COMFORTS

Most shark babies develop inside an egg, which is incubated inside a female shark. The mako shark, for example, uses this method. A few species of shark, including hammerheads, bull sharks and blue sharks grow inside the mother's womb, without the need of any kind of egg-sac, just like human babies.

Born in water
When sharks are born, they can swim and are ready to eat solid food.

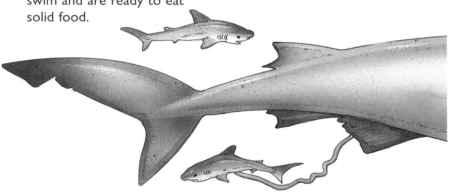

Internal egg developers
Sand tiger sharks grow in an egg inside their mothers. Unlike blue sharks, which are fed through an umbilical cord, sand tiger sharks feed from a special yolk-sac in their egg.

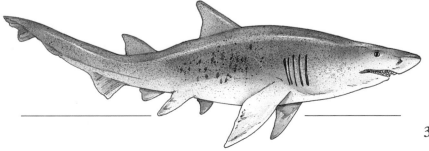

A SHARK'S BODY

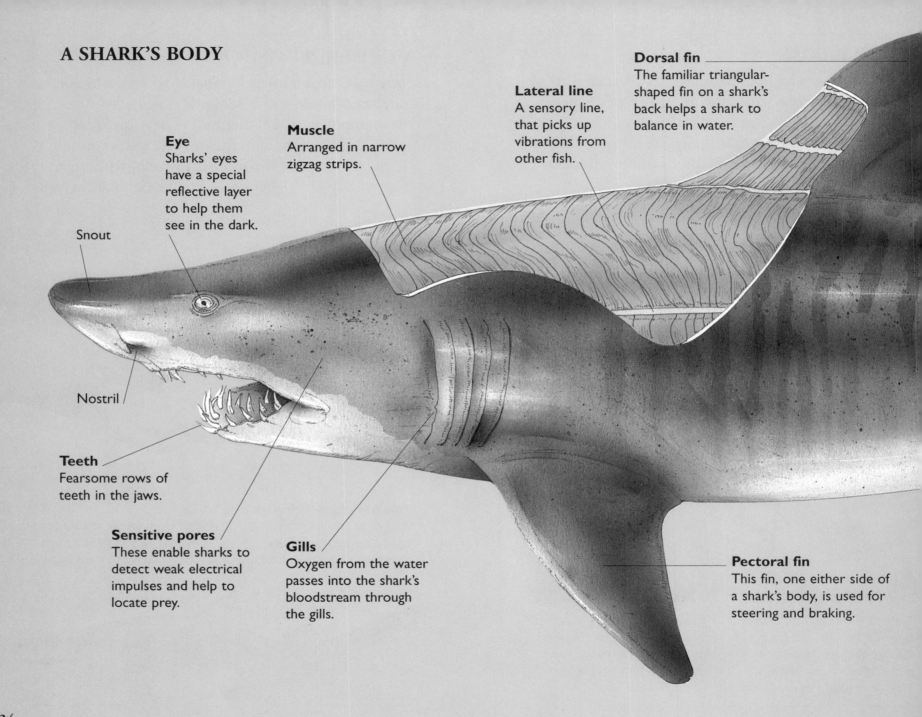

Eye
Sharks' eyes have a special reflective layer to help them see in the dark.

Snout

Nostril

Teeth
Fearsome rows of teeth in the jaws.

Sensitive pores
These enable sharks to detect weak electrical impulses and help to locate prey.

Muscle
Arranged in narrow zigzag strips.

Gills
Oxygen from the water passes into the shark's bloodstream through the gills.

Lateral line
A sensory line, that picks up vibrations from other fish.

Dorsal fin
The familiar triangular-shaped fin on a shark's back helps a shark to balance in water.

Pectoral fin
This fin, one either side of a shark's body, is used for steering and braking.

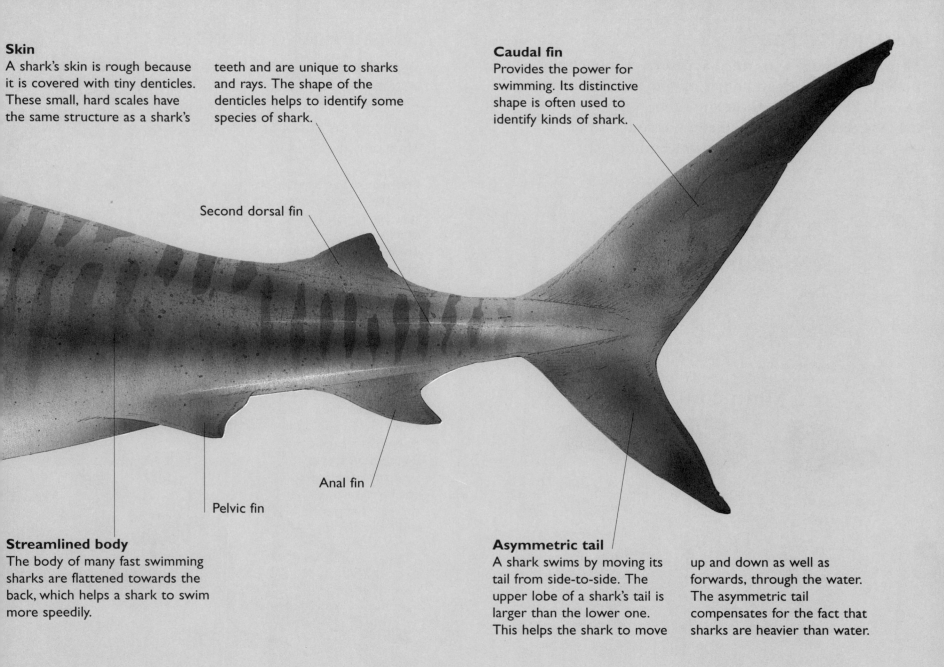

Skin
A shark's skin is rough because it is covered with tiny denticles. These small, hard scales have the same structure as a shark's teeth and are unique to sharks and rays. The shape of the denticles helps to identify some species of shark.

Caudal fin
Provides the power for swimming. Its distinctive shape is often used to identify kinds of shark.

Second dorsal fin

Anal fin

Pelvic fin

Streamlined body
The body of many fast swimming sharks are flattened towards the back, which helps a shark to swim more speedily.

Asymmetric tail
A shark swims by moving its tail from side-to-side. The upper lobe of a shark's tail is larger than the lower one. This helps the shark to move up and down as well as forwards, through the water. The asymmetric tail compensates for the fact that sharks are heavier than water.

A SHARK'S MEAL

Sharks have huge and varied appetites. Although they prefer fish, shellfish and other marine life, sharks often swim behind boats and eat any rubbish that is thrown overboard. This complete menu was found inside a grey shark, nearly four metres in length, caught in Australian waters.

Menu
Starters
1 Piece of sacking

1 Ship's scraper

Main course
8 Legs of mutton

Half a ham

135 kilograms of horse flesh

Dessert
Head and forelegs of a bulldog

Hind quarters of a pig

HAMMERS AND BONNETS

No one knows why the hammerhead shark has such a strangely shaped head. Its widely-spaced eyes and nose, and its typically flat head may allow the hammerhead shark to sense and swim after prey more easily.

Hammerhead shark
This shark has hundreds of sensitive pores on the underside of its strangely shaped head. These pores may help the shark sweep the seabed more efficiently, to detect buried prey like stingrays – one of its favourite meals.

Bonnethead shark
Another member of the hammerhead group is the bonnethead shark. From above, this shark's head resembles a car bonnet. Bonnethead sharks hunt small fish and sea creatures such as crab and squid, often in shallow seas.

GENTLE GIANTS

The largest fish in the sea are the mighty whale shark and the basking shark. Yet neither of these giants are a threat to people. Instead of teeth, both have special filters in their gills that sieve tiny animals called **zooplankton** from the water.

Surface skimmers
Some large sharks cruise slowly near the surface. Incredibly, they sometimes jump completely out of the water.

Whale shark
This shark feeds during the day in warm tropical oceans. The largest living fish, it can grow to eighteen metres and can weigh over twenty tonnes.

Basking shark
This shark can grow to be nearly fourteen metres long. About half a million litres of seawater flows through its gaping mouth every hour.

NEW SPECIES
*In 1976 a rare, new shark was discovered – the megamouth. It was found tangled in the anchor of an American warship. Only a few megamouths have ever been caught. Very little is known about this shark, but it is thought to tempt prey into its huge, **luminous** mouth, which contains more than one hundred rows of teeth.*
The megamouth lives in deep tropical waters.

37

MOVING RIGHT ALONG

Sharks are tailor-made for fast swimming. In fact, probably the only thing sharks cannot do, which most bony fish can, is swim backwards.

Streamlining
A shark's streamlined shape makes it very agile underwater and enables it to turn quickly. Also, its fins may curve slightly towards its tail, helping the animal to swim faster.

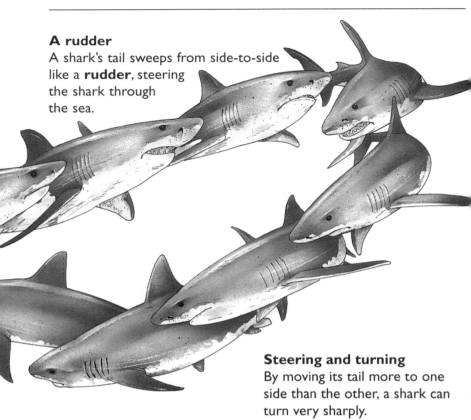

A rudder
A shark's tail sweeps from side-to-side like a **rudder**, steering the shark through the sea.

Fins for lifting
The **pectoral fins** act like an aeroplane's wings to help create 'lift' and move the shark up or down.

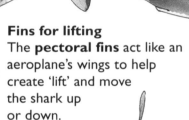

Steering and turning
By moving its tail more to one side than the other, a shark can turn very sharply.

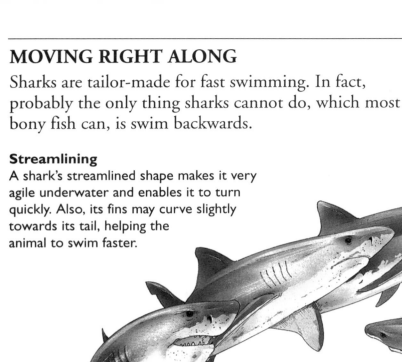

THE THRESHER SHARK

A shark's spine extends into the tail, giving it extra strength. The thresher shark's tail is actually longer than the whole of the rest of its body!

SHARK TAILS

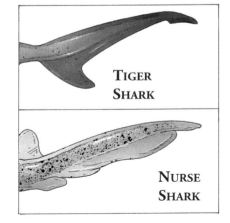

TIGER SHARK

NURSE SHARK

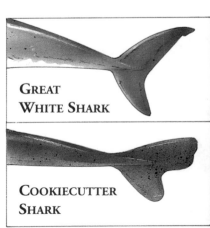

GREAT WHITE SHARK

COOKIECUTTER SHARK

SIX OF THE BEST KNOWN

Mako
This agile shark's high speed helps it to catch tuna and mackerel, its favourite foods. It swims near the surface and sometimes attacks boats.

Sand tiger shark
This shark's needle-sharp teeth make it look very fierce, but it is not a particularly dangerous one. In Australia it is called the grey nurse shark. It eats fish, smaller sharks, crabs and lobsters.

Leopard shark
This striking, black-spotted shark feeds mainly on clams. Common along the Pacific coast of North America, it is harmless to people.

Oceanic whitetip
A tuna may mistake the white tips of this shark's fins for small fish. When the tuna investigates, it finds itself lured into the shark's trap, and eaten.

Nurse shark
This large shark usually spends the day sitting on the seabed in shallow water. If disturbed, it may attack swimmers. At night it searches for crabs or small fish.

Lemon shark
A young lemon shark can be aggressive towards divers, but the adult lemon shark is extremely shy. A lemon shark eats fish that live on the seabed.

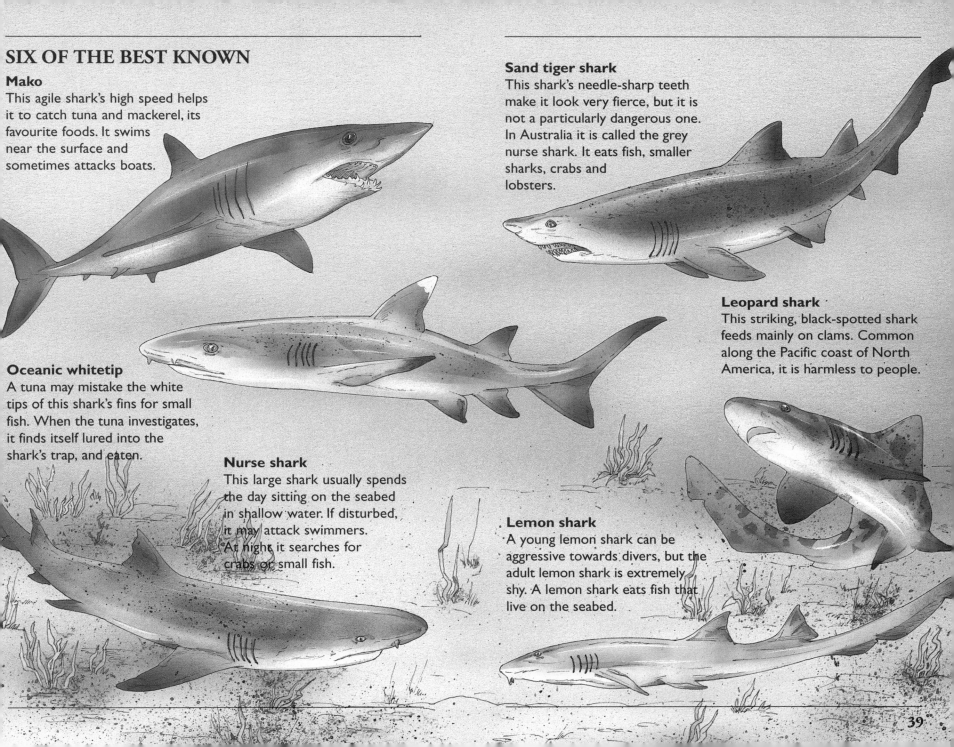

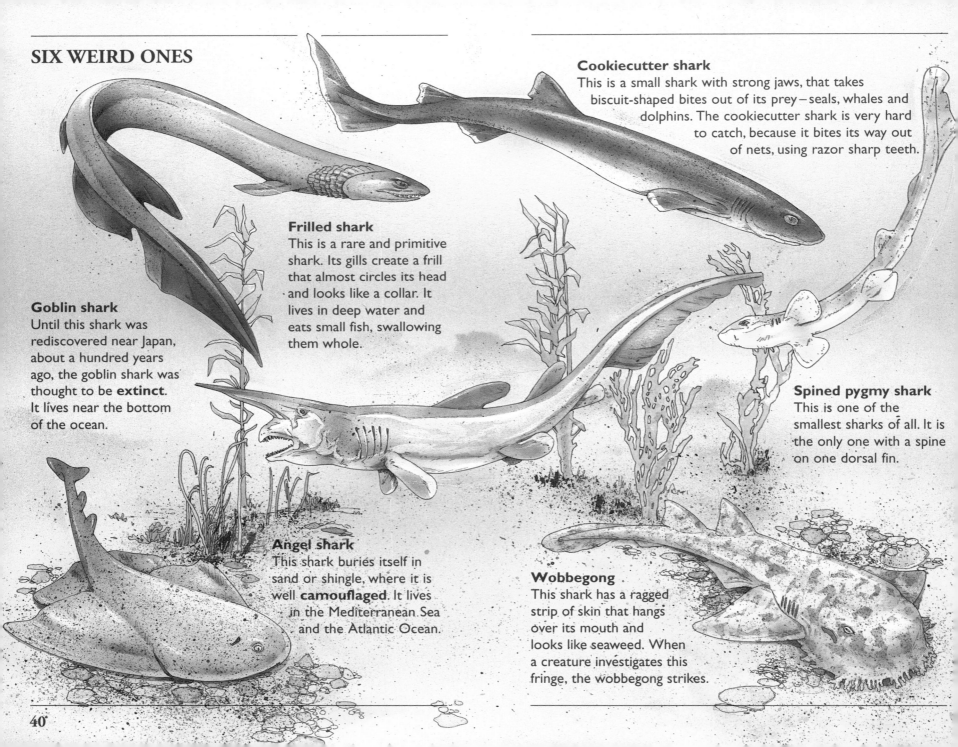

SIX WEIRD ONES

Cookiecutter shark
This is a small shark with strong jaws, that takes biscuit-shaped bites out of its prey – seals, whales and dolphins. The cookiecutter shark is very hard to catch, because it bites its way out of nets, using razor sharp teeth.

Frilled shark
This is a rare and primitive shark. Its gills create a frill that almost circles its head and looks like a collar. It lives in deep water and eats small fish, swallowing them whole.

Goblin shark
Until this shark was rediscovered near Japan, about a hundred years ago, the goblin shark was thought to be **extinct**. It lives near the bottom of the ocean.

Spined pygmy shark
This is one of the smallest sharks of all. It is the only one with a spine on one dorsal fin.

Angel shark
This shark buries itself in sand or shingle, where it is well **camouflaged**. It lives in the Mediterranean Sea and the Atlantic Ocean.

Wobbegong
This shark has a ragged strip of skin that hangs over its mouth and looks like seaweed. When a creature investigates this fringe, the wobbegong strikes.

THE SHARK'S GREATEST ENEMY

Shark attacks on humans are nearly always caused by divers annoying the sharks, or by the sharks mistaking swimmers or surfers for their usual prey. Researchers have tried out many safeguards against attack, one being a tube-shaped inflatable container, called a shark screen.

Protection
Divers sometimes wear a **chain-mail diving suit** to keep themselves safe from sharks.

Shark cages
Divers use shark cages to protect themselves when studying sharks at close range. Films of sharks are also often photographed in this way.

Seal   Turtle   Surfer

Deciphering an outline
To a shark, the outline of a person paddling on a surfboard must be very similar to the outline of a seal or turtle.

People kill a staggering 100 million sharks every year. Sharks cannot survive such a high rate of slaughter, especially as some of the larger species do not breed until they are eighteen years old. Happily, some countries are now actively trying to protect certain species.

Killed for food and sport
Many sharks are killed by the nets that protect beaches. Sharks become entangled in nets and drown.

AMAZING SHARK FACTS

- **River sharks**
Only two sharks may sometimes leave the sea and swim into freshwater rivers. They are the bull shark and the Ganges shark.

- **Light producing organ**
The lantern shark has small, special organs, set in its belly, which produce light. The lantern shark lives deep in the Atlantic Ocean, feeding on squid, crabs and similar creatures.

- **Cookiecutter sharks** These sharks swim about four kilometres each day. They move up from the depths of the ocean to feed near the surface.

- **White shark longevity** The great white shark may be the most long-lived of all sharks. It is thought that individuals may live for a hundred years.

- **The most common shark** The piked dogfish is thought to be the most common shark in the world. Between 1904 and 1905, 27 million were caught off the American coast alone. These sharks range widely through the world's oceans.

- **Having a ride** Remora fish stick very closely to sharks. They use a special sucker pad to hitch a ride, anchoring themselves to the shark's skin.

- **Horn shark eggs** Sharks' eggs come in an assortment of shapes and sizes. One of the strangest is the egg of the horn shark, which has its own screwthread, enabling the mother shark to fasten the egg securely in a rocky crack.

- **Taking a look** Great whites lift their heads out of the water to look at objects on the surface.

GLOSSARY

Bloodstream The name for blood flowing round a body.

Camouflage The way in which a creature can conceal itself because of its appearance. It also usually lies still.

Cartilage The flexible substance of which sharks' skeletons are made.

Chain-mail diving suit Interlocking metal loops, like armour, which can save a diver from being badly attacked by a shark.

Denticles The tooth-like covering on a shark's skin, which gives it a rough feel.

Dorsal fins The fins on the shark's back. A dorsal fin becomes visible above the water when the shark is swimming close to the surface.

Extinct A creature which is thought to no longer exist on the planet.

Luminous An object which glows in the dark. Deep water sharks may have luminous areas on their bodies.

Oxygen A gas present in air and in water which is essential to life.

Pectoral fin The fin present just behind the head, on either side of a fish's body. These fins help the shark to change direction as it swims.

Pore A tiny opening in the skin, which allows liquid or air to pass through.

Prey Animals which are eaten by other animals.

Ray A wide-bodied fish, related to the shark.

Rudder The part of a boat, at the back, which is used for steering.

Sandpaper Paper, usually with grains of sand stuck to it, used to rub down wood and other surfaces to make them smooth.

Skate A group of fish related to sharks, which are often caught by people for food.

Streamlined Having a curved body which allows quick and easy movement through the water.

Zooplankton Tiny floating creatures which live in the oceans and are eaten by much larger animals, including some sharks.

WHALES
AND DOLPHINS

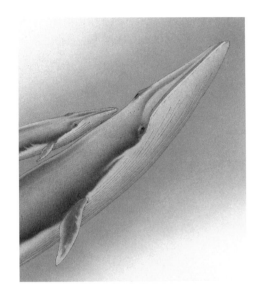

WHALES
AND DOLPHINS

CONTENTS

INTRODUCTION

Whales and dolphins are among the most well-loved creatures living in our seas. Whales can be huge and at the same time are gentle and mysterious. Dolphins are sleek and quick and appear playful and intelligent. Many of us may never actually see a whale or dolphin in the wild, but we can still learn much from these fascinating creatures and their lifestyles.

Sperm whale

Harbour porpoise

Right whale

Minke whale

Fin whale

Dusky dolphin

WHAT IS A WHALE?

Whales and dolphins may look like fish, but they are in fact **mammals**. Like humans, whales and dolphins are **warm-blooded**. The mothers give birth to their babies and feed the babies on milk. Whales, dolphins and porpoises together make up a group of sea creatures known as **cetaceans** (pronounced 'set-ace-ans').

Most experts agree that the earliest ancestors of today's cetaceans were wolf-like creatures which made their homes in estuaries, about fifty million years ago. At first these creatures hunted land animals but grew better at catching fish. They slowly changed as they left the land to live in the sea – all the oceans were theirs to explore.

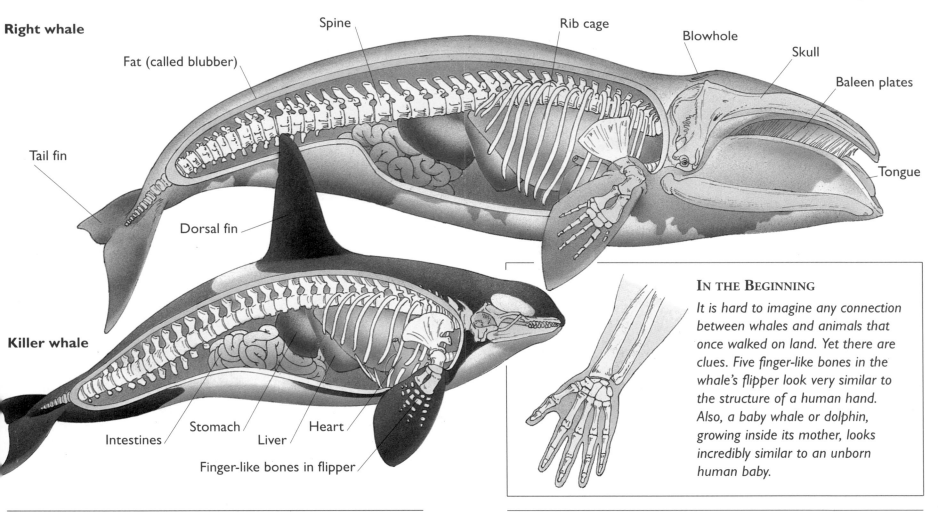

Right whale

Spine

Rib cage

Blowhole

Skull

Baleen plates

Fat (called blubber)

Tail fin

Dorsal fin

Tongue

Killer whale

Intestines

Stomach

Liver

Heart

Finger-like bones in flipper

IN THE BEGINNING

It is hard to imagine any connection between whales and animals that once walked on land. Yet there are clues. Five finger-like bones in the whale's flipper look very similar to the structure of a human hand. Also, a baby whale or dolphin, growing inside its mother, looks incredibly similar to an unborn human baby.

GRAZING WHALES

The ten species of **baleen whale** feed by filtering their food. Instead of teeth, their mouths have triangular **baleen plates** which sift tiny plants and animals from great scoops of sea water. A baleen whale's favourite food is **krill**, which are tiny shrimp-like creatures.

A whale without teeth
A humpback whale has grooves on its throat which stretch and allow the whale to take huge gulps of water.

BALEEN PLATES

Baleen plates have a hairy fringe and are made from keratin, the substance that makes our fingernails hard.

TOOTHED WHALES

Apart from the baleen whales, all other whales and all dolphins and porpoises are hunters and have teeth. Most have sharp pointed teeth to catch and hold onto **prey**, which a whale or dolphin will swallow whole. The teeth of whales and dolphins are all the same size and shape. Toothed whales eat fish, squid, octopus and cuttlefish.

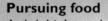

Pursuing food
A dolphin's teeth are designed for grasping prey – fish which are usually swallowed in one go.

GOING PLACES

Most fish swim by moving their tails and bodies from side-to-side, but cetaceans move through the water with a powerful up-and-down motion. Their sleek and streamlined bodies and their specially shaped fins help these graceful animals to cut through the water at speed.

Dolphins are fast swimmers. They can reach speeds of up to 55 kilometres per hour – as fast as a speedboat. The larger whales can reach 30 kilometres per hour for short bursts.

Blowhole
A whale has a blowhole for breathing, which is covered by a valve.

Ears
Whales can hear extremely well, although they don't have any earflaps, like we do.

Eyes
A whale can see both in and out of the water.

No noticeable neck
A whale's backbones are often fused together, which provides a streamlined shape.

Adapted for sea life
Water glides smoothly over a whale's slippery skin.

Fins
A whale's fins are thicker nearer their bodies and thinner towards the back.

Additional streamlines
Grooves in the skin help a whale to swim faster.

STRONG, MUSCULAR TAIL
*The power to swim fast is provided by the wide tail fins or **flukes**, which move up and down. Toothed whales depend on their speed to catch their prey.*

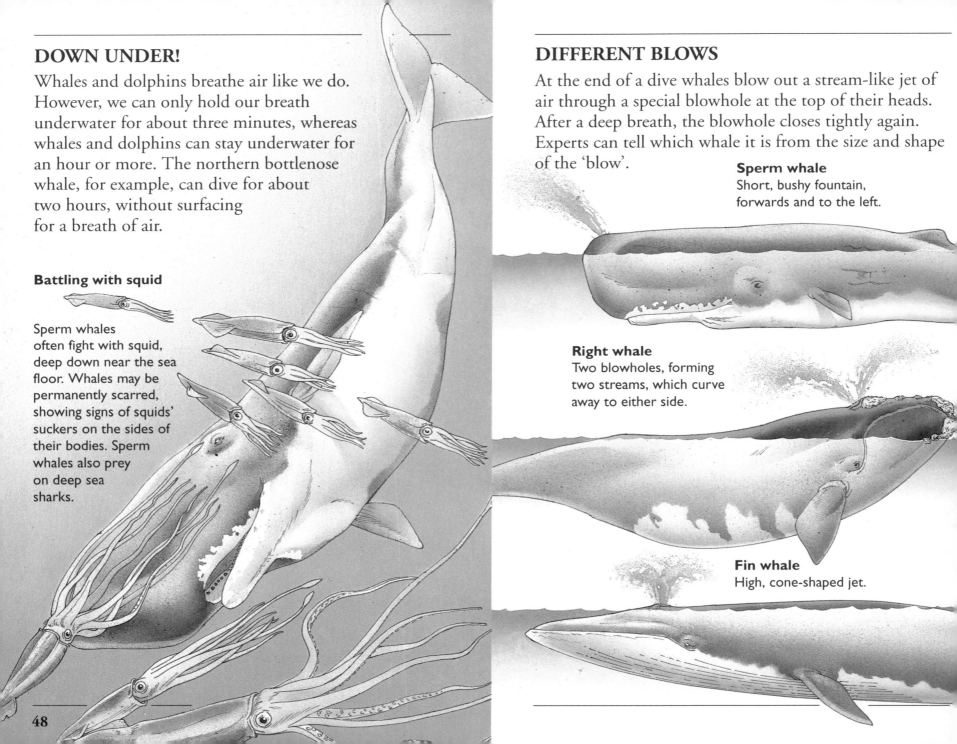

DOWN UNDER!

Whales and dolphins breathe air like we do. However, we can only hold our breath underwater for about three minutes, whereas whales and dolphins can stay underwater for an hour or more. The northern bottlenose whale, for example, can dive for about two hours, without surfacing for a breath of air.

Battling with squid

Sperm whales often fight with squid, deep down near the sea floor. Whales may be permanently scarred, showing signs of squids' suckers on the sides of their bodies. Sperm whales also prey on deep sea sharks.

DIFFERENT BLOWS

At the end of a dive whales blow out a stream-like jet of air through a special blowhole at the top of their heads. After a deep breath, the blowhole closes tightly again. Experts can tell which whale it is from the size and shape of the 'blow'.

Sperm whale
Short, bushy fountain, forwards and to the left.

Right whale
Two blowholes, forming two streams, which curve away to either side.

Fin whale
High, cone-shaped jet.

SENSES

As the sea is usually dark, cetaceans do not need good eyesight. However, sounds travel well through water and cetaceans have an excellent sense of hearing. Sounds pass up from the lower jaw to the inner ear, inside the head. Their lack of an earflap may prevent some cetaceans from hearing sounds in air.

Sniffing, tasting and touching
Whales have a poor sense of smell, and probably little taste, but their sense of touch is good. Dolphins often nudge each other with their noses.

Asleep and alert
Cetaceans put only half of their brains to sleep at a time and so avoid the danger of sinking or stopping breathing while in water.

ECHOLOCATION

Toothed cetaceans have a special sense, called **echolocation**. This sense helps cetaceans to find food. A dolphin emits a clicking sound that bounces back off solid objects like squid or fish. The echo tells the dolphin where an object is, its size and its shape. A dolphin even knows if the object is solid or hollow.

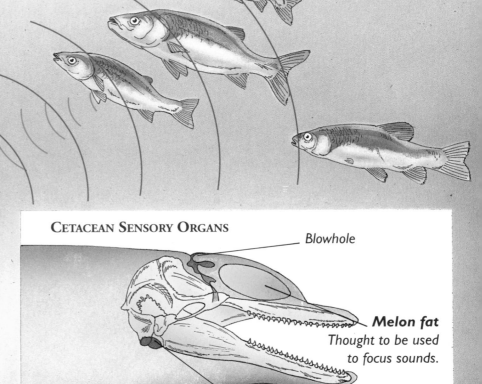

CETACEAN SENSORY ORGANS

Blowhole

Melon fat
Thought to be used to focus sounds.

Inner ear

49

STRANDINGS

Experts believe that whales and dolphins use invisible **magnetic lines** in the seabed for **navigation**. Sometimes these lines cross from sea to land, which is confusing for whales and dolphins. This may explain why large groups of whales sometimes become stranded on the shore. Sadly, rescue attempts do not often succeed and some whales immediately re-strand themselves.

SENDING MESSAGES

Whales and dolphins communicate using their voices and other sounds. Some whales leap out of the water crashing down on the surface. Others slap the water with their tails or flippers. Baleen whales bellow, rumble and whine and can be heard over one hundred kilometres away.

Breaching and lobtailing
These are actions used by whales to make a noise which can be heard by other whales, many kilometres away.

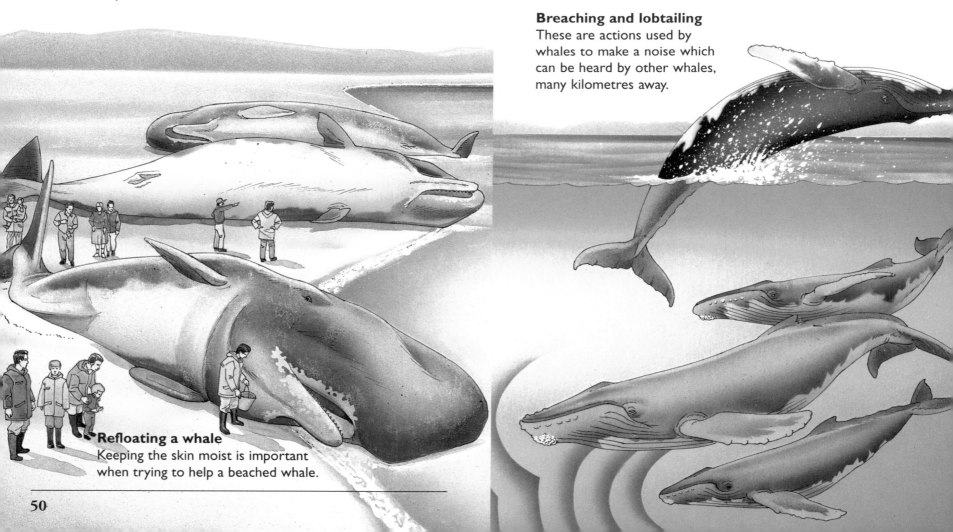

Refloating a whale
Keeping the skin moist is important when trying to help a beached whale.

MOTHER AND BABY

Underwater birth

A baby whale is born tail first. The baby must quickly swim to the surface for its first breath of air. When the baby is born it has floppy fins and tail flukes, which stiffen in the first few days.

Nurturing a baby blue whale

A baby blue whale suckles from its mother underwater, with milk being squirted into the baby's mouth. A baby blue whale drinks about 100 litres of milk in a day.

A fully grown female blue whale has her first calf when she is around five or six years old. She carries the baby for eleven months and then gives birth in midwinter in the warm seas near the Equator. Like us, mother whales usually give birth to only one baby at a time. In the spring the female and her calf migrate from the warm seas near the Equator towards the polar waters which have plenty of food. They stay there until the summer ends.

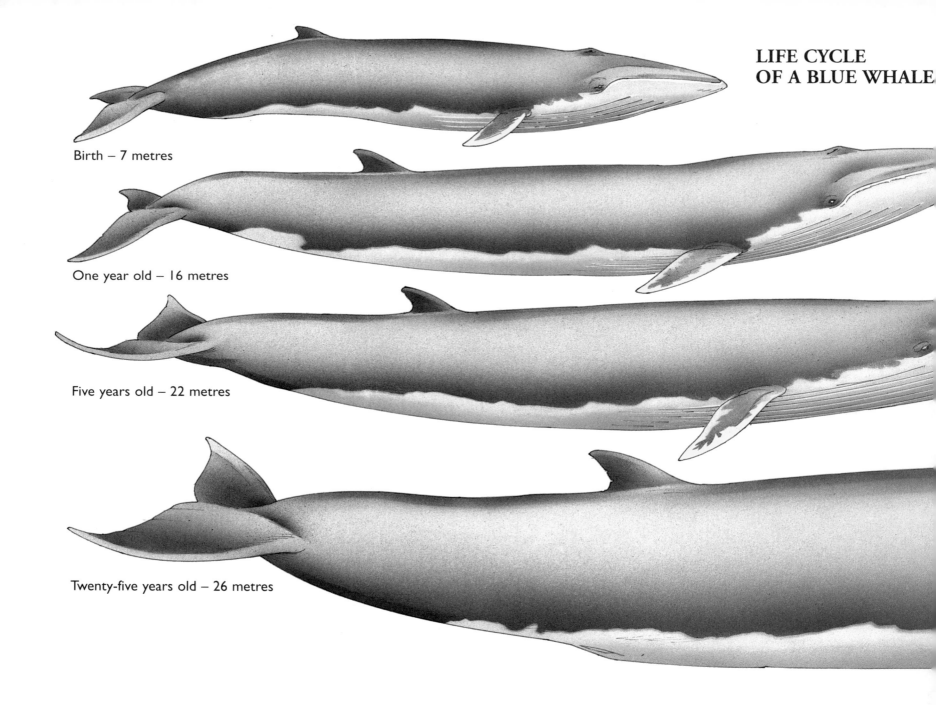

LIFE CYCLE
OF A BLUE WHALE

Birth – 7 metres

One year old – 16 metres

Five years old – 22 metres

Twenty-five years old – 26 metres

52

Birth
At birth, a baby blue whale weighs as much as an elephant! The baby is fed on its mother's milk. Together, they journey to summer feeding grounds near the poles.

One year old
The baby grows steadily. A one-year old blue whale may already be two-thirds of its full adult size.

Five years old
When a blue whale is four or five years old, it has a growth spurt, but it does not reach adult size.

An adult blue whale
An adult whale reaches its maximum size when it is about twenty-five to thirty years old.

THE LARGEST CREATURE ON EARTH

The most spectacular baleen whale is the mighty blue whale. It weighs more than the largest known dinosaur. Its heart is about the size of a small car, and its tongue is heavier than an elephant!

53

INTELLIGENCE

Whales and dolphins are intelligent creatures. In captivity whales and dolphins have proved that they are clever enough to learn difficult tricks. In one experiment one dolphin passed instructions to another dolphin in a separate pool, telling it which of two paddles to press to find food.

**Swimming
with dolphins**
Many people will only get to see a whale or dolphin in captivity.

BEHAVIOUR

Many whales and dolphins love to nudge or rub against each other, sometimes touching while swimming. Some even give their **calves** piggy-backs. Many male dolphins and porpoises argue over who is in charge by clapping their jaws, slapping their tails and sometimes ramming and biting each other.

Playful porpoises
Porpoises have rough skin on their backs, which may be specially designed for giving calves piggy-backs.

Dolphins have fun
Dolphins appear to enjoy playing, sometimes jumping, chasing, tossing dead fish or seaweed, or speeding alongside boats.

WHALE WATCHING

Whales and dolphins are found in all oceans, from the warm waters of the **tropics** to the icy waters of the **poles**, and in a few rivers, too. Whale watching is a popular hobby and people travel around the world in the hope of seeing or touching whales and swimming with dolphins.

There are many millions of whales, dolphins and porpoises in the world's oceans. Some species live close to the coastline while others live far out at sea. Some tend to stay in one area whereas others, like the baleen whales, migrate long distances to breed.

☐ = Where whales live

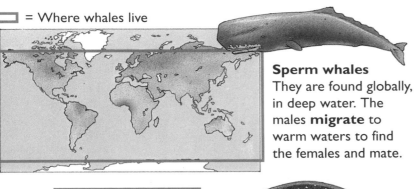

Sperm whales
They are found globally, in deep water. The males **migrate** to warm waters to find the females and mate.

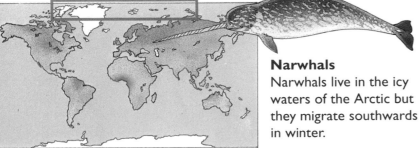

Narwhals
Narwhals live in the icy waters of the Arctic but they migrate southwards in winter.

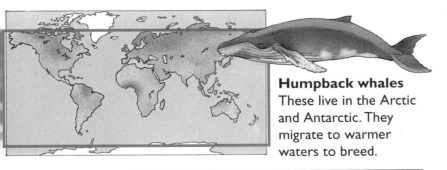

Humpback whales
These live in the Arctic and Antarctic. They migrate to warmer waters to breed.

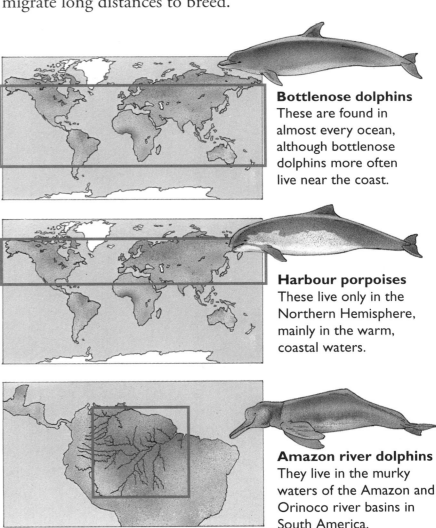

Bottlenose dolphins
These are found in almost every ocean, although bottlenose dolphins more often live near the coast.

Harbour porpoises
These live only in the Northern Hemisphere, mainly in the warm, coastal waters.

Amazon river dolphins
They live in the murky waters of the Amazon and Orinoco river basins in South America.

WHALES OF THE WORLD

Right whale
This big, stocky whale was named by early whalers, who thought it was the 'right' whale to catch – it was slow and provided lots of valuable oil and bone. The pattern of pale, horny growths around the head and face is different for every whale. Many **parasitic** worms and lice live on these whales.

Dwarf sperm whale
This is the smallest of all whales. It is under three metres long. Like other sperm whales, a dwarf sperm whale has a squarish head, but also has a tall dorsal fin. Dwarf sperm whales are secretive and rarely seen by people, except when stranded.

Killer whale
This is the only whale which attacks and kills other whales and dolphins, including blue whales, which are many times a killer whale's own size. Surprisingly, a killer whale has never been known to attack humans. The huge fin on the male's back can be up to two metres high. This striking, black and white whale is also known as an orca. It lives in the same **pod** all its life and is found in all oceans.

Grey whale
Named after its colour, the grey whale lives close to the coast and feeds by sifting through the sand or mud on the seabed, filtering out tiny creatures. A grey whale has a distinctive long, narrow head shape.

56

Beluga whale

Early sailors called this whale a 'sea canary' because of the squeaking and whistling noises it made to other belugas. This small white whale lives mainly within the Arctic Circle and is often mistaken for blocks of drifting ice by killer whales! Belugas are very sociable whales, usually living in groups of up to fifteen, but sometimes, where there is plenty to eat, they are found in thousands. At birth, a beluga is dark brown. This colour fades to grey and then turns white as the whale matures.

Narwhal

The male narwhal's long, spiral-shaped tusk makes it one of the strangest animals on the planet. The tusk is actually a tooth that has grown out through the narwhal's lip, usually from the left side. Sometimes, but very rarely, two teeth develop into a tusk, creating a two-tusked narwhal. It takes a year for young males to grow their tusk. An adult male can have a tusk as long as three metres.

Straptooth whale

This whale is named after the two strange curved teeth which males grow from either side of their lower jaw. The male straptooth whale cannot open its mouth fully, but it is still able to feed.

Northern bottlenose whale

Found mainly in the North Atlantic and Arctic oceans, this whale has a rounded forehead, and males have two large **conical** teeth in their lower jaw. A northern bottlenose whale lives in deep water, eating its favourite food, squid. This whale would often swim up to whaling ships and stay with its injured companions, making itself an even easier target for whalers. In 1977, the International Whaling Commission listed these large whales as a protected species.

57

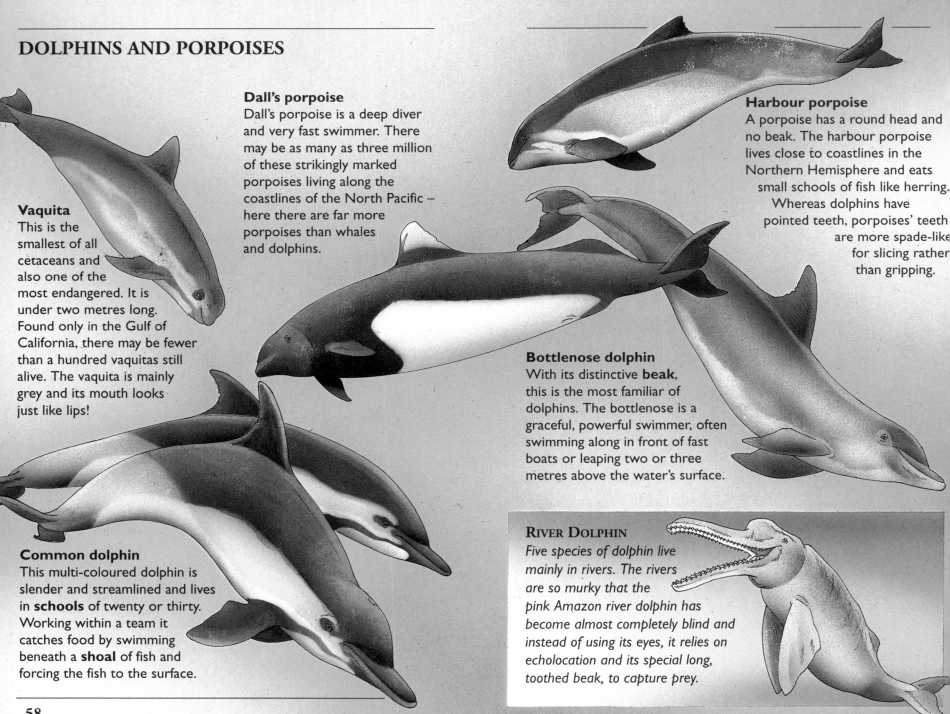

DOLPHINS AND PORPOISES

Dall's porpoise
Dall's porpoise is a deep diver and very fast swimmer. There may be as many as three million of these strikingly marked porpoises living along the coastlines of the North Pacific – here there are far more porpoises than whales and dolphins.

Harbour porpoise
A porpoise has a round head and no beak. The harbour porpoise lives close to coastlines in the Northern Hemisphere and eats small schools of fish like herring. Whereas dolphins have pointed teeth, porpoises' teeth are more spade-like for slicing rather than gripping.

Vaquita
This is the smallest of all cetaceans and also one of the most endangered. It is under two metres long. Found only in the Gulf of California, there may be fewer than a hundred vaquitas still alive. The vaquita is mainly grey and its mouth looks just like lips!

Bottlenose dolphin
With its distinctive **beak**, this is the most familiar of dolphins. The bottlenose is a graceful, powerful swimmer, often swimming along in front of fast boats or leaping two or three metres above the water's surface.

Common dolphin
This multi-coloured dolphin is slender and streamlined and lives in **schools** of twenty or thirty. Working within a team it catches food by swimming beneath a **shoal** of fish and forcing the fish to the surface.

RIVER DOLPHIN
Five species of dolphin live mainly in rivers. The rivers are so murky that the pink Amazon river dolphin has become almost completely blind and instead of using its eyes, it relies on echolocation and its special long, toothed beak, to capture prey.

PAST, PRESENT AND FUTURE

For hundreds of years, whales were hunted for oil, baleen and meat. As whaling ships became faster, the number of whales killed grew higher and higher. People then began to realise that some species might disappear altogether. In recent years whaling has gradually been cut back, and now whales are protected by most countries. The number of whales in the sea is slowly increasing.

Killing big and small whales
At one time, only the largest whales were chased, but today even the small minke whale attracts whalers. Whale meat is considered a delicacy in some parts of the world.

Protecting whales
In the 1930s as many as 40,000 whales a year were being killed, most of them blue whales. In 1946 the International Whaling Commission set quotas, establishing the number of whales that could be killed.

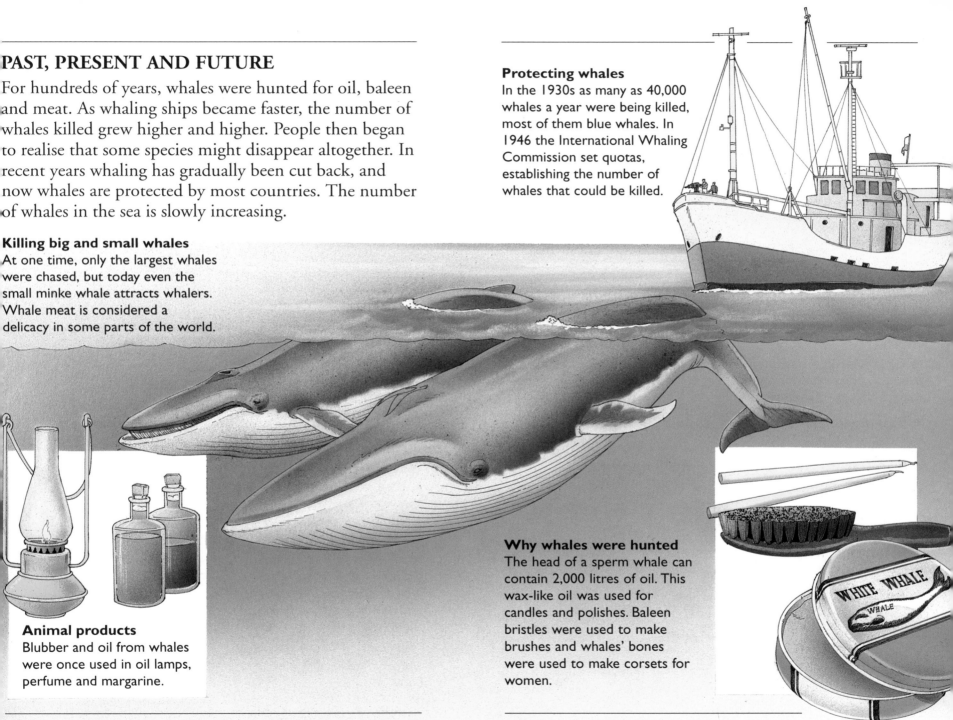

Animal products
Blubber and oil from whales were once used in oil lamps, perfume and margarine.

Why whales were hunted
The head of a sperm whale can contain 2,000 litres of oil. This wax-like oil was used for candles and polishes. Baleen bristles were used to make brushes and whales' bones were used to make corsets for women.

WHITE WHALE
WHALE

AMAZING CETACEAN FACTS

- **Whales' heartbeat** The rate of a whale's heartbeat is halved during a deep dive. A sperm whale can dive as deep as 3,000 metres when searching for squid.

- **Dolphins can drown** Dolphins often become tangled up in fishing nets and drown. About seven million dolphins have accidentally died in this way, over the past thirty years.

- **Endangered** Chinese river dolphins are probably the most endangered cetaceans in the world. There are less than 300 surviving in the wild. **Pollution** and lack of food are the reasons for the decline in numbers of Chinese river dolphins.

- **Growth** Blue whale calves can grow to a length of nine metres in just seven months. This is the fastest rate of growth for any animal on the planet.

- **Singing whales** Humpback whales may sing for thirty minutes at a time.

- **Speedy and sleepless** Dall's porpoises are the world's fastest marine mammal and they never go to sleep.

- **Whale lice** Tiny crab-like creatures called whale lice live around the eyes and other parts of whales' bodies.

- **Unicorns** Legends about unicorns sprang from sightings, by early sailors, of the long tusk on the head of male narwhals.

- **Appetite** Whales eat about four tonnes of krill from the sea in a single day.

GLOSSARY

Baleen plate Sieve-like plates in a whale's mouth. These plates allow the whale to take food out of water.

Baleen whale A whale which feeds on small sea creatures, which it filters out from sea water.

Beak The nose of a dolphin.

Calf The name for a young whale or dolphin.

Cetacean A name given to all whales, dolphins and porpoises.

Conical The cone-like shape of the teeth of some whales.

Echolocation A sense which cetaceans use to locate nearby objects by making clicking sounds that bounce off objects, and return as echoes.

Fluke The flat, curved part of a whale's tail, which moves as the whale swims.

Krill A tiny sea creature protected by a hard shell.

Magnetic line A magnetic force in the Earth which whales and dolphins can sense, and which they use to find their way through the oceans.

Mammal A warm-blooded animal. The female feeds her baby on milk.

Migrate To move regularly from one place to another at a certain time of the year.

Navigation Finding a way in the sea from one place to another.

Parasitic A name for a creature which lives and feeds on another creature.

Pod A group of whales, porpoises or dolphins.

Poles The most northern and southerly parts of the Earth.

Pollution Damaging the environment with chemicals and waste.

Prey An animal which is eaten by other animals.

School A large number of fish or sea mammals swimming together as a group.

Shoal A group of fish swimming together.

Tropics The warmer part of the world surrounding the Equator.

Warm-blooded The name for a creature which does not depend on the temperature of the environment to keep warm. It can maintain its own internal temperature.

RAIN FOREST
A N I M A L S

CONTENTS

◖ This symbol represents animals that live in South and Central America.

◓ This symbol represents animals that live in Africa.

◕ This symbol represents animals that live in Asia. More than one symbol represents animals which can be found in several continents.

WHAT IS A RAIN FOREST?

The world's rain forests grow round the central part of the Earth, in the **tropics**. Rain forests are hot and humid places, but little sunlight passes down through the dense cover of trees and vines to the ground. Here, it is quite dark and there are lots of shadows.

Where are the rain forests?

Rain forests cover about one tenth of the world's surface, but they are home to nine out of ten of the world's plants and animals.

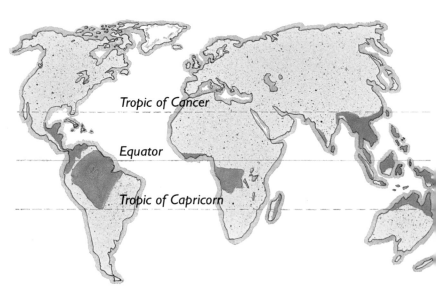

Tropic of Cancer

Equator

Tropic of Capricorn

Rain forests are found in the hottest parts of the Earth – between the Tropic of Cancer and the Tropic of Capricorn. In this equatorial region there are no seasons. The weather is always hot and humid. It always becomes dark, quickly, at about 6 pm, every day of the year. The main rain forests are found in the Americas, Africa and Asia. They are the green parts of the map.

THE WATER CYCLE

If you fly over a rain forest in a plane, the forest below will look like a green carpet. There are no seasons here, and the trees have leaves and fruit throughout the year. When it rains, water drips down through the dense **canopy** into the lower parts of the rain forest.

Water everywhere

Rain forests are very wet places. It rains almost every day. But the clouds clear quickly and then it becomes sunny. There is a lot of water **vapour** in the air. This is why being in a rain forest feels sticky. The Sun's heat dries up some of the rain, which then forms clouds. These clouds will produce more rain, and so the water cycle continues.

PLANTS

Some of the most unusual plants in the world grow in the rain forests. More than a quarter of the medicines we use today first came from rain forest plants, along with many of the fruits we eat, like bananas. A number of other plants from the world's rain forests, such as begonias, have found their way into our homes as houseplants.

Lianas
These are woody vines which use the trees like a scaffold to climb up, clinging on with tendrils. Some lianas are thin, others are thick and as strong as a rope.

Rafflesia's giant blooms
The rafflesia produces the largest flowers of any plant in the world. These can measure one metre across, and smell like rotten meat.

Rosy periwinkle
This plant grows in Madagascar, off Africa, and is used to help cure leukaemia, a type of cancer.

CREEPY CRAWLIES

No one knows how many insects and similar creatures live in the rain forests of the world. A large number, especially those whose home is up in the forest canopy, have still to be discovered. Some scientists believe there could be as many as 50 million different animals living in the canopy of trees.

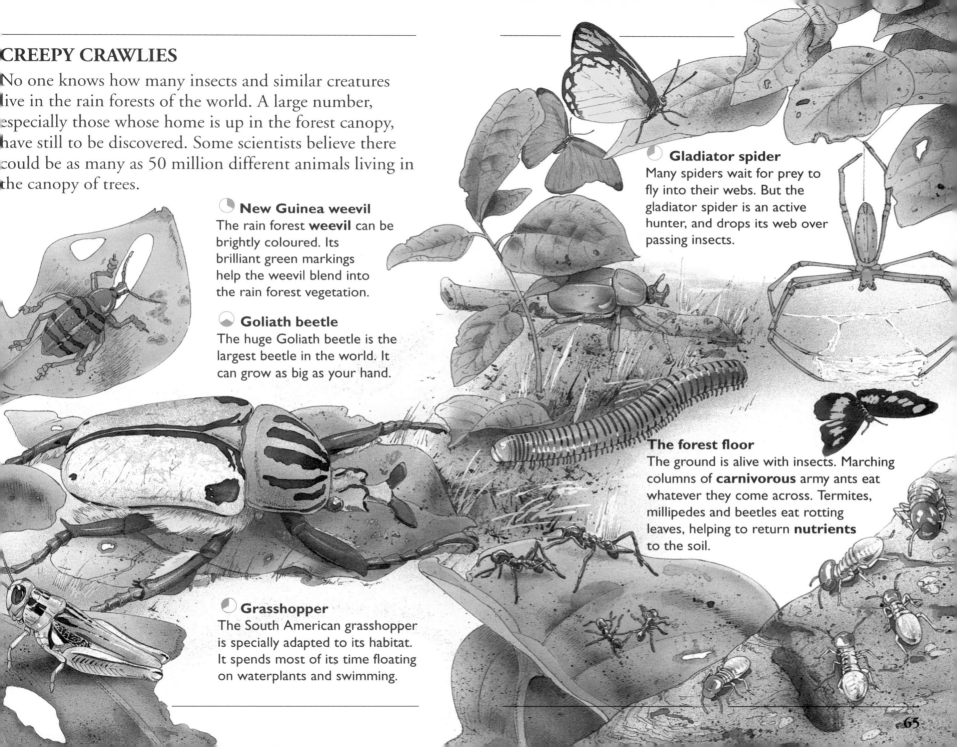

New Guinea weevil
The rain forest **weevil** can be brightly coloured. Its brilliant green markings help the weevil blend into the rain forest vegetation.

Goliath beetle
The huge Goliath beetle is the largest beetle in the world. It can grow as big as your hand.

Grasshopper
The South American grasshopper is specially adapted to its habitat. It spends most of its time floating on waterplants and swimming.

Gladiator spider
Many spiders wait for prey to fly into their webs. But the gladiator spider is an active hunter, and drops its web over passing insects.

The forest floor
The ground is alive with insects. Marching columns of **carnivorous** army ants eat whatever they come across. Termites, millipedes and beetles eat rotting leaves, helping to return **nutrients** to the soil.

FISH

The rivers and streams in rain forests contain fish of many different shapes and sizes. Fish face many enemies, and not all are in the water. Fishing bats, for example, can even locate fish from the air and use a special toe which is shaped like a hook to lift fish out of water.

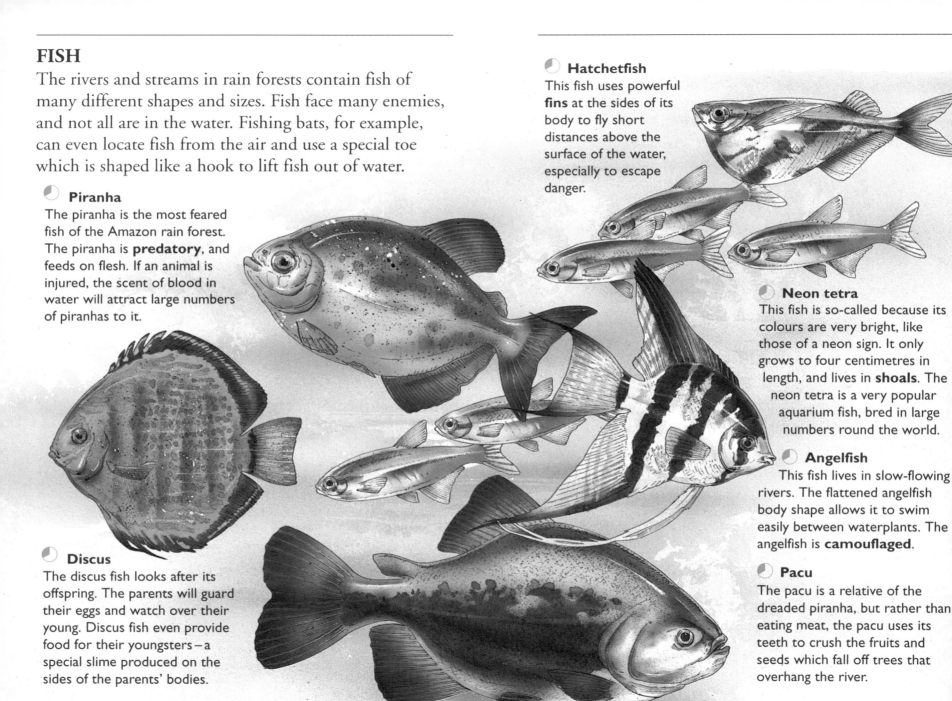

Piranha
The piranha is the most feared fish of the Amazon rain forest. The piranha is **predatory**, and feeds on flesh. If an animal is injured, the scent of blood in water will attract large numbers of piranhas to it.

Discus
The discus fish looks after its offspring. The parents will guard their eggs and watch over their young. Discus fish even provide food for their youngsters—a special slime produced on the sides of the parents' bodies.

Hatchetfish
This fish uses powerful **fins** at the sides of its body to fly short distances above the surface of the water, especially to escape danger.

Neon tetra
This fish is so-called because its colours are very bright, like those of a neon sign. It only grows to four centimetres in length, and lives in **shoals**. The neon tetra is a very popular aquarium fish, bred in large numbers round the world.

Angelfish
This fish lives in slow-flowing rivers. The flattened angelfish body shape allows it to swim easily between waterplants. The angelfish is **camouflaged**.

Pacu
The pacu is a relative of the dreaded piranha, but rather than eating meat, the pacu uses its teeth to crush the fruits and seeds which fall off trees that overhang the river.

FROGS, TOADS, LIZARDS AND CROCODILES

Frogs thrive in the moist surroundings of the rain forest. Here, some frogs no longer **spawn** in water, but lay their eggs in leaves, where the eggs are kept moist. A number of interesting **reptiles** have also adapted to rain forest life.

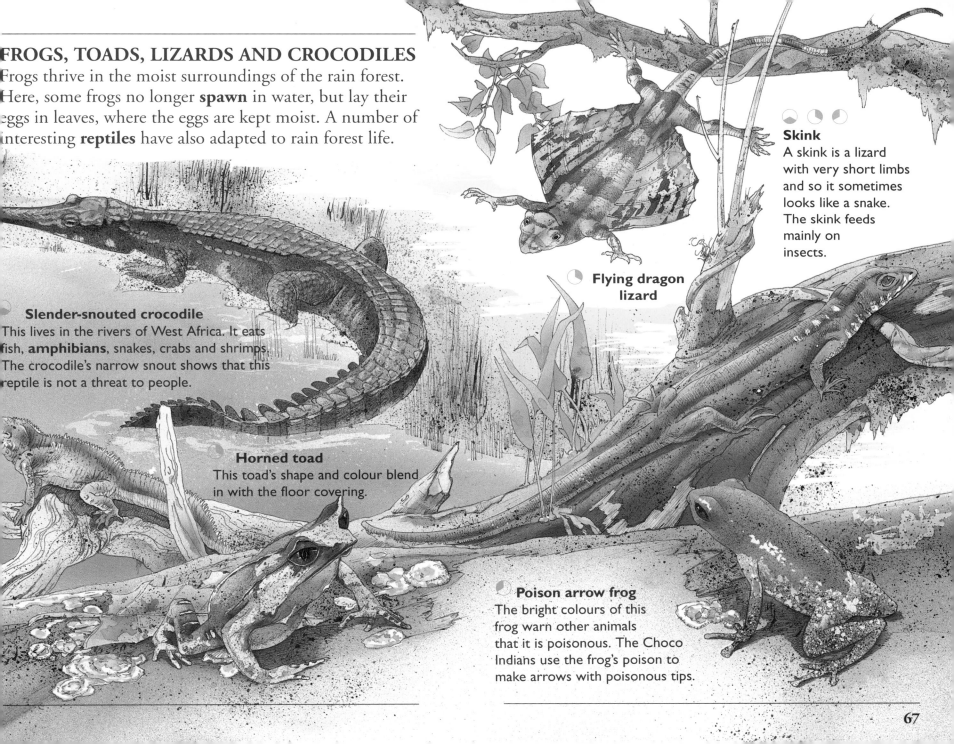

Skink
A skink is a lizard with very short limbs and so it sometimes looks like a snake. The skink feeds mainly on insects.

Flying dragon lizard

Slender-snouted crocodile
This lives in the rivers of West Africa. It eats fish, **amphibians**, snakes, crabs and shrimps. The crocodile's narrow snout shows that this reptile is not a threat to people.

Horned toad
This toad's shape and colour blend in with the floor covering.

Poison arrow frog
The bright colours of this frog warn other animals that it is poisonous. The Choco Indians use the frog's poison to make arrows with poisonous tips.

SNAKES

Snakes can be seen anywhere in the rain forest, from the canopy down to the floor and in the rivers too. The sensitive, forked tongues of these reptiles help them to find their prey. Poisonous snakes have grooved teeth which inject poison. Boas squeeze their prey to death.

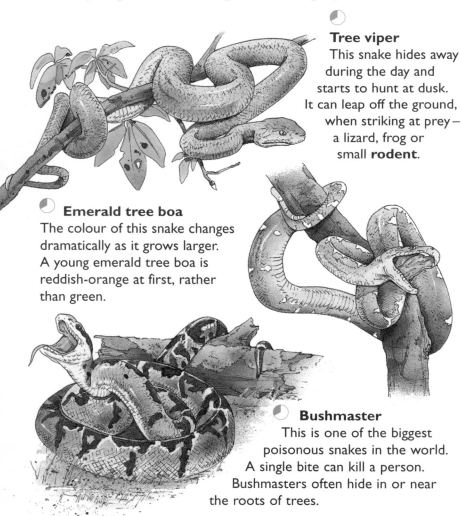

Tree viper
This snake hides away during the day and starts to hunt at dusk. It can leap off the ground, when striking at prey— a lizard, frog or small **rodent**.

Emerald tree boa
The colour of this snake changes dramatically as it grows larger. A young emerald tree boa is reddish-orange at first, rather than green.

Bushmaster
This is one of the biggest poisonous snakes in the world. A single bite can kill a person. Bushmasters often hide in or near the roots of trees.

RAIN FOREST LAYERS

The tallest trees in the rain forest are called emergents. These trees can grow as tall as 35 metres, which is as tall as a twenty-storey building. The uppermost layer is called the canopy.

Trees which make up the forest canopy have long, bare trunks with branches at the top. Most of the treetops form a roof-like layer which prevents sunlight from reaching the forest floor.

Under the thick canopy, there is just enough light for smaller trees and ferns to grow. This layer is called the **understorey**.

The floor of the forest is covered with a layer of fallen leaves, mosses, fungi and dead wood.

RAIN FOREST CREATURES
FROM AROUND THE WORLD

Eclectus parrots

Hummingbird

Tarsier

Tiger

Slender-snouted crocodile

Gorilla

Stick insect

Capybara

Goliath beetle

Golden toad

Iguana

70

OTHER RAIN FOREST ANIMALS

It is often difficult to see animals in the rain forest, even when they are quite big. This is partly why new animals are still being discovered here. The rain forest is also dense, which means that it can be both difficult and dangerous to walk far into the forest, because you could end up lost.

Lemur
This strange monkey-like animal lives only on the island of Madagascar, which is near the tip of Africa.

Okapi
A relative of the giraffe, the okapi was not discovered until 1901. The okapi feeds on plants in the rain forest, and is hard to spot, in spite of its large size. It is about as tall as a person.

Capybara
A capybara is a large rodent and related to a guinea pig. Capybaras live near to water and feed on plants.

TURTLES AND TORTOISES

Tortoises live on the forest floor and eat the fallen fruit and plants found here. Turtles may spend much of their time in rivers and streams. They tend to be carnivorous, and eat creatures like worms and fish. Turtles and tortoises lay eggs, just like birds and other reptiles.

Red-footed tortoise
This tortoise can grow as long as your arm. It is hunted and eaten by people in the forest and faces few other enemies. Some red-footed tortoises have very brightly coloured feet.

Spiny turtle
The sharp spines around the edge of the shell of this turtle are thought to protect it from snakes. It spends some of its time in water, but also wanders on land, finding fruit to eat.

AMAZON RIVER TURTLE
*This turtle grows to a large size, weighing more than a fully-grown person. It lays its eggs on **sandbanks**, when the water level in rivers is low. The young turtles hatch quickly, in a few weeks, before the area is flooded again.*

BIRDS

Most of the thousands of different rain forest birds live in the canopy where there is plenty of food for them to eat – fruit, nuts, flowers and insects. The trees can also be used as nesting sites. Rain forest birds are usually brightly coloured, but their plumage blends in with the background, making birds hard to see in their natural surroundings.

Macaw
The macaw is the biggest of all the world's 330 kinds of parrot.

Toucan
The toucan's bright and distinctive bill hides its long, feather-like tongue. The bill has a honeycomb structure and is light but strong. The toucan's long bill allows it to pick fruits which otherwise could be out of reach.

Parrot
A parrot uses its strong, hooked beak to crack nuts. It holds food in one claw, then bites into the food.

Hummingbird
The hummingbird is the smallest bird in the world. It can beat its wings so fast that it can **hover** like a helicopter. It is the only bird that can fly backwards.

Bird of paradise
A male bird of paradise uses his magnificent plumage to show off to females in special display areas in the forest. The loud calls of the males attract the females.

Hoatzin
The hoatzin is one of the most primitive of all living birds. A young hoatzin hatches with claws on its wings. A hoatzin eats leaves and shoots.

RAIN FOREST CATS

Several wild cats live in the world's rain forests. Wild cats have good eyesight and hearing and a keen sense of smell. They move quietly through the rain forest, becoming most active at night. Wild cats are always hard to spot, in spite of their size, because their markings give them excellent camouflage.

Tiger
A tiger is the largest and strongest wild cat in the world. The tiger is also the only wild cat with a striped coat. A tiger lives on its own and hunts large animals like deer and even baby elephants.

Ocelot
An ocelot climbs trees and sleeps in tree hollows, but it usually prefers to hunt on the ground. The ocelot coat patterning varies from one ocelot to another and no two ocelots have the same markings.

Leopard
A leopard can be spotted or plain black. The black leopard is rare. It was first called a black panther because of its dark coat.

Jaguar
A jaguar will often live close to rivers. A jaguar is a good swimmer and may catch fish, turtles and **caimans** in the water. Young jaguars will stay with their mother for up to two years, while she teaches them to hunt.

THE ELEPHANT AND THE MANATEE

Although it may seem strange, Asian elephants and Amazonian manatees are closely related to each other! Asian elephants have smaller tusks and ears than elephants that live in Africa. Some tame Asian elephants are still used today to help people move timber out of the forests. Amazonian manatees are found in the River Amazon in South America. Manatees spend their whole lives in water.

Asian elephant
There are only about 50,000 of these elephants left, due to their homeland being cut down.

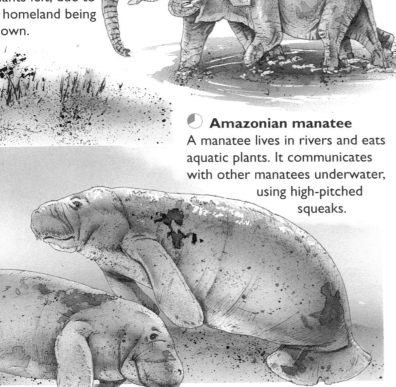

Amazonian manatee
A manatee lives in rivers and eats aquatic plants. It communicates with other manatees underwater, using high-pitched squeaks.

MARMOSETS AND MONKEYS

Having a long tail is very useful for most monkeys and **marmosets**. A monkey's tail is like an extra arm or leg, helping a monkey to hang on a branch as it jumps and swings through the rain forest canopy. But, even so, accidents do happen and occasionally a monkey may fall and injure itself. Youngsters are most likely to get hurt.

Howler monkey
A howler monkey screeches so loudly that its call can be heard over three kilometres away.

Spider monkey
A spider monkey is one of the most acrobatic monkeys. It can use its tail to pick fruit.

Golden lion marmoset
The silky golden marmoset's mane looks like a lion's mane. The marmoset lives in Brazil.

APES

This group includes our closest living relatives in the animal kingdom. The great apes are the gorillas, chimpanzees and orangutans. The gibbons are known as lesser apes. All apes live in family groups. They have powerful arms and expressive faces, but they cannot walk on two legs for any distance.

Gorilla

The plant-eating gorilla is the largest of all apes. Gorillas talk to each other using noises and gestures. The gorilla lives on the ground and sleeps in its forest floor nest.

Orangutan

Sometimes called the 'old man of the woods', the orangutan is more solitary than other apes. Its long, powerful arms and weak legs make the orangutan more at home in the trees than on the ground.

Gibbon

The smallest and most active ape. It lives high up in the treetops.

Chimpanzee

A chimp eats fruit and vegetables, and will hunt for insects and birds' eggs. A chimp may also kill small animals.

RAIN FOREST PEOPLE

Many different groups of people live in the world's rain forests. They are **hunter-gatherers**. Until recently the forest provided all their needs – food, shelter, medicine and clothes. But now their way of life has been disrupted as people from cities have cleared large areas of forest.

The Yanomani
The Amerindians in Brazil live together in a large, round building called a **yano**.

The Penan
Some Penan people still live in the traditional way in the forests of Sarawak, which is part of Malaysia. The Penan hunt animals by creeping up on them and firing poisonous darts from their blowpipes. They also gather plants and fruit. The Penan build their homes out of branches, logs and plants. They use forest plants for medicines.

VANISHING RAIN FORESTS

An area of rain forest the size of a football pitch is being cut down every second of every day. The wood from the trees is being sold and the land is used for farming or mining. This means that the homes of rain forest people, animals and plants are being destroyed for ever. Some **species** have almost certainly become extinct because of forest clearance, before we even knew they existed.

Bird of paradise
Some of the most unusual animals live in rain forests. This bird of paradise is called Wallace's standard wing. It is found on just two Indonesian islands. If it loses its forest home, there will be nowhere else for it to live.

Gone forever
Roads slash through vast areas of former forest. In **deforested** areas, the thin soil covering will blow or wash away in the rain.

AMAZING RAIN FOREST FACTS

- **Largest rain forest** Amazonia is the world's largest area of rain forest. It covers an area of six-and-a-half million square kilometres, which is larger than the whole of Western Europe.

- **Poisonous birds** The first known poisonous birds were discovered in the rain forests of Papua New Guinea in 1992. Hooded pitohuis produce a poison which is similar to that of the poison arrow frogs.

- **Big leaps** Gibbons can leap over ten metres from one tree to another without falling, which is about the same as three cars lined up end-to-end.

- **Big and poisonous** King cobras are the biggest poisonous snakes in the world. Living in Asia, they can grow to a length of nearly six metres.

- **Slowest mammals** Three-toed sloths, which live in the rain forests of South America, are the slowest of all mammals. They move, on the ground, at about two metres per minute.

- **Deadliest spiders** The most deadly spiders in the world live in the rain forests of Brazil. They often hide in shoes and clothes.

- **Killer frogs** Poison arrow frogs can each produce enough poison to kill fifty people.

- **Endangered** The golden lion marmoset is a highly endangered animal. This is because of the destruction of its rain forest homeland.

GLOSSARY

Amphibian A cold-blooded animal which lives on land and in water. Frogs and toads are amphibians.

Caiman A type of crocodile which lives in Central and South America. Unfortunately its skin is often used to make handbags.

Camouflage The way in which an animal hides itself, using its body shape or colour to blend into the background.

Canopy The tallest layer of trees in the rain forest.

Carnivorous An animal which feeds on meat or fish.

Deforest To cut down trees in such large numbers that the forest eventually disappears.

Fin The limb of a fish, used for swimming.

Hover To fly without moving forwards or backwards.

Hunter-gatherers People who live by hunting animals and gathering food.

Marmoset A long-tailed monkey, living in South and Central America. They have silky fur and sharp claws.

Nutrients Foodstuffs which are necessary for life.

Predator An animal which hunts other animals.

Reptile A cold-blooded animal with a scaly skin, such as a crocodile, lizard, tortoise or snake.

Rodent A small mammal characterised by its sharp front teeth.

Sandbank A raised area of sand on the river bottom, which can become exposed when the water level is low.

Shoal A large group of fish.

Spawn Fish or amphibians producing eggs.

Species A group of animals which are related to one another and which only breed within their own kind.

Tropics The hottest part of the world, around the Equator.

Understorey The lower level of the rain forest, beneath the canopy.

Vapour A gas in the atmosphere.

Weevil A type of beetle, with quite a small head and a large body.

Yano The name of the building built as a home by the Yanomani people in Brazil.

POLAR
ANIMALS

CONTENTS

◖ This symbol represents animals that live in the Arctic.
◗ This symbol represents animals that live in the Antarctic.
◖◗ These symbols represent animals that live both in the Arctic and Antarctic.

WHERE ARE THE POLES?

The north and south poles lie at the very ends of the Earth. They are the coldest, windiest, most icy places on our planet. The **North Pole** is in the middle of the frozen Arctic Ocean. The **South Pole** is at the centre of the huge, ice-covered continent of Antarctica.

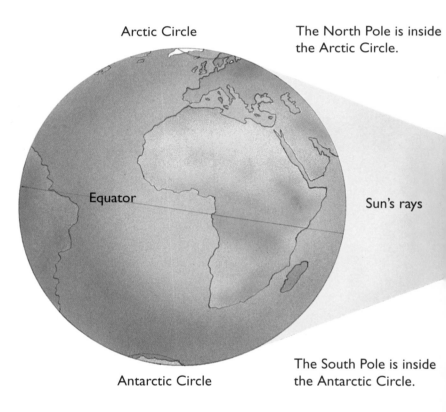

Arctic Circle

The North Pole is inside the Arctic Circle.

Equator

Sun's rays

Antarctic Circle

The South Pole is inside the Antarctic Circle.

The Sun's rays are strongest at the Equator, which is the broadest part of the Earth. The rays are weakest at the poles because the Earth is curved. This means that the poles are always colder than the rest of the Earth.

THE ARCTIC

The landscape in the Arctic is bleak because there is ice everywhere. No trees grow because it is too cold. The North Pole is an important geographical point. It lies on the nought degree line of longitude, an imaginary line that encircles the Earth.

The Arctic Circle
Here there is an area of land called **tundra** where most of the Arctic animals are found.

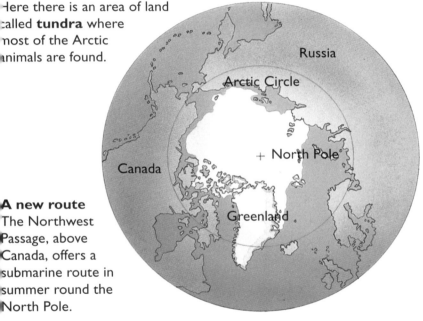

A new route
The Northwest Passage, above Canada, offers a submarine route in summer round the North Pole.

Perpetual darkness
In polar lands, during winter, the Sun never rises. It is dark for months. When it is winter in the Arctic, then it is summer in the Antarctic.

THE ANTARCTIC

The nought degree line of longitude runs round the Earth from the North Pole through to the South Pole. Antarctica is the fifth largest of the world's continents, but it is the only one where there are no local people. It is thought that no one had ever walked here until 1895.

The coldest place on Earth
Temperatures at the South Pole fall as low as -80°C. In spite of this, a number of scientists live and work here.

A remote place
Antarctica is separated from the rest of the world by more than 1,000 kilometres of rough, dangerous seas.

The midnight Sun
During the polar summer, the Sun never sets – it always shines even at midnight. When it is summer in the Antarctic, then it is winter in the Arctic.

ICE ALL AROUND

There is ice everywhere at the poles, as far as the eye can see. In the Arctic, an ice sheet covers most of the island of Greenland. Here the Quarayaq Glacier moves at a speed of up to twenty metres per hour every day. It is the fastest flowing glacier in the world.

The ice sheet covering the continent of Antarctica is up to four kilometres thick and millions of years old. It contains 90 per cent of all the ice on Earth, and it never melts. If it did, the sea level round the world would rise by up to one hundred metres, causing gigantic floods.

1 Growlers
These are small icebergs that have broken off from a big iceberg or the end of a glacier.

2 Tabular icebergs
These are huge and are characterised by flat tops and sides.

3 Glaciers
Over thousands of years rivers of ice flow very slowly down a mountain or an ice cap, forming a glacier. Many glaciers eventually reach the sea.

4 Crevasses
Crevasses are deep cracks in the ice that are formed as a glacier moves along.

5 Bergy bits
Bergy bits are chunks of ice that have broken away from large icebergs.

6 Icebergs
Icebergs are gigantic chunks of ice that have broken off from an ice shelf or the end of a glacier. Only about one-eighth of an iceberg shows above the water.

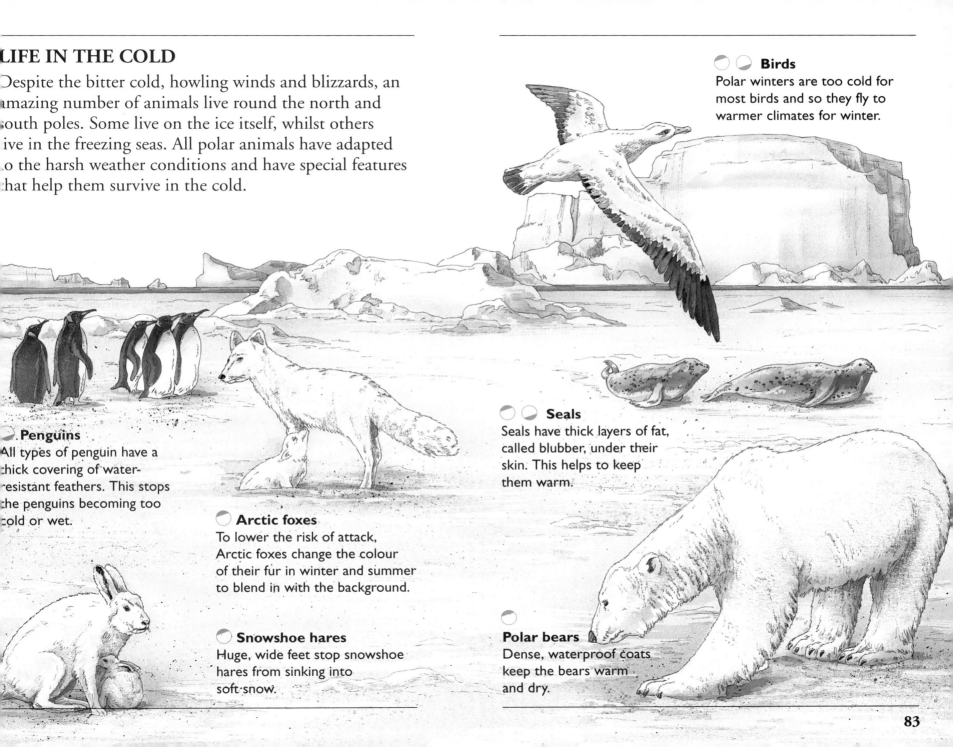

LIFE IN THE COLD

Despite the bitter cold, howling winds and blizzards, an amazing number of animals live round the north and south poles. Some live on the ice itself, whilst others live in the freezing seas. All polar animals have adapted to the harsh weather conditions and have special features that help them survive in the cold.

Birds
Polar winters are too cold for most birds and so they fly to warmer climates for winter.

Seals
Seals have thick layers of fat, called blubber, under their skin. This helps to keep them warm.

Penguins
All types of penguin have a thick covering of water-resistant feathers. This stops the penguins becoming too cold or wet.

Arctic foxes
To lower the risk of attack, Arctic foxes change the colour of their fur in winter and summer to blend in with the background.

Snowshoe hares
Huge, wide feet stop snowshoe hares from sinking into soft snow.

Polar bears
Dense, waterproof coats keep the bears warm and dry.

ANIMALS OF THE POLES

Southern elephant seal

Albatross

Arctic fox

Caribou

Penguin

Walrus

Polar bear

Weddell seal

85

SEALS

Seals live in both the Arctic and the Antarctic. They spend most of their time swimming and diving for fish and other seafood. Seals are well equipped for swimming – they have strong flippers, and their sleek, streamlined bodies cut through the water easily.

○ Southern elephant seal
This giant is the largest of all seals and can weigh up to 4,000 kilograms – as much as a small truck – and can be up to six metres long.

Diving for food
Although they are **mammals** and breathe air, seals can hold their breath for long periods as they dive underwater for food.

Arctic seals

Antarctic seals

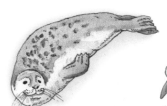

○ Harp seal
Harp seal pups are born with fluffy, white fur that darkens as the seal grows older.

○ Hooded seal
The 'bag' on the nose of the male swells when the seal becomes excited.

○ Ringed seal
The smallest of the polar seals, the ringed seal is only about one metre long.

○ Leopard seal
The leopard seal is a fierce hunter and uses its sharp teeth to catch penguins.

○ Weddell seal
The Weddell seal uses its teeth to gnaw **breathing holes** in the ice.

○ Crabeater seal
Despite its name, this seal mainly eats **krill**, sieving them through its teeth.

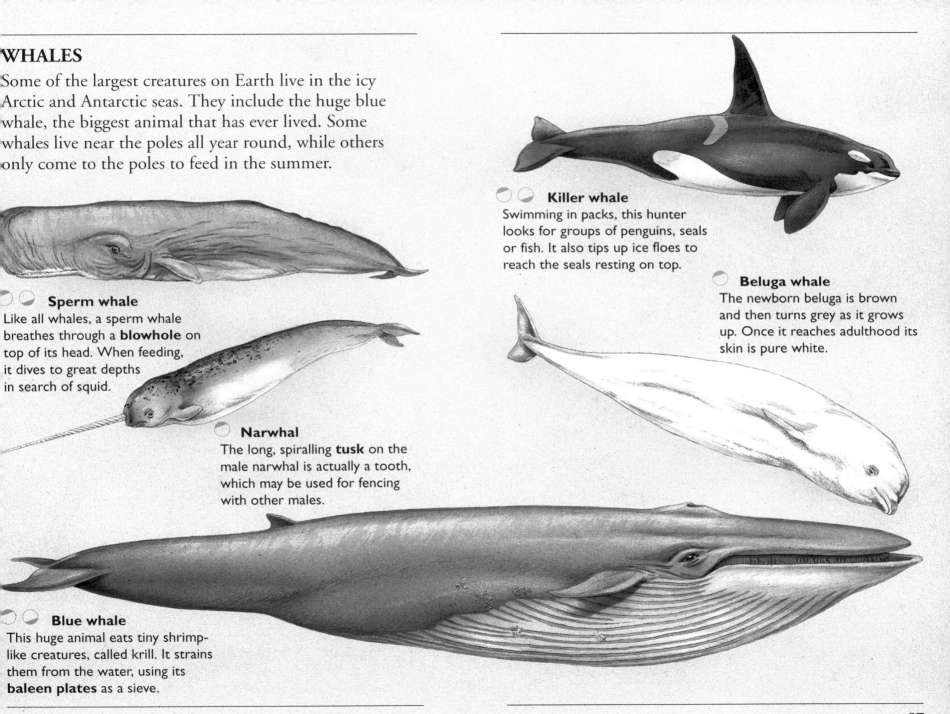

WHALES

Some of the largest creatures on Earth live in the icy Arctic and Antarctic seas. They include the huge blue whale, the biggest animal that has ever lived. Some whales live near the poles all year round, while others only come to the poles to feed in the summer.

Sperm whale
Like all whales, a sperm whale breathes through a **blowhole** on top of its head. When feeding, it dives to great depths in search of squid.

Narwhal
The long, spiralling **tusk** on the male narwhal is actually a tooth, which may be used for fencing with other males.

Killer whale
Swimming in packs, this hunter looks for groups of penguins, seals or fish. It also tips up ice floes to reach the seals resting on top.

Beluga whale
The newborn beluga is brown and then turns grey as it grows up. Once it reaches adulthood its skin is pure white.

Blue whale
This huge animal eats tiny shrimp-like creatures, called krill. It strains them from the water, using its **baleen plates** as a sieve.

PENGUINS

There are no penguins in the Arctic, but several different types can be found in Antarctica. Although penguins cannot fly and they may look clumsy on land, their sleek bodies, partly webbed feet and flipper-like wings make penguins fast, graceful swimmers.

Speedy divers
Penguins can swim really fast and shoot out of the sea onto rocks.

The Emperor
After the female lays the egg, the male looks after the egg until it hatches. Standing in the cold and wind for two months in the winter, the male emperor penguin eats nothing and hardly moves. He balances the egg on his feet with a flap of furry skin.

The Adelie
One of the few birds native to Antarctica.

The Gentoo
The gentoo breeds in huge colonies.

The Rockhopper
It can climb steep rocks by hopping.

The Chinstrap
This penguin defends its young fiercely.

The Macaroni
Lays two eggs; only the larger one hatches.

The King
This big penguin eats fish, squid and krill.

BIRDS

Some birds live at the poles all year round. Others nest and breed at the poles in their millions in the spring and summer when there is plenty of food. The most famous Antarctic birds are penguins. But petrels, skuas and albatrosses also nest on islands along the Antarctic coast.

Arctic tern
Each year the Arctic tern flies from the Arctic to Australia and back again, a distance of more than 40,000 kilometres. This is the longest journey made by any animal in the world.

Kittiwake
Building its nest on cliffs keeps the kittiwake safe from foxes and bears.

Puffin
A puffin can hold as many as fifty herrings at the same time in its colourful beak.

Little auk
This is one of fourteen species of auk, and lives on the Arctic cliffs.

In winter, some birds survive by eating roots and berries found under the snow, or small mammals and insects.

Wandering albatross
Soaring effortlessly over southern seas on its long, narrow wings, the albatross nests on islands along the Antarctic coast.

Gannet
The gannet catches fish by diving into the sea at speed, its wings neatly folded.

Guillemot
The guillemot breeds in the summer when there are plenty of fish to feed on.

Snowy owl
Unlike most owls, the snowy owl hunts during the day rather than at night.

POLAR BEARS

Polar bears live in the Arctic all year round, roaming along the coasts or floating out to sea on ice floes. Polar bears are twice as big as tigers and are powerful hunters. They eat mainly seals. A bear will wait by a seal's breathing hole until it comes up for air. Then the bear pounces, killing the seal with a single blow using its powerful paw.

WALRUSES

Walruses live in large **colonies** along the coasts of the Arctic Ocean. They hunt for food on the seabed, using their bristly moustaches to feel for clams, crabs and sea urchins. Walruses root food out with their tusks and snouts. Their tusks can grow longer than your arm. On land, walruses bask in the Sun to warm themselves.

Small ears reduce heat loss.

● **Polar bear**

Excellent sense of smell to detect food.

The polar bear's fur is thick, warm and waterproof.

Fur on the bottom of the paws stops the bear from slipping on the smooth ice.

Large, sharp claws help the bear to grip the ice and hold on to slippery seals.

Partly webbed toes help the bear to swim well.

The walrus uses its tusks, which are long teeth, for self-defence and for making air holes in the ice.

A walrus has very small eyes because the polar waters are too murky to see clearly and so it doesn't need large eyes.

Pinky-brown skin turns deeper pink as the walrus sunbathes.

● **Walrus**

Walruses sometimes sleep in the water, hooking themselves onto the ice with their tusks. Large males can grow over four metres long and weigh up to 1,800 kilograms.

LIFE BELOW THE ICE

There is an amazing, unseen world under the polar ice, where hundreds of different kinds of fish, shellfish and tiny creatures live. Tiny plants grow on the undersides of the ice and are eaten by small creatures such as krill. These, in turn, are eaten by larger animals such as fish and whales.

PINK ICE FIELDS

Only a few very hardy plants can grow round the South Pole. Crusty **lichens** and tiny plants called **algae** turn patches of the ice pinky-red.
A pink pigment helps to protect the algae from the Sun's harsh glare.

Krill

The krill is a tiny **crustacean** that lives in huge swarms. It is an important part of the **food web** and is the main food of the blue whale.

Sea slug

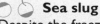

Despite the freezing temperatures of the polar seas, the sea slug, shellfish, sponge and sea urchin live under the ice.

Starfish

The Arctic starfish does not grow as big as starfish in warmer seas.

Antarctic ice fish

Many polar fish, such as the Antarctic ice fish, have a kind of antifreeze in their blood to stop them from freezing solid.

Jellyfish

Some jellyfish have poisonous tentacles that they use to kill small fish.

Cod

Found in the warmer Arctic waters, the cod is caught by people, for food.

SURVIVING ABOVE AND BELOW THE ICE

Little auk

Arctic tern

Puffin

Walrus

Gannet

Penguin

Narwhal

Beluga whale

Killer whale

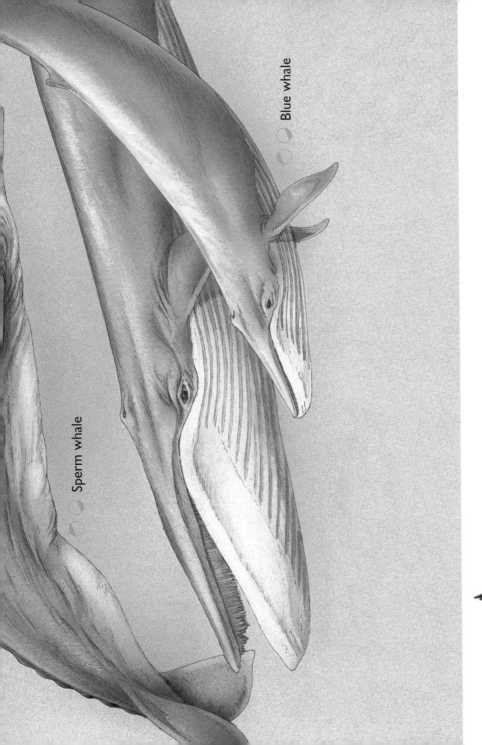

Blue whale

Sperm whale

SAVING THE POLES

The poles are fragile areas, and need to be protected for the future. The poles are among the last unspoilt places on Earth, and home to some of the world's rarest animals. They are also rich in resources such as fish, oil and valuable metals.

In the past, millions of whales, seals and penguins were killed for their meat, skins and other products. Several types of whales were almost hunted to extinction. Today, most countries have banned whaling.

The poles are being spoilt by rubbish left behind by scientists and tourists. Environmentalists would like to clean up the litter, which is ugly and dangerous to the polar wildlife.

Oil spills from tankers are a threat to wildlife. Scientists are worried that the Antarctic will be spoilt by exploration for oil and minerals. Scientists would like the Antarctic to be a protected World Park.

EXPLORING THE POLES

Polar explorers face many problems. They must take the right clothes and supplies for the harsh conditions, and cope with hazards such as shifting ice and hungry polar bears. The most successful explorers are those who copy the ways Arctic people survive.

HUSKIES

Using husky dogs made Amundsen's journey much easier. Scott's men used up a lot of energy by pulling their own sledges.

Robert Peary

The American explorer Robert Peary was probably the first person to reach the North Pole. He got there in 1909. Some people claim, however, that another American, Frederick Cook, beat Peary to it.

Robert Scott

Robert Scott led the British expedition to the Antarctic. The team arrived at the South Pole on 17 January 1912, just thirty four days after Amundsen. On their way back to base camp, Scott and his entire team died. Scott wrote a diary that was found later.

Roald Amundsen

Amundsen was the first person ever to reach the South Pole. With his party of four Norwegian explorers and a pack of fifty two dogs to pull sledges, he set out in October 1911. The party arrived at the Pole two months later, on 14 December 1911, almost a century after the continent of Antarctica was first discovered.

Ranulph Fiennes

In 1993, two British explorers, Ranulph Fiennes and Michael Stroud, walked farther across Antarctica than anyone else had ever been. But, even with the help of hi-tech clothing and equipment, this two-man team suffered from severe **frostbite** and starvation.

PEOPLE OF THE POLES

The local Arctic people, called the Inuit, have lived near the North Pole for thousands of years and are experts at Arctic survival. They used to wander from place to place, hunting seals and polar bears. Today, many Inuit live in small towns.

Some Inuit remain **nomadic** and continue their traditional ways, living from the land and sea.

Many Inuit live in settlements and use modern **skidoos** for transport.

Inuit lifestyle

The Inuit hunted seals as a source of food. They also used the seal skins for making clothes and tents, and the seal blubber for oil to burn in lamps.

The Inuit travelled by husky sledge and **kayak**. Igloos, built of blocks of ice, were used for shelter on hunting trips – igloos are surprisingly warm and cosy.

Education in schools for Inuit children is now an important part of daily life.

Warm clothes, often made from animal skins, protect the Inuit against the cold.

AMAZING POLAR FACTS

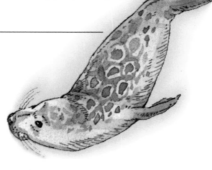

- **Penguins** Penguins can dive to depths of 265 metres. They may stay underwater without coming up to breathe for as long as eighteen minutes.

- **Narwhals** The long, twisted tusk of narwhals was once thought to be the horn of a unicorn. Only male narwhals have a tusk. This grows out of their lips and can reach a length of nearly three metres.

- **Killer whales** Killer whales can break through ice sheets which are a metre thick. They do this to throw seals resting on top of the ice sheet, into the sea. The whales can then catch the seals more easily in water. A killer whale may eat as many as twenty four seals in one meal.

- **Blue whales** Baby blue whales are the fastest growing creatures on Earth. They grow in weight from less than a milligram to twenty six tonnes in under two years. The calls of adult blue whales can be heard by other whales, from one end of an ocean to the other. These calls are the loudest sound made by any living animal.

- **Polar bears** Polar bears have no fear of people. They will hunt us if they are hungry. This makes polar bears the most dangerous mammals on the planet.

- **Icebergs** The largest iceberg ever recorded had an area of 31,000 square kilometres, making it bigger than the country of Belgium.

- **Arctic terns** An Arctic tern had a ring fitted to its leg when it was a chick in July 1955. The bird was then found less than a year later in Australia. It would have flown a distance of 22,530 kilometres to reach this continent.

GLOSSARY

Algae Tiny plants that grow in water or on wet land.

Baleen plates Sieve-like plates in a whale's mouth. These plates allow it to take food out of the water.

Blowhole A small hole in the top of a whale's head that the whale breathes through.

Breathing hole A hole that a seal makes in the ice so that it can breathe.

Colony A large collection of birds or animals that lives in one area.

Crustacean An animal that is covered in a hard, protective shell.

Food web A term that describes the food cycle between plants and animals. For example, insects eat plants, birds eat insects, foxes eat birds, and when the fox dies, its body decomposes and fertilizes the plants.

Frostbite Freezing of parts of the body, often fingers and toes. This happens if a person is in a cold climate for too long, without suitable clothes.

Kayak A type of canoe where a person sits enclosed in the boat.

Krill A tiny creature that is covered in a hard shell and which lives in huge numbers.

Lichen A small plant that grows clinging to rocks and stones.

Mammal An animal that breathes air and can regulate its temperature.

Nomadic A way of life where people move around a large area with their homes and never settle in one place for longer than a few months.

North Pole The North Pole is an imaginary point that lies on the sea floor and not on the surface of the ice. It marks the northernmost point of the Earth's axis.

Skidoo A motorised sledge that can travel across the snow and ice at high speeds.

South Pole The South Pole is an imaginary point, marking the southern point of the Earth's axis.

Tundra An area of land in the Arctic that is frozen in winter but thaws on the surface during summer.

Tusk A long tooth of an animal that has grown outside the mouth.

QUEST FOR NEW
ANIMALS

CONTENTS

FINDING NEW ANIMALS

Every year, new creatures are being discovered on Earth. These can include quite large animals. Some amazing discoveries have been made over the past 100 years, and more finds, perhaps even a living dinosaur, may still await discovery.

White rhinoceros

White rhinoceroses are among the largest animals on Earth, so they should be easy enough to spot. Until 1900 however, they were believed to live only in southern Africa. Then a group was spotted over 3,000 kilometres away, proving that there are at least two sets of white rhinos in Africa.

Neon tetras

In any shop that sells tropical fish, you will see neon tetras. They are now such popular aquarium fish that it is surprising to learn that they were not discovered until 1936. Neon tetras originally come from the river Amazon in South America.

Yemeni monitor lizard

Sometimes you don't even need to go out to wild places to find new animals today. This lizard was recognised as being unknown to science by a **zoologist** who saw it in a television programme in 1985.

A BIG MISTAKE

Once it was thought that all the world's big animals had been found, but we now know better. In order to be officially recognised, a new animal must be obtained – either dead or alive – so that it can be described in detail and **classified**. This means giving it a scientific name, and fitting it in with other animals, as part of the animal kingdom. The first new animal so classified is called the **type specimen**.

Baron Cuvier
This famous zoologist said in 1812 that he felt it was unlikely there were any large animals still undiscovered. He was wrong! Today, the search for new animals continues. It is called cryptozoology, from the Greek word *cryptos* meaning hidden, and *zoology*, the study of animals.

The tapir's nose can be used like a hand to pull down branches.

Malayan tapir
The existence of this tapir was confirmed by Diard, a pupil of Baron Cuvier's, just seven years after the Baron had suggested there were no more such animals to be found. Although there had been earlier reports of Malayan tapirs dating back to 1772, Cuvier himself had not believed them.

Giant panda
When the French explorer Père David was travelling through China in 1869 he saw a skin of a black and white animal which he assumed had been a bear.

It was, in fact, a giant panda which has since become one of the best-known animals in the world, although today it is highly **endangered** in the wild.

Okapi
Local African stories about forest donkeys led Sir Harry Johnston to search for these animals. He thought they might be a new type of zebra. Then he learnt that they had two hooves on each foot, unlike zebras and other members of the horse family, who have one. In 1901, when the okapi was discovered, it turned out to be a relative of the giraffe.

THE SCOPE OF THE SEA

Stories about sea monsters have been told for thousands of years. The world's oceans are some of the least-known areas on the planet, and they may well hide large creatures in their depths. Only if a body is washed up on a beach, or caught in the nets of a fishing boat can the existence of such animals be proved beyond doubt.

The kraken

This monster was believed to live in the seas off the coast of Norway. The kraken had many large arms, called tentacles, and was greatly feared. It was said to drag sailors overboard, and even destroy ships' masts with its powerful tentacles. Stories about the kraken may have been based on early sightings of giant squids.

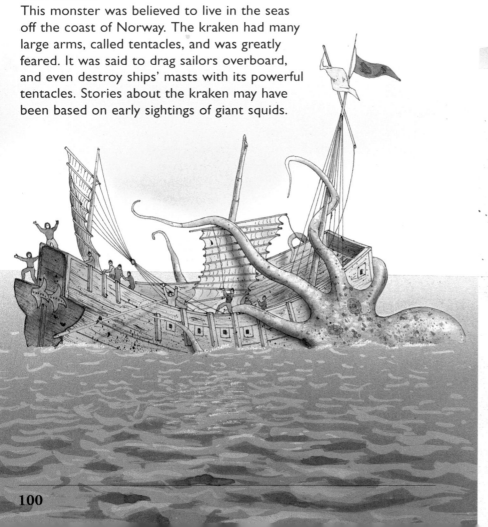

A MYSTERY IN A JAR

Scientists have recently tested samples from a huge, unidentified carcass which was washed ashore on a North American beach in 1896. The tests showed that the animal was a previously unknown giant octopus. Its body was known to have been 30 metres long.

Giant squid

The biggest giant squid ever found was eighteen metres long. Even bigger squids – perhaps ten times as large – may live in the world's oceans. Scars thought to be caused by their tentacles have been seen on dead whales.

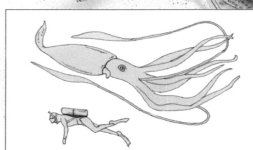

RELATIVE SIZE

Giant squids can be nine times as long as a large adult, and can have tentacles twice as long as their own bodies.

MYSTERIES OF THE DEEP

Recent deep sea exploration has meant that completely new types of fish have been found in the ocean depths. Some have proved to be living fossils, such as the goblin shark. Fossils of this shark were first found in the mid-1800s. Each had a strange protrusion, like a shovel, on the head above the jaws. Amazingly, a living example of a goblin shark was then caught in deep water close to the Japanese island of Yokohama in 1897. These sharks probably use their shovel-like projections to dig for worms on the seabed.

Coelacanth

Coelacanths were thought to have become **extinct** about 60 million years ago. Then in 1938, a trawler caught a strange fish which none of the fishermen on board could identify. This mysterious fish finally proved to be a coelacanth. It was fourteen years before another specimen was caught.

Megamouth shark

So called because of its huge mouth, the megamouth shark was discovered in 1976 as the result of a freak accident. One of these massive fish became caught up in a ship's anchor, and was hauled to the surface from a depth of about 150 metres. This megamouth shark was caught near the Hawaiian islands, off the west coast of America. Since then, others have been caught near Japan and Australia. The shark's mouth contains more than 100 rows of teeth which it uses to sieve tiny plankton.

RELATIVE SIZE

A megamouth shark is about three times the size of a large adult person, but only half the size of a great white shark. It is not dangerous to people.

Parasitic angler fish

One of a group of strange, ugly deep-sea fish, this particular angler fish is actually made up of three fish. The large female has two much smaller males permanently attached to her body. Part of the dorsal fin on the back of other angler fish has changed into a lure, looking rather like a fishing rod. This hangs down in front of the mouth and attracts small fish, which can then be snapped up.

WHALES AND SEALS

Although giant whales used to be heavily hunted by whaling fleets, smaller whales were not killed in such large quantities. This may explain why several types of smaller whales remained unknown until very recently. Unlike fish, however, these marine **mammals** must come up to the surface to breathe, so they are perhaps more likely to be seen.

Shepherd's beaked whale

In 1933, one of these whales became stranded on the western coast of North Island, New Zealand. Others have since been washed up on the coast of South America. They can grow to over six metres long.

Andrew's beaked whale

This whale was also first found on a New Zealand beach. Only eight specimens are known to scientists at present, with the first being identified in 1904.

They are thought to live in cool waters, and can grow to a length of at least four metres. They have distinctive beaks by which they are recognised.

Hawaiian monk seal

Living near the Hawaiian islands, this is the most recent seal to have been discovered, in 1905. Unfortunately, since then it has been heavily hunted for its fur, and probably no more than 1,000 remain alive. These seals sometimes look slightly greenish, because of microscopic **algae** growing on their fur.

Baja California porpoise

Found only in the Gulf of California, on America's western coast, this porpoise was unknown to science until 1950. It is the smallest known member of the whale family, growing to a size of a tall child and weighing less than a large dog!

SECRETS OF FROGS AND TOADS

Frogs and toads (**amphibians**) must live in damp surroundings because they breathe through their skins, which have to be kept moist. Many frogs and toads can be found in the world's rain forests, where it rains almost every day and the air is very humid.

Hairy frog

Living in the rain forests of West Africa, male hairy frogs grow folds of skin, which look rather like hairs, during the breeding period. The folds help these frogs to breathe more easily. Hairy frogs were first found in 1900.

Goliath frog

The rain forests of West Africa are also home to goliath frogs, the largest frogs in the world. Goliath frogs swim in fast flowing streams and were discovered in 1906.

RELATIVE SIZE

Poison arrow frogs

No one knows how many different types of poison arrow frogs there are in Central and South America. This deadly one lives in Colombia, and was first recorded in 1973.

Mallorcan midwife toad

Fossilized remains of these toads were first discovered in 1977, on the island of Mallorca in the Mediterranean. Scientists believed they were extinct, but living examples were then found in 1980. These toads are very secretive, hiding in cracks in cliff faces. The males wrap the eggs around their back legs.

DEADLY DARTS

Darts tipped with the poison from some frogs are used by hunters to kill animals.

Gold toad

This is perhaps one of the most beautiful toads in the world, living in a valley in Panama, Central America. Gold toads first became known in 1929, but since then their numbers have fallen greatly, and they may soon become extinct.

BEWARE OF THE DRAGON

All reptiles are **cold-blooded**, so they are most common in tropical parts of the world. There they can remain active throughout the year, without having to **hibernate** over the winter. Some reptiles are confined to small islands. The Indonesian island of Komodo, for example, is home to the largest lizard in the world, the Komodo dragon, first heard of in Europe in 1912.

Weber's sailfin dragon

These lizards are found on two of the Moluccan islands, off the coast of southeast Asia. They grow to more than one metre long, and are so called because of the crest running down the centre of their back and tail. They were first discovered in 1911.

Komodo dragon

These huge **carnivorous** lizards can grow to over three metres long. They are fearsome hunters, eating pigs, goats and sometimes even people. Why such large lizards should have **evolved** on the small island of Komodo is unknown. They may have originally preyed on **pygmy** elephants which once lived there.

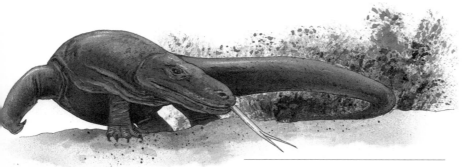

Pancake tortoise

Tortoises usually have hard, domed shells, but that of the pancake tortoise is very flat and soft. These particular tortoises, discovered in 1903, live in rocky areas of East Africa. They use their flattened shape to hide under stones and escape **predators**.

Light shells allow pancake tortoises to move very fast.

New Guinea crocodile

In 1908 a skull found in Papua New Guinea was proved to belong to the New Guinea crocodile. Up until then everyone had believed that the only crocodile living in the area was the Indo-Pacific crocodile. The New Guinea crocodile is smaller than its Indo-Pacific relative, only growing to four metres in length, and is also less aggressive.

HEAD OF A NEW GUINEA CROCODILE

The jaws of this crocodile are narrow, suggesting that it feeds mainly on fish.

NEW BIRDS

Birds that live in remote parts of the world – even quite large birds – have remained unknown, although they may be familiar to local people. Reports of new birds come every year, and almost certainly there are more birds to be discovered, especially in the world's rain forest regions.

Congo peacock pheasant

While in Zaire, central Africa during 1913, an **ornithologist** called Dr Chapin saw a strange feather in a local headdress which he did not recognise. It came from a bird known locally as *mbulu*, but on his return to America, Dr Chapin still could not identify it. Many years later, in a Belgian museum, he saw two stuffed birds whose feathers matched the one in the headdress. He returned to Zaire in 1937, and found a living Congo peacock pheasant for the first time.

Mikado pheasant

Unknown tail feathers in another local headdress, on the island of Taiwan, near China, started the search for this Asian pheasant. Its magnificent tail feathers make up about half the mikado pheasant's total length. It was finally found in 1906.

Ribbon-tailed bird of paradise

Only the cock bird has these long, trailing tail feathers, which can be up to one metre long. They are about three-and-a-half times as long as the bird's body. This bird of paradise was unknown outside its Papua New Guinean homeland until 1936.

Long-whiskered owlet

This tiny owl's home is in the Andean mountains of northern Peru, where it was only discovered in 1976. The long-whiskered owlet is so called because of the whisker-like feathers on the sides of its face.

Imperial and Vo Quy's pheasants

Both these pheasants live in Vietnam, southeast Asia. The imperial was first found there in 1923, and has since been bred in **aviaries**. Vo Quy's pheasant remains more mysterious. It was originally seen in 1964. It is hoped that these pheasants will be bred at Vietnam's Hanoi Zoo.

Imperial

Vo Quy's

EXCITING SIGHTINGS

Some animals are very secretive and hard to spot, which may make people think that they have died out. Those animals which live in trees and rarely, if ever, come down to the ground, can be particularly hard to see.

Celebes palm civet (Asia)
Looking rather like a dog, this mammal lives on the island of Sulawesi, which used to be called Celebes, in Indonesia. No sightings were made for over 30 years, and people believed it was extinct. Then one was seen and actually photographed in a palm tree in 1978.

Pygmy hog (Asia)
In 1971, a pygmy hog caught in India, provin that it was not extinct as scientists had thou

Tasmanian wolf
(Australia)
This is not really a wolf, but a **marsupial**, related to the kangaroo. Blamed for attacks on sheep, it was heavily hunted and was believed to be extinct by 1936. Recently, so many Tasmanian wolves have been seen and even photographed that zoologists are convinced they still survive in parts of Australia.

Taipan (Australia)
This deadly snake was first seen in 1867, but it was not until 1923 that more were found.

Yellow-tailed woolly monkey (Americas)
Zoologists had been looking for this
primate for a long time. They finally
found it in 1974, when they came across
one being kept as a pet in a village in Peru,
South America.

Thin-spined porcupine (Americas)
This rat-like creature lives in the trees
of southeastern Brazil. First seen in
1818, there had recently been fears about
its survival, until two were sighted in 1986.

Leadbeater's possum (Australia)
Leadbeater's possum was once believed to have
become extinct. But in 1961, two zoologists carrying
out a survey in the state of Victoria found one in a tree.
After more searching, they came across three others.

BIRDS BACK FROM THE BRINK

Some birds have been rediscovered many years after they were believed to have become extinct. If the numbers of a specific bird or animal fall below a certain level however, they will not be able to breed properly. They are then almost certainly doomed to extinction.

Bermuda petrel (Americas)
This sea bird lives today on the small Castle Harbour islands, close to the island of Bermuda in the Atlantic Ocean. During the 1620s this petrel was thought to have been wiped out due to hunting by sailors and black rats eating the birds' eggs. Amazingly – more than 300 years later – the Bermuda petrel is still alive.

Madagascan serpent eagle (Africa)
After the last sighting of this snake-eating eagle was made in 1930, it was not seen again until the summer of 1988. A dead Madagascan serpent eagle was then found two years later, and finally, in 1993, a live eagle was caught and photographed. Conservation work is now being carried out to help these rare eagles to survive.

Takahe (Australasia)
Living on South Island, New Zealand, the takahe was first seen alive by European settlers in 1849. No further sightings were recorded for nearly 30 years, and this was followed by a further gap until 1948. In that year, a doctor called Geoffrey Orbell set out in search of the takahe, with help from the local Maori people. He found the valley where these birds still live, and today they are fully protected.

PARROTS' PARADISE

There are 330 different types of parrots in the world today. In less than ten years, three new parrots have been found in South America alone, and there is still a strong chance that more new ones may be found.

El Oro conure
This parrot is named after the part of Ecuador in South America where it was first seen in 1980. The El Oro conure feeds on figs and other fruits in the treetops, and lives in flocks of between four and twelve birds.

Kawall's Amazon parrot
This mysterious parrot differs from other Amazon parrots by having a bald patch of skin round its lower bill. Until 1989, it was confused with the mealy Amazon, which it otherwise looks like.

Amazonian parrotlet
Parrotlets are among the smallest of all parrots, and they are hard to spot in the trees, because of their mainly green coloration. The Amazonian parrotlet was originally sighted in 1985. It lives in eastern Peru.

ANIMALS IN HIDING

Many large animals have been in existence for thousands of years but have only recently been discovered. This is often because they live in remote parts of the world. Some smaller animals have simply not been noticed.

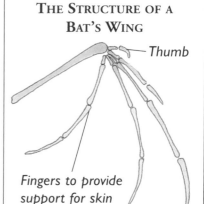

Thumb

Fingers to provide support for skin

Mountain gorilla
From the 1860s onwards, stories of monstrous apes were brought back by European explorers. But it was not until 1902 that scientific proof of their existence was finally obtained.
A mountain gorilla is larger than its lowland relatives. Sadly, this vegetarian ape is now endangered because it is being hunted.

Kitti's hog-nosed bat
This bat is one of the world's smallest mammals. It is no bigger than a bumblebee, with a nose which looks like the snout of a pig! These bats were first found in a cave in Thailand, southeast Asia, in 1973.

Giant forest hog
Living in the dense rain forest areas of Africa, this giant hog is the largest pig in the world. It stands nearly a metre tall at the shoulder, and can be over two metres long. The existence of the giant forest hog was confirmed in 1904.

Pygmy chimpanzee
A new type of chimpanzee was discovered in Africa during the 1920s. The pygmy chimpanzee is slimmer than the ordinary chimpanzee, with a blacker face. It lives in tropical forests, gathering fruit and other food in the trees, and uses its long arms to swing from branch to branch.

Donkey pig
The real name of this wild pig is the chacoan peccary. Local people call it the donkey pig because of the shape of its ears. It was thought to have died out during the last ice age, over 10,000 years ago. But in 1974 it was discovered that the chacoan peccary had actually survived.

STEALTHY HUNTERS

Quiet and secretive by nature, wild cats are never easy to spot. Most wild cats are **nocturnal**, hunting at night, which means they are less likely to be seen. Tracks, and signs of their kills, are the best clues to their presence in an area. During the 1980s, several new cats were found.

King cheetah
As well as spots, the king cheetah's coat is marked with black stripes. It was first reported in 1926, from the African country of Zimbabwe. It was not until the 1980s that the king cheetah was proved to be a rare tabby form of the ordinary cheetah.

Iriomote cat
The Iriomote cat was unknown until 1967, and is very rare indeed. It is named after the island of Iriomote, to the south of Japan, where it lives. Only about 100 of these cats live on the island, and they are sometimes caught and eaten by local people.

Tshushima cat
This cat lives on the island of Tshushima, between Japan and South Korea. It is thought that less than 100 of these cats live there. The Tshushima cat was first discovered in 1988, but little is known about its habits so far.

Onza
Back in the early 1500s, the first Spanish explorers wrote about a large, long-legged wild cat which lived in Mexico. It wasn't until 1986 that the existence of the onza was at last confirmed. These cats hunt deer, and probably other large animals.

111

GATHERING THE CLUES

Finding new animals is not just a matter of luck. Listening to people talking about their local wildlife can give clues. Studying **hunting trophies**, carvings and paintings for evidence of unknown animals are all useful methods of locating new species. These factors helped to find the **herbivorous** animals on this page.

Vu Quang ox

In 1992, zoologists working in Vietnam in southeast Asia, saw some unusual horns in the homes of local hunters. Those horns came from the Vu Quang ox, which may be a relative of the cow and the antelope.

Kouprey

This ox, also from Asia, may be truly wild, or it may be a **domesticated** animal that has gone back to the wild. Carvings of the kouprey are known to date back over 800 years, but its existence was only officially confirmed in 1937.

Mountain buffalo

This tiny buffalo lives in the mountainous forest on the large island of Sulawesi, off the southeast coast of Asia. It is about as high as an adult's shoulder, and was first recorded in 1910.

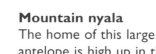

Mountain nyala

The home of this large antelope is high up in the Sahatu mountains of Ethiopia in the northeast of Africa. There it lives and grazes on the flat areas called plateaus. It too was discovered in 1910.

BAMBOO LEMUR

The only place this lemur is found is on the island of Madagascar, off the southeastern coast of Africa. Golden bamboo lemurs were seen for the first time in 1985. They are so called because they feed only on bamboo. Another, larger type of bamboo lemur, thought to have become extinct in the early 1900s, was rediscovered on Madagascar in 1972.

DO THEY EXIST?

The search goes on for mysterious creatures that may live on our planet. So far we have no proof that any of the animals shown here do actually exist, but each one is claimed to have been seen a number of times. One of the most likely to be found in the future is probably the Congo swamp monster, which may be a living **sauropod**-type of dinosaur. It is said to live in water, using its long neck to feed on the hard rain forest chocolate fruits which grow along the riverbanks.

Congo swamp monster

This animal has been reported in a part of Africa which has hardly changed at all since dinosaurs died out, about 65 million years ago.

It is called *mokele-mbembe* by the local people, who say it is reddish in colour and up to nine metres in length.

Bigfoot in North America

This massive creature might prove to be a large ape, which lives in small family groups like gorillas. The Indian people of the heavily forested region it is believed to inhabit call it *sasquatch*. Over 10,000 sightings have been recorded, and there is also a film which claims to show a living bigfoot.

FOOTPRINTS
Further evidence of bigfoot's existence is based on footprints

Supposed bigfoot footprint   *Human footprint*

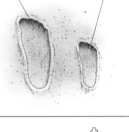

The Loch Ness monster

Britain's most famous mysterious animal is said to live in Scotland's Loch Ness, a large and very deep lake. Sightings of creatures like sea serpents have been made over hundreds of years, but there is little real evidence of them.

Mysterious cats

For the past twenty years, there have been reports of large wild cats from various parts of Britain. Some people believe that pumas or panthers that have escaped from zoos are now breeding in the wild.

Cat footprint

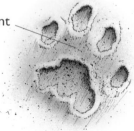

AMAZING NEW ANIMAL FACTS

- **Mystery swallow** In 1984, the body of an unknown swallow was found on an island in the Middle East. It has become known as the Red Sea cliff swallow. No similar swallows have ever been recorded.

- **The aggressive ape** Although no apes are believed to live in South America, a strange ape-like creature was once photographed there. This was in 1920, close to the border between Colombia and Venezuela. The animal was shot dead as it was about to attack a group of scientists.

- **A rare find in a squashed snake** In 1992, when Graham Armstrong examined a snake that had been run over on a road close to the town of Burra, South Australia, he recognised this reptile's last meal. It had been a pygmy blue-tongued skink, thought to have been extinct since 1959. Searching the area nearby, he then rediscovered a group of these lizards. Some are now being bred at Adelaide Zoo.

- **Mystery giant Asian elephants** Tall elephants with large domed swellings on their foreheads were reported from a remote part of western Nepal in 1992. They may be a new type of elephant, possibly the living descendants of an extinct form called *Stegodon*.

- **Millions of insects** Zoologists think that there could be as many as 50 million different invertebrates living in the world's rain forest areas. This would mean that a huge number still await discovery.

- **A predicted discovery** The famous naturalist Charles Darwin predicted the existence of a butterfly or moth with a very large tongue. No one believed him at the time, but in 1903 – over forty years after Darwin suggested the idea – the Madagascan long-tongued hawk moth was finally found.

GLOSSARY

Algae Tiny plants that live in or near water.

Amphibian An animal that can live on land but must return to water to breed.

Aviary A place for keeping birds.

Carnivore An animal that only eats meat.

Classified An animal that has been recorded and given a scientific name.

Cold-blooded An animal whose body temperature changes with the temperature of its surroundings.

Domesticate To make an animal able to live with people.

Endangered When a species of animal is in danger of dying out completely.

Evolve To change gradually over many years and adapt to new conditions.

Extinct When an animal has died out and no longer exists.

Herbivore An animal that feeds on grass and plants.

Hibernate To go into a long sleep during the winter.

Hunting trophy The head or skin of an animal that has been mounted on a wall as a decoration.

Mammal An animal that is fed, when young, on milk from its mother's body.

Marsupial An animal that carries its young in a pouch.

Nocturnal Happening or active at night.

Ornithologist A scientist who studies birds.

Predator An animal that lives by killing and eating other animals.

Primate A member of a group of mammals that includes humans and monkeys.

Pygmy A species of animal that is smaller than usual.

Sauropod A plant-eating dinosaur with a long neck and tail.

Type specimen The first example from which all animals of the same kind are described.

Zoologist A scientist who studies the behaviour and habitats of animals.

PLANTS

CONTENTS

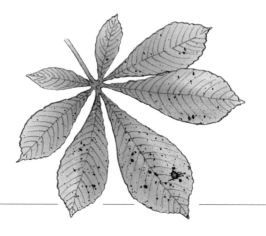

THE ORIGINS OF PLANTS

Plants first appeared on Earth about 630 million years ago, long before animals came into existence. The earliest plants developed in water, and then, around 400 million years ago, vegetation began to grow on land.

Cycads
These ancient plants, which look like a cross between ferns and trees, were already present on Earth over 200 million years ago, at the time of the dinosaurs. Cycads grow from seeds, which can be as large as a hen's egg.

Algae
The first plants were very small and simple. They were similar to **algae**, being made up of single cells. Algae are very adaptable, and can grow almost anywhere on Earth in a damp environment.

Giant sequoias
These trees are among the largest plants in the world. They can grow to over 80 metres – taller than a skyscraper. They grow mainly in northwestern America. People have cut tunnels through sequoia trunks that are wide enough to drive a car through.

WHAT ARE PLANTS?

There are over 275,000 different kinds of plants in the world today. These include mosses and liverworts, which were the first plants on land. The most important plants today are the flowering plants, which are the ones that produce seeds.

CHLOROPHYLL
*This is the substance in leaves that makes them green. It also helps to make the plant's food through **photosynthesis**.*

Flowers
Flowers contain sweet nectar to attract insects.

Stalk
The plant is supported by the stalk.

Leaves
These contain chlorophyll to make the plant's food.

PHOTOSYNTHESIS
Chlorophyll makes the plant's food in the leaves by combining carbon dioxide from the air, hydrogen from water and energy from the Sun.

Roots
Water and minerals from the soil are taken up by the roots.

FLOWERING PLANTS
*Flowers attract creatures, such as insects, bats and birds, to **pollinate** them. Seeds form as the flower dies. The seeds then start to grow – a process called **germination** – and produce new plants.*

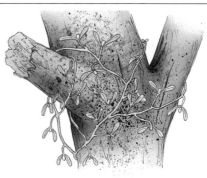

Large, colourful petals

Anthers contain pollen granules

Sepals which covered the bud

Carpel where seeds form

Parasitic plants
Mistletoe grows on the branches of trees like apple and poplar. It uses its roots to reach the tree's **xylem**, drawing off water and mineral salts from the tree rather than from the soil.

Epiphytes
Epiphytes grow on the sides of other plants. They have no roots in the soil. Instead they obtain mineral salts from rain. Bromeliads have leaves which form special cups at their centres. The cup fills up when it rains and provides the plant with water.

Mushrooms
Mushrooms and toadstools (called fungi) are not true plants. They have no chlorophyll, so they cannot produce food by photosynthesis. Instead, they feed on rotting vegetation.

THE WORLD'S FORESTS

Almost three-quarters of the Earth's land is covered with trees. They form forests which are home to many other plants and animals. Although trees exist in a wide range of **habitats**, some parts of the world, such as the far north or deserts, are too cold or dry for trees to survive.

Tropical rainforests
These are found near the Equator, where it is hot and wet. In rainforests, there can be as many as 300 different types of trees in just two square kilometres.

Deciduous forests

Deciduous trees shed their leaves in autumn, and then grow them again in spring. Deciduous forests grow where there are distinct seasons, and the weather becomes colder during the winter.

Coniferous forests

Conifers grow in cold climates. They have needles rather than leaves so that snow falls off them more easily. Conifers grow so thickly that little light can penetrate to the forest floor, and few other plants can grow there.

SURVIVAL IN THE HEAT

The burning heat of the Sun, the freezing temperatures at night and the lack of rain mean that hardly any plants can live in the world's deserts. But cacti and succulents have **evolved** to survive in these hot, dry places, and other plants spring into life in the sandy soil when it rains.

Lack of leaves
Cacti have spines rather than leaves. These reduce the amount of water lost by **transpiration**. They also give good protection against animals which might otherwise eat the cacti.

Under the ground
The roots of cacti are often shallow and extend over a wide area. This helps them to absorb the moisture which forms in the early morning as dew.

The effect of rain
There is no regular rainfall in the desert, and some places stay dry for many years. But when the rains do come, the desert landscape is transformed into a mass of colour. Seeds which have been lying in the sand since the end of the last rain germinate. They must produce plants, followed very quickly by flowers and more seeds if they are to survive until the next rain.

Long-lived plants
Succulents grow in the desert. They have thick, fleshy leaves where they store water. These desert plants grow slowly, and some can live for well over 100 years. If pieces of cacti and succulents break off, they can take root in the desert sand and grow into new plants.

119

SURVIVAL IN THE COLD

The ground is permanently frozen in cold northern parts of the world. During the very short summers, the top layer of soil thaws and the ground then becomes marshy. Trees cannot grow because of the frozen ground and cold summers, and the landscape looks bleak. There may be a few willow or alder bushes, and small flowering shrubs. The ground is covered with low-growing grasses, mosses, herbs and lichens.

Lichens

Lichens are the most common form of plant life in the southern continent of Antarctica, which is the coldest place on Earth.

They grow very slowly wherever there is moisture and are surprisingly colourful, often being shades of pink or red.

FLOWERS

Flowering plants grow close to the ground so that the fierce winds will not damage their blooms. Annual plants which flower and die in a year are very rare in cold climates, because they cannot produce seed in time, before the snow buries them.

True partnership

Lichens are remarkable, because they are a combination of algae and fungi. The algae, which contain chlorophyll, can photosynthesise and produce food, while the fungi provide protection and minerals, so that both can survive. This kind of cooperation is called symbiosis.

Vital food

Plant-eating animals such as reindeer and Arctic hares depend on tiny plant life to survive in the cold Arctic environment.

ENJOYING THE WATER

Some plants live entirely underwater, whereas others have leaves and flowers above the surface. The roots of water plants are important since they act as anchors. Water plant leaves are often long and thin or feathery.

GIANT WATER LILY

This plant grows in the river Amazon in South America. Its leaves can grow to be as wide as a bus and are strong enough to support the weight of a child sitting on them.

Pond plants

Different plants grow at different depths in water. Those round the edge are called marginals.

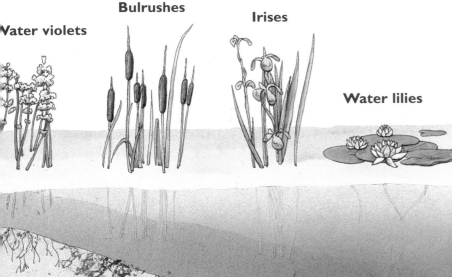

Water violets

Bulrushes

Irises

Water lilies

MANGROVE SWAMPS

These marshy areas are connected to the sea, so the mangrove trees here must grow in salty water. Some of their roots stick upwards, out of the mud, to obtain oxygen from the air at low tide.

Coastal scene

Grasses often grow in sand leading down to the seashore. They produce shoots called **rhizomes** which burrow down into the sand, stopping the plant from blowing away. Once the sand is firm, flowering plants that can live in the salty environment will start to grow. On the rocks, seaweeds (which are algae) cling fast as the tide moves in and out.

THE MEAT-EATERS

In parts of the world where the soil is boggy and has a low mineral content, strange meat-eating plants have evolved. They lure unsuspecting insects into their traps, with enticing scents and offers of sweet nectar. Even small mammals can fall into some of the larger of these plants. There they drown, and their remains are slowly digested by the plant.

Venus fly trap
Found in the swamplands of the Carolinas in America, this plant attracts flies to its open leaves, in the centre of which there are special trigger spikes. When the spikes are brushed by the insect, the leaves spring shut in a fraction of a second, trapping the fly.

Sarracenia
This plant is like a hollow tube. Flies and other insects crawl onto the rim of the plant. They lose their grip and tumble down inside, unable to escape.

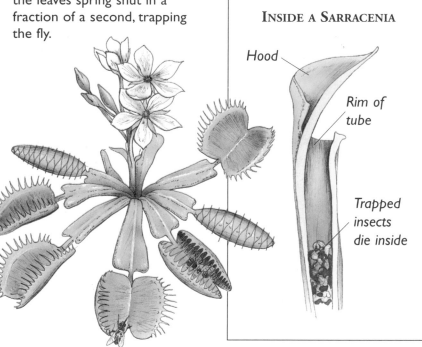

INSIDE A SARRACENIA
Hood

Rim of tube

Trapped insects die inside

Sundews
This group of plants grows throughout the world. Their sticky appearance lures insects down onto their leaves. But once a fly lands here, it will be unable to escape. It dies, and its body is slowly digested by the plant.

Pitcher plants
These plants come in many different shapes and sizes to attract insects into their pitchers, and they may fill up with rainwater. Some pitcher plants may grow to a height of 40 metres by climbing up trees, whereas others stay much closer to the ground.

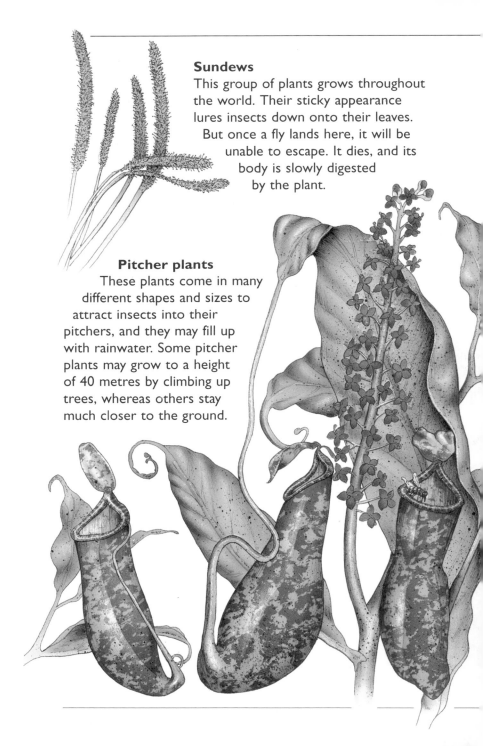

THE FLOWERING CYCLE

For a seed to form, pollen from the male part of the plant must reach the female part. This can be done within the same plant, and is called self-pollination. More often, two plants are involved, which is known as cross-pollination. Insects often help to pollinate plants, and other creatures also play a part, such as nectar-feeding birds that transfer pollen between flowers. When you look inside a flower, you can usually see the pollen. This is present on the **stamen**, and looks like powder.

Wind pollination

Some plants such as grasses and many trees depend on the wind rather than insects for pollination. Their flowers are very small and they have no nectar. The pollen granules are very light, and are produced in huge quantities. You can become allergic to this type of pollen, and suffer from hay fever as a result.

Insect pollination

Many flowers have coloured petals to attract insects. When an insect comes to feed on the flower's nectar, its head brushes against the male anther, collecting pollen. When the insect lands on another flower of the same species, it rubs this pollen onto the female **stigma** and pollination occurs.

Sycamore seeds　**Sycamore leaves**　**Oak leaves**

Pine needles

Seed dispersal

Sycamore seeds are kept in capsules that fly long distances in the wind. Pine cones fall to the ground and the seeds spill onto the soil. Squirrels carry acorns away from the oak tree to places where they may grow.

Acorns

Pine cones

Coconuts

Some seeds can be carried long distances. A coconut is the seed of a palm tree, which often grows near the sea. The coconut may fall into the sea and be washed up on an island, where it grows.

Helpful birds

Birds often eat fruits, and although they digest the soft part, the seeds are left intact. The bird will then pass the seeds out in its droppings, often a long way from where it ate the fruit. This helps plants to spread.

123

A SILVER FIR TREE

A silver fir tree, like most conifer trees, does not change through the year. Its leaves do not lose their green coloration and they do not fall off. Conifers are most common in colder parts of the world. Conifers grow taller than any other trees. A redwood in the Redwood National Park in California, America, is the tallest tree on Earth. It measures over 111 metres in height – more than eighteen giraffes! Conifers also live longer than most other trees. Bristlecone pine trees could have a maximum lifespan of about 5,500 years.

PLANTATIONS
Conifers are grown commercially in plantations both as a source of timber and for the paper industry. They are also grown as Christmas trees, a fashion started by Queen Victoria's husband, Prince Albert, in the 19th century.

NEEDLES
These grow instead of leaves, and help to distinguish conifers from other trees. Pine needles are not shed in the autumn, but they are all replaced gradually over many years.

CONES
Pine cones come in different shapes and sizes. When they are ripe and the weather is warm, they open up and the seeds drop out. Squirrels and some birds feed on pine cones.

Cone

Seeds

BARK SEGMENT

You can work out the age of a tree from the growth rings in its trunk. It is also possible to tell how much a tree grew in a particular year. The most recent rings are on the outside. This technique is called **dendrochronology**.

THE SHAPE

The downward, triangular shape of many conifers means that snow falls off their branches easily. Otherwise, the snow could accumulate on their branches, causing them to break under its weight.

BARK

This tough, protective covering on the outside of the tree has minute holes in it, known as centicels, through which gases can move in and out of the tree's stem.

Cork cambium from which the bark develops.

ROOTS

The roots help to anchor the tree in the ground, as well as providing it with a source of nutrients from the soil. They may spread out a considerable distance from the tree itself.

125

A HORSE CHESTNUT TREE

A horse chestnut tree changes through the year, as the seasons change. In the autumn, the leaves lose their green coloration. Growth and photosynthesis both stop, as the weather becomes colder. The link between the leaves and branches weakens and the tree loses its leaves, especially in windy weather. In time, the leaves will start to rot away in the ground, and release valuable nutrients into the soil, which the tree may take up again through its roots. The tree is dormant over the winter, before growing new leaves again in the spring.

Sapling

At this stage, the small tree, called a sapling, could be trampled underfoot or destroyed by grazing animals. But if it survives, a horse chestnut tree may live for 150 years or more.

Taking root

Left lying on the surface of the soil, the conker starts to germinate, with a root and shoot growing through its outer covering.

Conkers

The spiky seed capsule of the horse chestnut splits apart when it hits the ground. There may be one to three conkers inside. Some are round in shape, whereas others can have flat sides.

LEAF

Horse chestnut leaves are compound leaves because they are made up of a number of leaflets.

SCALE

The base of a horse chestnut may be wider than a truck. It can grow as tall as a ten-storey building.

LIFE CYCLE OF A HORSE CHESTNUT TREE

WINTER
The tree has now lost all of its leaves. Sticky winter buds form at the ends of branches.

AUTUMN
The leaves start to become more yellow, and begin to fall off. Conkers also fall to the ground.

SUMMER
At first the conker's outer casing is quite smooth. It becomes more spiky as the conker grows.

SPRING
Leaves start to appear in late March or early April in the Northern Hemisphere.

GROWING AND SPREADING

Many flowering plants use seeds to reproduce. Some plants can also divide from their roots or stems, buds or leaves, to reproduce. This is called **vegetative reproduction**. It allows plants to spread more rapidly than is possible from seed.

Bulbs
An onion is a bulb. If you slice it in half, you will see it is made up of tightly-packed leaves. A bulb is actually a type of bud. Roots grow out from the base of the bulb, with new bulbs developing on the sides.

Tubers
Some plants, like potatoes, have underground stems which swell at their ends to form **tubers**. If you look closely at a potato, you will be able to see the scar where it was attached to a stem when it was underground.

Creepers
Epiphytic orchids grow by creeping along tree branches, using their roots to anchor themselves to the tree.

PROTECTION AND WEAPONS

Plants cannot move like animals can – they are held in the ground by their roots. So they must develop other ways to protect themselves and avoid being eaten by grazing animals. Many plants have sharp spines to stop animals eating them.

Bramble
The spikes on bramble shoots form a thick barrier, which allows the plant to grow over a wide area.

Sharp spikes break off like splinters.

Even the leaves have small spikes on their undersides.

ACACIAS
Acacias grow quickly, protected by a dense covering of vicious spines. Once the acacia is mature, with no lower branches, only the tall giraffe can reach its leaves. The giraffe's mouth is not injured by the spikes.

Deadly nightshade
Some plants protect themselves by being poisonous. The poisonous berries of deadly nightshade may look tempting, but they can kill you if swallowed.

Nettles
The caterpillars of some butterflies feed on stinging nettles. This might give them some protection against predators.

WHY NETTLES STING
This close-up picture shows the sharp spiky hairs on a nettle leaf. If you touch the leaf, the hairs break off and release painful formic acid into your skin. Cutting nettles back regularly strengthens their stinging power.

PLANTS UNDER THREAT

Whole communities of plants are being destroyed every day all over the world, particularly in tropical parts. Huge areas of forest are being cleared to supply timber, often for furniture, and little is being done to replant these forests. The trees take many years to grow, so some of them are becoming endangered. Trees are also often cut to provide firewood.

Growing firewood

Some trees are now being planted specially for the purpose of providing fuel, to conserve forests. The neem tree was taken to Ghana in Africa from India in the early 1900s. Today it is widely grown, and bats feeding on its fruits have spread its seeds and helped to establish it over a large area.

Firewood

In many areas trees are vital as the only available fuel. Wood is still frequently used for cooking and heating, particularly in developing countries.

PLANT BREEDING

People have been breeding plants and selecting the best ones for many years. This has led to a wide range of cultivated crops and plants which we have in our gardens and homes. **Strains** have been developed which are more resistant to disease, and will grow well in colder parts of the world. Crosses between two strains produce what are called first generation **hybrids**. These often grow better and produce bigger crops.

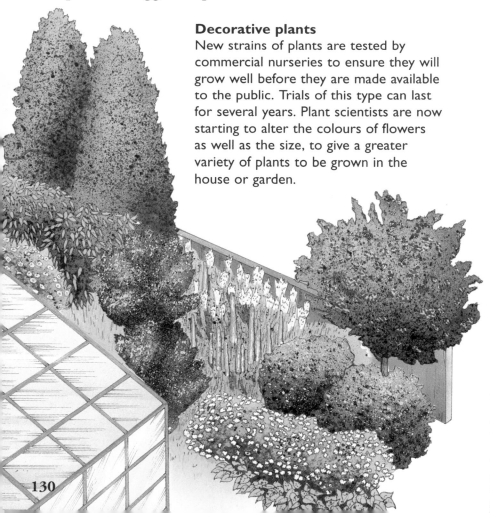

Decorative plants
New strains of plants are tested by commercial nurseries to ensure they will grow well before they are made available to the public. Trials of this type can last for several years. Plant scientists are now starting to alter the colours of flowers as well as the size, to give a greater variety of plants to be grown in the house or garden.

ORCHID CULTIVATION
*Certain plants are much harder to grow from seed than others. Orchids will grow best on a special chemical mix, rather than in soil. The seeds are grown in sealed flasks, and germination may take from a few days to several months. The **seedlings** remain in the flask for up to a year before being planted out into pots.*

New crops
Cereal crops are very important sources of food, and farmers prefer strains which have high yields. But it is still important to keep older less productive seeds available, in case the crops of today are hit by diseases and new strains have to be developed.

Seed banks
These have been established to store rarer varieties of cereals and plants which could be needed in the future. The International Maize and Wheat Improvement Centre in Mexico keeps 120,000 different strains of these two cereals.

PLANTS WE USE

We depend on plants in many areas of our lives. People still use reeds and timber to build their homes in some parts of the world, and baskets, bags and other household objects can be woven from plant materials, as can floor coverings. Plants are used in many of our drinks, ranging from ginger beer to tea leaves and coffee beans. Hops are grown specially to make beer. There is still much to be learnt about plants, in terms of their medicinal uses. Western scientists are now working with rainforest people to learn about the plants they use for healing purposes. This is called **ethnobotany**.

Crops

For thousands of years, people all over the world have grown crops to provide a variety of foods. These range from wheat for making bread to sunflowers for sunflower oil. The crops are grown in huge fields and are harvested at the end of the summer.

Medicines

Many of the drugs used to treat illnesses today originated from plants. Digitalis, which is found in foxgloves, is actually very poisonous but is used to treat some heart patients. The use of plants for healing purposes is called **herbalism**.

Perfumes

Roses and some other plants contain special oils which can be distilled and concentrated into perfumes. A number of these 'essential essences' are also used in lotions and ointments to help people with stress.

Insecticides

Plants have developed ways of avoiding attacks by insects. Pyrethrin is a chemical present in a type of flower called a chrysanthemum. It is deadly to insects, but does not cause serious harm to most other creatures. It is now used as an **insecticide**.

Clothing and dyes

For centuries, plant fibres such as cotton and flax have been made into clothes. Some plants, such as woad, produce dyes which are used to colour cloth and, in some cultures, for body painting.

AMAZING PLANT FACTS

- **Deadly competition** Guayle plants, which grow in groups in the desert areas of Mexico, produce an acid from their roots which kills off other vegetation, preventing other plants growing near them.

- **Drought resistant** Both the caper plant, which grows in the Sahara desert in Africa, and the American pygmy cedar can live without taking up any water at all through their roots. They are able to absorb water vapour directly from the air.

- **Under threat** More than 25,000 of the world's flowering plants are now in danger of extinction, which is about one in ten of the total number of plants on the planet.

- **Tree house** The baobab tree has a huge swollen trunk, which is quite soft. In parts of Africa and Australia, people sometimes hollow this out, so that they can make a home inside the tree.

- **Largest leaves** The raffia palm, which grows on islands in the Indian Ocean, has leaves up to twenty metres long.

- **Biggest seed** The Coco de Mer palm, which grows only on the Seychelles islands off the coast of Africa, produces huge nuts which can weigh twenty kilograms. There are both male and female forms of this palm. Only the females produce these huge nuts, with pollen being produced by the male palms.

- **What a stinker!** The flowers of the rafflesia plant, which grows in the rainforests of southeast Asia, smell like rotting flesh. The flowers are huge – the biggest flowers in the world.

- **Old timer** A bristlecone pine tree in the White Mountains of California, America, is thought to be around 4,700 years old.

GLOSSARY

Algae Microscopic plants which often grow in water.

Dendrochronology The technique of finding a tree's age by counting the rings in its trunk.

Epiphyte A plant that grows on the branches of another plant and doesn't take root in the soil.

Ethnobotany The study by scientists to discover new medicines from plants.

Evolve To change gradually over many years.

Germinate The process which results in seeds sprouting and growing.

Habitat The area where a plant naturally grows.

Herbalism The use of plants for healing purposes.

Hybrid A plant which is produced by crossing two similar but different plants.

Insecticide A chemical used to kill harmful insects and pests which often damage crops.

Photosynthesis The process which allows plants to make their food from sunlight.

Pollinate The transfer of pollen to the stigma which fertilizes the flower.

Rhizome An underground stem present in some plants which helps them to spread.

Seedling A young plant, grown from a seed.

Stamen The male part of a flower where pollen is produced.

Stigma The female part of the flower where pollination takes place.

Strain A plant which has been grown under special conditions for a particular purpose.

Transpiration Evaporation of water from tiny holes, called pores, in the leaves.

Tuber A short, fleshy underground stem.

Vegetative reproduction The way in which some plants can increase in numbers by growing from existing parts of the plant.

Xylem The system that carries water and mineral salts from the roots to other parts of the plant.

FOOD

CONTENTS

WHY DO WE EAT?

We eat when we are hungry because food is a necessity of life. Food acts as our fuel, and so gives us the **energy** we need to carry out our lives. It also provides us with the materials for the growth, repair and general health of our bodies. Without enough food, we would be tired, weak and unhappy.

A balanced diet
The variety of food we need every day to keep us fit and healthy is shown here. A balanced **diet** includes fruit, vegetables, fish, **cereals** and milk products.

WHAT IS FOOD MADE OF?

Food is made up of five main groups of **nutrients**: proteins, carbohydrates, fats, **vitamins** and minerals. We should eat a variety of food to make sure our diet contains all the nutrients. We also need water.

Proteins
Proteins are used to build and repair our bodies. Meat, fish, milk, beans and cereals are good sources of protein.

Carbohydrates
Carbohydrates give our bodies energy. Potatoes, bread, rice and sugar contain carbohydrates.

Fats
Fats provide us with twice as much energy as carbohydrates. We can store extra fats in our bodies to use later. We should avoid eating too many fats because they can cause obesity and heart problems.

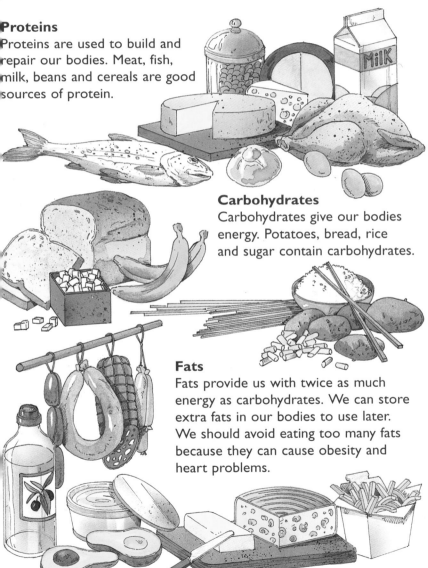

Vitamins
Vitamins are needed in very tiny amounts to help our bodies to work properly. Vitamin C, for example, helps wounds to heal. Fresh fruit and vegetables, liver and fish are rich in vitamins.

Minerals
Minerals are needed in small amounts by different parts of our bodies. Calcium is used for building bones and teeth, and iron helps our blood to carry oxygen round our bodies. Eggs, liver, fish and milk contain lots of minerals.

Water
Almost two-thirds of our bodies are made of water. We need about two litres of water a day. One litre comes from drinks and the other from food.

OUR STAPLE FOODS

Staple foods form a large part of our diet and we eat them every day. In many places they are made from types of grasses that have been grown since prehistoric times, and that we now know as cereals. The seeds we eat are called **grains**. They mostly contain carbohydrates.

Wheat
This is grown all over the world. It is usually ground into flour, which is used for making bread. Pasta and noodles are also made from wheat flour.

Rice
Rice grows best in warmer parts of the world. It is an important staple food in Indonesia, India, China and other countries in Asia.

Over half the people in the world eat rice at every meal. Most rice is grown in flooded fields, called rice paddies, and is often sown and picked by hand.

Oats
Oats grow in cool climates and are eaten as porridge in many parts of Northern Europe.

Maize
One type of maize produces the head of seeds that we know as sweetcorn, or corn on the cob. The other, which has more starchy grains, is a staple food in East Africa, where it is ground and made into porridge. In Mexico and South America, the ground corn is used to produce a flat, pancake-like bread called a tortilla.

Millet and sorghum
These are important cereal crops in Africa because they grow quickly in hot, dry climates. They are ground to make flour for porridge or bread.

Rye
This grows in cold climates like Scandinavia and Russia where other cereals will not survive. It is made into flour which produces a dark and heavy bread.

FOOD FROM PLANTS

All fruit and vegetables come from plants. Fruit and vegetables contain vitamins and minerals and lots of **fibre**. Fibre is important in our diet as it helps us to get rid of waste from our bodies.

Vegetables

We eat many parts of vegetable plants, such as the leaves of cabbages, the roots of carrots, the flowers of cauliflower and broccoli, the stems of celery and the seeds of peas and beans. The potato is a swollen stem which grows underground, known as a **tuber**. Yams and sweet potatoes are also tubers.

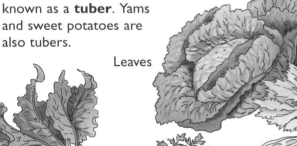

Stalks

Leaves

Roots

Seeds

Tubers

Flowers

Fruits

Fruits are juicy foods which contain the seeds of plants. There are a huge variety of fruits available, and they can be eaten raw, cooked or dried. They can also be crushed or squeezed into juices.

SEEDS

Many fruits contain seeds or pips. Tomatoes are often called vegetables but in fact they are fruits because they have seeds inside. The seeds of many other fruits are edible, such as pomegranates, kiwifruit and strawberries.

FOOD FROM WHEAT

It is surprising how many foods can be made out of wheat. Wheat is one of our most important cereal crops, and wheatfields can be seen in many areas of the world. The Prairies of America and the Steppes of Russia are important wheat growing areas.

An ear of wheat
Wheat consists of grains, clustered at the top of a stalk.

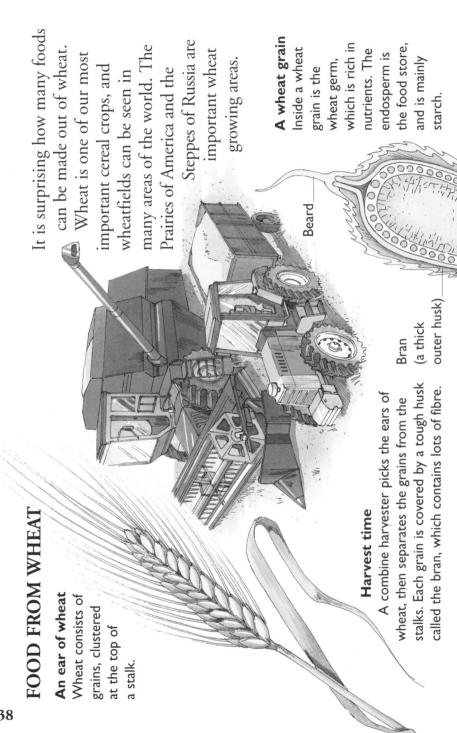

Harvest time
A combine harvester picks the ears of wheat, then separates the grains from the stalks. Each grain is covered by a tough husk called the bran, which contains lots of fibre.

Milling of wheat
The wheat grains are torn open, then crushed and ground down into flour by mechanical rollers. Different types of flour can be made by sieving out coarser particles of bran.

Actual size of wheat grain

A wheat grain
Inside a wheat grain is the wheat germ, which is rich in nutrients. The endosperm is the food store, and is mainly starch.

Beard

Bran (a thick outer husk)

Endosperm (a food store)

Wheat germ (a seed)

Three main types of flour

Wholemeal flour
The whole wheat grain is used for this flour. It contains lots of fibre, and all nutrients from the grain.

Brown flour
Some of the bran layer (the fibre) is removed from the wheat grain during milling.

White flour
All the bran and the wheat germ are removed. Only the endosperm is used.

Cereals
Wheat can be made into breakfast cereals, which are a healthy food if the whole wheat grain is used. Cereals are often fortified with extra vitamins and minerals.

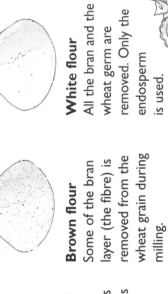

Pasta
Pasta is made out of flour from a special type of wheat known as durum wheat. This has a high protein content. Pasta is made into many shapes.

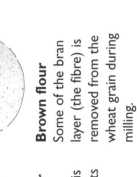

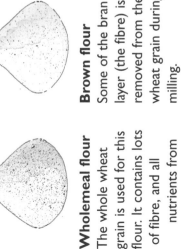

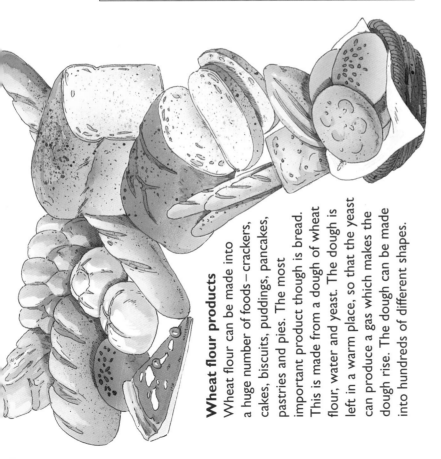

BREAD
This is an important food all around the world – it is even sometimes called 'the staff of life'. Different countries have their own special breads. From sandwiches to toast, bread is eaten at almost every meal.

Composition of bread	
Vitamins/Minerals	1%
Protein	9%
Fat	2%
Carbohydrate	42%
Water	38%
Fibre	8%

Wheat flour products
Wheat flour can be made into a huge number of foods – crackers, cakes, biscuits, puddings, pancakes, pastries and pies. The most important product though is bread. This is made from a dough of wheat flour, water and yeast. The dough is left in a warm place, so that the yeast can produce a gas which makes the dough rise. The dough can be made into hundreds of different shapes.

EGGS

We eat many kinds of birds' eggs – from tiny quails' eggs to huge ostrich eggs. All are rich in protein, vitamins and minerals, especially iron. The yolk of an egg is a food store, surrounded by a protective egg white and shell. The colour and shape of eggs vary from **species** to species and has nothing to do with the diet of the bird.

Quails' eggs   Hens' eggs   Ostrich egg

Inside an egg

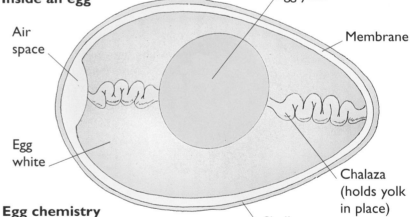

Air space

Egg yolk

Membrane

Egg white

Chalaza (holds yolk in place)

Shell

Egg chemistry
When eggs are cooked, the proteins set or **coagulate**. By using different ingredients, or various methods of cooking, eggs are used in a huge variety of dishes throughout the world.

Eggs can go bad easily if they are not stored properly. The air space inside an egg grows bigger as an egg becomes older. This makes a fresh egg sink in water, but a stale egg will float! If eggs are really rotten, hydrogen sulphide gas is formed, which has a horrible smell.

139

FOOD FROM THE SEA

There is an enormous variety of fish and shellfish found in the sea, and these have traditionally been used as food for thousands of years.

Fish for healthy eating

Fish is a healthy part of our diet because it contains proteins, vitamins and minerals, and is low in fat.

Fishing

A fishing trawler drags a huge, bag-like net behind it in the sea. Weights keep the mouth of the net open, trapping fish. Large fishing industries provide fish to feed lots of people. The biggest fishing nations are Japan, Russia and China. Recently, international laws have been passed to prevent overfishing our seas.

Shellfish

Crabs, prawns, scallops and mussels are collectively called shellfish. They have a hard outer cover that has to be removed to reach the tasty food inside.

Seaweed

Seaweed is a popular food in many parts of the world. In Japan it is dried in the Sun before being sold in flat sheets, shredded into strips or ground into powder.

Fish fingers

Most fish fingers are made from a large fish called cod. The flesh is cut up into strips, then dipped in breadcrumbs and frozen. Fish fingers are known as a 'convenience food' because they are quick and easy to prepare.

DAIRY PRODUCTS

Milk has been part of our diet for centuries and we consume millions of litres of it every year. It is produced by all mammals, but we mostly use domesticated, vegetarian animals for milk. It is either drunk as it is or **processed** into dairy foods like cheese.

Cows

Cows are kept in dairy herds and milked every day. Milk used to be a common source of **bacteria**. Today, milk is heat-treated to kill germs and to make it safe to drink.

A milking parlour

Special cups gently squeeze the cow's milk from the udder into pipes. The pipes lead to a cold tank where the milk is kept fresh. It takes about ten minutes to milk a cow.

Camels

Milking a camel is quite a tricky job! Camels are easily annoyed and may bite or kick when they become angry. But their milk is rich in fat and protein.

Buffalo

In large parts of Asia and some parts of Africa, milk comes from buffalo. Their milk has more protein and fat than cows' milk.

Reindeer

In northern countries where it is very cold, reindeer are kept for their milk. Reindeer milk is much higher in fat and protein than any other milk.

Goats and sheep

Goats are kept in hilly areas and in deserts. They will eat almost anything – including brambles, shrubs and weeds. Goats' milk is often made into cheese.

Sheep are milked in Central Europe. Their milk is made into a distinctive tasting cheese. Pigs are not milked because it is difficult to milk a sow.

MILK PRODUCTS

*Milk contains a sugar called lactose which is easily changed into an acid by bacteria. This is called **souring** and causes the protein in milk to curdle. We use this natural change to make cheese and yoghourt.*

WHAT HAPPENS TO MILK

Most milk that we drink comes from cows. Different kinds of cows have been specially bred for their milk yield. Jersey cows, for example, produce milk which is very creamy and high in fat.

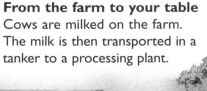

From the farm to your table
Cows are milked on the farm. The milk is then transported in a tanker to a processing plant.

NUTRIENTS IN MILK

Milk consists mainly of water, with tiny droplets of fat dispersed in it. If unprocessed milk is left to stand, the fat rises to the top, and can be seen as the cream layer. Milk is a good food because it contains many nutrients.

Composition of milk	
Vitamins/Minerals	0.7%
Protein	3.3%
Fat	3.8%
Carbohydrate	4.7%
Water	87.5%

Skimmed milk
All the fat (cream) is removed from the milk by machine. Skimmed milk is healthier than whole milk as it has less fat and fewer **calories**.

Pasteurised milk
The milk is heated to kill any harmful bacteria, and then cooled quickly.

Long life milk
The milk is heated to a very high temperature to kill all bacteria.

Dried milk
The milk is sprayed into hot air and dried into a powder. The powder is then sealed into an air tight container.

Evaporated milk
Some of the water is evaporated from heat-treated milk. It is then sealed into cans.

Condensed milk
This is like evaporated milk but with sugar added to make it thick.

142

The pasteurisation plant

Here the milk is heated to a temperature of 72°C for fifteen seconds and then rapidly cooled to 4°C. After strict tests for quality, the milk is poured into steam-cleaned bottles or cartons ready for delivery.

Cheese

Turning milk into cheese is a traditional way of preserving it. During this process, milk is allowed to become slightly sour. A special **enzyme** called rennet is added, and this 'sets' the milk proteins into thick curds. The liquid produced, called whey, is drained off, leaving the cheese to be salted and then packed into moulds to ripen. Cheeses are matured and flavoured in many different ways. Blue cheese has special types of harmless mould growing through it, which gives it the blue veins.

Composition of cheese	
Vitamins/Minerals	3%
Protein	26%
Fat	33%
Water	38%

Cream

Cream is made by separating out the creamy part of milk. Nowadays this is normally done by machine. Double cream has a higher fat content (48%) than whipping (35%) or single (18%) cream.

Composition of cream	
Vitamins/Minerals	0.5%
Protein	1.5%
Fat	48%
Carbohydrate	2%
Water	48%

Butter

The traditional butter churn has now been replaced by a complex machine. This makes fat droplets in cream stick together to produce butter. Butter milk, a by-product, is drained away. The butter is then cut and wrapped in foil or waxed paper.

Composition of butter	
Vitamins/Minerals	1.5%
Protein	0.5%
Fat	83%
Water	15%

Yoghourt

Harmless bacteria in milk, called *lactobacilli*, are left to produce lactic acid at a warm temperature. This sours the milk, which then sets into yoghourt. Sugar or fruit are often added.

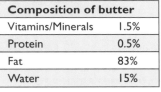

Composition of yoghourt	
Vitamins/Minerals	2%
Protein	5%
Fat	0.5%
Carbohydrate	12%
Water	80.5%

MEAT

Animals like chickens, cows, pigs, sheep, goats and rabbits are kept on farms for their meat, milk and eggs. Over many years animals have been specially **bred** to produce more milk or leaner, less fatty meat.

Pigs

Pigs are kept by farmers almost all over the world, although in some areas, such as the Middle East, pork is not eaten for religious reasons. Most parts of a pig can be eaten, including its feet or 'trotters'. Smoked or salted pork meat is called bacon or ham. Pigs are easy to feed— they eat almost anything.

Sheep

Sheep can live happily in hilly areas as they eat short, tough grass. Meat from adult sheep is called mutton. Meat from young sheep is called lamb.

Cows

Cattle are farmed on grasslands in many areas of the world. In some countries cattle are injected with drugs to produce more meat, as well as being fattened by grazing. Most male calves are reared for meat. Herds of female dairy cows are kept by some farmers to supply milk.

Ducks

Ducks are a popular food in China, where large flocks are kept on rough pasture land. Many different parts of the duck, including the feet, liver and fat, are eaten.

Unusual meats

In some areas of the world, a variety of animals are kept to be eaten. For example, snakes and frogs are a delicacy in China, and snails in France. Ostriches are now farmed in many countries.

Geese

Geese are kept in flocks in China, providing plenty of meat and large eggs. Geese make excellent guards as they hiss loudly if anyone approaches.

Chickens

Battery chickens are kept in large sheds in small wire cages with very little room to move. Free range chickens live outdoors in plenty of open space.

COOKING FOOD

Some foods are eaten raw, such as carrots, lettuce and fruit, and in Japan many people enjoy raw fish. Other food needs to be cooked to soften it and make it easier to chew. Cooking also improves the taste of food and changes its shape and appearance. The heat of cooking kills bacteria, which could otherwise make us ill.

Cooking on an open fire

This is a traditional way of cooking and we still barbecue food in the same way. The heat from the fire cooks the outside of the food first. A spit is often used to rotate the food and so prevent burning in one place.

Frying

Batter, made from flour and water, can be cooked on a hot metal plate to make pancakes. We often use a frying pan to conduct heat into food. Besides pancakes, we fry many other foods like meat, fish and vegetables.

Cookers in kitchens

A modern cooker allows us to control heat. Hot air circulating inside an oven means that we can bake bread and cakes, or roast meat. We can also use the top of the cooker to boil, simmer, steam and fry food.

Microwave ovens

Microwaves penetrate food, giving energy to the food particles which generates heat quickly. Microwaves bounce off metal and so glass, china or plastic dishes are used in microwave ovens.

HERBS AND SPICES

Herbs are plants with sweet smelling leaves, like rosemary, mint, and basil. Some plants have seeds which are spicy and hot, like chili peppers.

145

PRESERVING FOOD

Bacteria are microscopic living creatures that can be found all round us. They grow well in food, but can make the food rotten and poison us. There are many ways to prevent this from happening. Freezing, canning, pickling, drying and freeze-drying are some of the ways of preserving food.

Freezing

The temperature in a freezer is too cold for bacteria to grow and so we freeze food to keep it fresh for longer. Food is frozen quickly, usually with blasts of very cold air. Once frozen, food must be stored in a freezer at a temperature below -18°C.

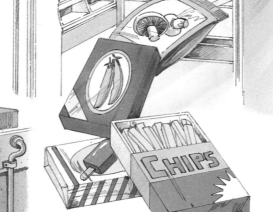

Canning

The food is prepared and filled automatically into cans. The air at the top of the can is sucked out before the lid is sealed. The cans are then heated in a **sterilizer** to high temperatures to kill all bacteria. The food then lasts for years.

Pickling

Some foods, usually vegetables, are soaked in vinegar and then bottled in an airtight container. The vinegar is an acid and this stops bacteria from growing, so the food is preserved. Eggs, onions and gherkins are popular pickled foods.

Drying

Bacteria cannot grow without water, so dried food lasts for a long time without going bad. In some countries, food is laid out to dry in the Sun — fish in China and fruits in the Philippines. More modern methods use hot air, generated in a factory, to **evaporate** water. Instant packaged potatoes and soups are produced in this way.

Freeze-drying

This method dries food quickly, making it porous and easy to **rehydrate** by adding water. Once fast-frozen, the food is put into a vacuum chamber. Here the ice crystals in the food change to steam, leaving the food dry.

LET'S CELEBRATE

Food is often served on special occasions. Holy days, weddings and birthdays are celebrated all over the world with a feast. These feasts can take a lot of preparation. For example, the Sardinian dish 'Cobbler's Bull' is roasted, for several hours, in a deep ditch dug out of the ground.

Japan
At the New Year festival in Japan, many sorts of fish, simmered or fried, are served with vegetables, soya beans, seaweed rolls and rice.

Africa
A traditional West African celebration dish is a big casserole of chicken and beef with lots of rice and vegetables.

India
At an Indian wedding the main dish is semolina dough fried in balls and flavoured with sugar and saffron.

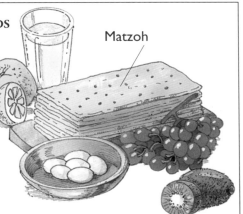

RELIGIOUS FESTIVAL FOODS
Jewish people celebrate Passover with unleavened bread called matzoh, a hard boiled egg, a lamb bone, some parsley, bitter horseradish and a sweet mixture of apple, almonds and raisins. All these foods are symbolic of events in the Bible.

Matzoh

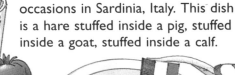

Italy
'Cobbler's Bull' is served on special occasions in Sardinia, Italy. This dish is a hare stuffed inside a pig, stuffed inside a goat, stuffed inside a calf.

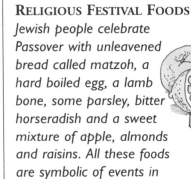

America
When Americans celebrate Thanksgiving, they eat roast turkey followed by pumpkin pie.

France
The centrepiece of a French wedding feast is often a huge pyramid of cream-filled profiteroles with caramel poured over. The pyramid can be a metre high.

Different kinds of bread
In Greece, at Easter, bread is baked into a variety of shapes and flavoured with cardamom seeds.

147

MARKETS AND SUPERMARKETS

There are lots of different ways of buying and selling food, and many kinds of food shops. Some sell only one kind of food – a baker sells bread and cakes. But other shops, like supermarkets, sell a wide variety of food.

Outdoor markets
There are outdoor markets in every country in the world where shoppers can choose from a wide selection of foods: fruit, vegetables, herbs, spices, and sometimes fish and meat too. The produce is always well displayed and very fresh.

Supermarkets
In a supermarket, most of the food is already weighed and packed in boxes, packets or jars. Carrots, for example, may be sold raw or canned or frozen. Supermarkets usually have a huge selection of different foods.

It is better to buy unprocessed foods because some packaged and tinned foods, though quick and easy to prepare, contain additives, like flavourings and colourings, and these can be harmful to our health.

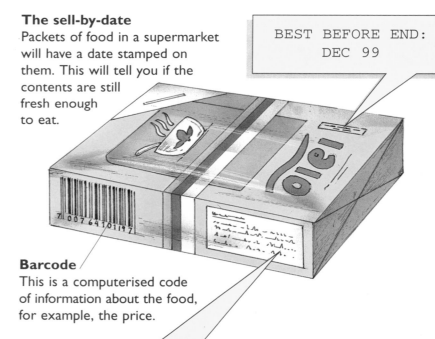

The sell-by-date
Packets of food in a supermarket will have a date stamped on them. This will tell you if the contents are still fresh enough to eat.

BEST BEFORE END: DEC 99

Barcode
This is a computerised code of information about the food, for example, the price.

Sugar
Starch
Gelatine
Dextrose
Salt
Flavouring
Colouring (E124, E102, E123)
Preservative (E220)

Ingredients
A list of ingredients is always displayed on packaged food, with the main ingredients first. The packaged dessert shown here contains mainly sugar. There are chemicals added to colour, flavour and preserve the food, and you should avoid too many of these.

FOOD FOR ALL

In some parts of the world there is hunger and **famine**. It may happen because of disasters like a drought or a flood. Poverty and wars are also causes of famine. Without food, children cannot grow properly and have no energy to move or resistance to disease. Adults also become ill and weak.

The importance of food

The child shown in the inset picture on the right is starving—little more than skin and bones, after a long time with hardly any food. The main picture shows the same child a few weeks after eating nourishing food, looking much healthier.

Scientists and farmers are working together to try to prevent famine. Improvements to water supplies and farming methods will help to prevent famine in the future. Farmers are now encouraged to use fertilizers and pesticides to help produce more crops. Also, new crops are being developed that are more resistant to drought and disease.

New crops

These are specially bred to give a higher yield of grain.

Maize

Rice

Wheat

Improved wheat

Improved maize

Improved rice

SPACE FOOD

Astronauts eat freeze-dried food in space. Freeze-dried meals are very light, but they keep their shape and colour. The taste is not as good as fresh food but it is a good supply of energy and nutrients.

149

AMAZING FOOD FACTS

- **Poisonous food** Some food contains natural poisons which can make us ill. In Japan, the liver of the puffer fish, a popular food, is highly poisonous and has to be cut out by specially trained people before the flesh of the fish is eaten.

- **Edible insects** Insects are a nutritious food and considered a delicacy in some countries. Ants and grasshoppers are popular in parts of South America, as are beetles in Asia. In Africa, insects are an important part of the daily, staple diet.

- **Cheese variety** France produces over 400 different kinds of cheese, including the famous ones such as Brie and Camembert. Britain, Holland, Denmark, Switzerland and America also have big cheese industries. Yet some countries eat very little cheese – the Chinese diet for example does not traditionally include dairy products.

- **Do carrots help us to see?** There is a saying that carrots help us to see in the dark. Carrots do contain plenty of vitamin A, which is needed for healthy eyes, but eating lots of carrots will not help us to see more clearly in the dark.

- **Soya beans** Soya beans are an amazing food as they have a huge variety of uses. These beans are very nutritious, and provide calcium, iron and B vitamins as well as having a higher protein content than most other foods.

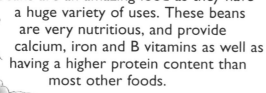

- **Breakfast cereals** These are one of the few new foods. Breakfast cereal was invented in 1904 and has revolutionised our breakfast eating habits.

GLOSSARY

Bacteria Tiny forms of life that live all around us. They can make food go bad.

Breeding Choosing certain animals and plants which are stronger or better than others to go on to produce young.

Calories A measure of energy supplied by food.

Cereal A plant like wheat, whose seeds are used for food.

Coagulate The hardening of proteins when they are cooked.

Diet Food and drink that you eat regularly. Some people use 'diet' to mean that they are eating less to lose weight.

Energy You need energy to do everything, even sleeping.

Enzyme A protein that is produced by living cells.

Evaporate When water changes into steam, usually by being heated.

Famine When there is not enough food for people to eat.

Fibre A substance found in plants. It cannot be digested, but it is vital in our diet to help us to get rid of waste.

Grain The seeds of cereal crops such as wheat, corn, rice, barley and oats.

Nutrients Materials we obtain from food which are needed for our health. They are protein, carbohydrate, fat, vitamins and minerals.

Processed Food which is made in a factory. It often contains colourings and preservatives, to make it look more appealing and to last longer.

Rehydrate To restore water that has been lost when the food was dried.

Souring The change, caused by acids, that occurs in fresh milk after a few days.

Species A group of animals or plants which are alike in certain ways.

Sterilize To kill all the germs or bacteria in a food.

Tuber The short, thick part of some plant stems which grow underground. Potatoes are tubers.

Vitamins They are needed by your body to work smoothly.

THE BODY

CONTENTS

THE OUTER BODY

The outer covering of an animal's body is very important. It forms a barrier, protecting the animal from infection. Fish and reptiles have a body casing of scales. Birds have feathers which help them to fly and maintain their body temperature. Mammals have body hair, which, like feathers, traps air close to the skin and helps them to keep warm.

Hedgehogs
Hedgehogs' sharp spines are actually modified hairs. There may be 7,500 spines on an adult hedgehog's body. Newborn hedgehogs have about one hundred white spines.

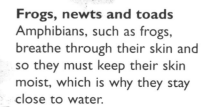

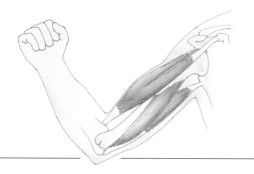

Frogs, newts and toads
Amphibians, such as frogs, breathe through their skin and so they must keep their skin moist, which is why they stay close to water.

Tortoises and turtles
Body armour can help to protect slow moving animals, like tortoises, from attack. The shells of tortoises may be hard, but they can still be damaged.

THE BRAIN AND NERVOUS SYSTEM

The brain coordinates all your body's movements and is active even while you are asleep. The brain is connected to nerves throughout the body by the spinal cord, which runs up your back, protected within your backbone. Information passes very quickly up and down this pathway, to and from the different parts of your body, in the form of electrical impulses.

Saltasaurus

The human brain

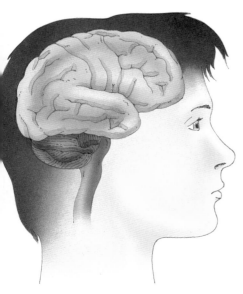

Two-brained dinosaurs
Fossilized sauropod dinosaur remains suggest that these dinosaurs had two small brains. They probably had one brain located above their hind legs plus a small brain in their heads.

The two sides of your brain
The brain controls our bodies. It regulates all our movements and thoughts. The left half of our brain controls the actions of the right side of our body, and the right half of our brain controls the actions of the left side of our body.

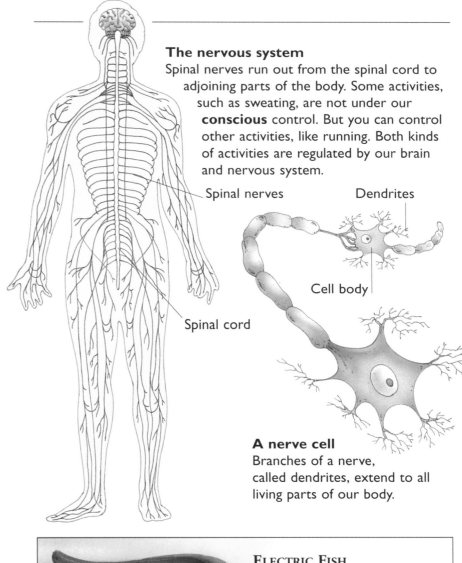

The nervous system
Spinal nerves run out from the spinal cord to adjoining parts of the body. Some activities, such as sweating, are not under our **conscious** control. But you can control other activities, like running. Both kinds of activities are regulated by our brain and nervous system.

Spinal nerves

Dendrites

Cell body

Spinal cord

A nerve cell
Branches of a nerve, called dendrites, extend to all living parts of our body.

ELECTRIC FISH
Some fish can produce electricity from their nervous systems. The deadly electric eel can generate as much as 650 volts – enough electricity to kill a large animal.

153

MUSCLES AND NERVES

Muscles control the body's movements. The most active **skeletal muscles** are those controlling the eyes. These move about 100,000 times every day, even when we are asleep.

Most muscles are paired, with the contraction of one muscle extending its opposite partner. They are called antagonistic because one muscle works against the other.

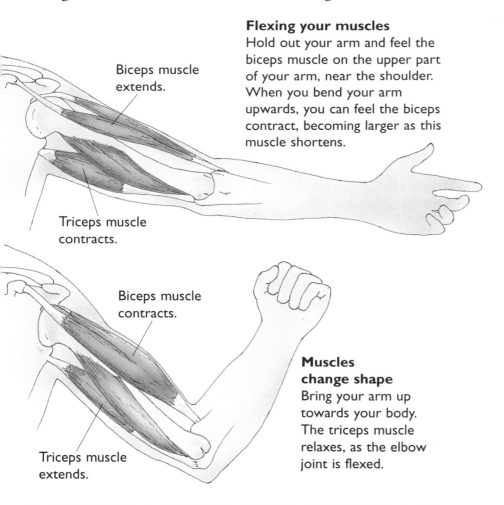

Flexing your muscles
Hold out your arm and feel the biceps muscle on the upper part of your arm, near the shoulder. When you bend your arm upwards, you can feel the biceps contract, becoming larger as this muscle shortens.

Biceps muscle extends.

Triceps muscle contracts.

Biceps muscle contracts.

Triceps muscle extends.

Muscles change shape
Bring your arm up towards your body. The triceps muscle relaxes, as the elbow joint is flexed.

When we want to flex our elbow **joint**, a signal is sent from the cerebral cortex in the brain. This message travels down through the spinal cord and triggers the nerves to the appropriate muscle.

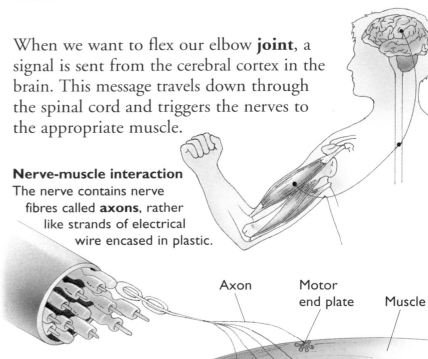

Nerve-muscle interaction
The nerve contains nerve fibres called **axons**, rather like strands of electrical wire encased in plastic.

Axon   Motor end plate   Muscle

Nerve impulses
Each motor axon divides into branches leading to motor end plates, where the nerve meets the muscle.

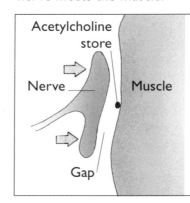

Acetylcholine store

Nerve   Muscle

Gap

THE SYNAPSE
*In the nerves at the motor end plates, there are tiny stores of a chemical transmitter called acetylcholine. This chemical is released by the electrical impulse from the nerve and travels across a gap called a **synapse** to reach the muscle, causing the muscle fibres to contract.*

EYES

Our eyes provide us with our main source of information about the world we live in. All mammals have a pair of eyes set in sockets in the skull, but the position of their eyes varies greatly. Animals, such as rabbits, which are likely to be attacked by other creatures, have their eyes positioned on the sides of their head. This allows them to locate danger easily.

How we see

Light passes through the pupil, which is the black area at the centre of our eye, and reaches the retina at the back of the eye. The retina relays the image of what we see to our brain, along the optic nerve.

A human eye

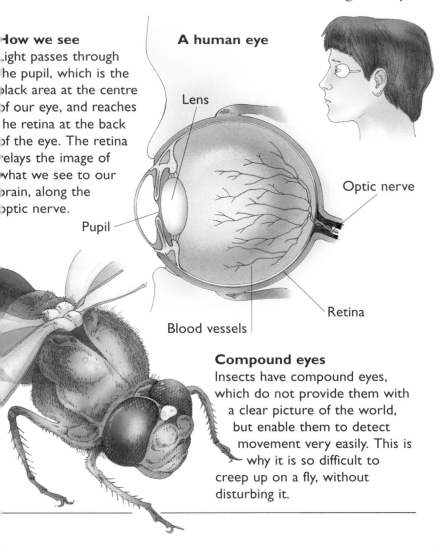

Lens

Optic nerve

Pupil

Retina

Blood vessels

Compound eyes

Insects have compound eyes, which do not provide them with a clear picture of the world, but enable them to detect movement very easily. This is why it is so difficult to creep up on a fly, without disturbing it.

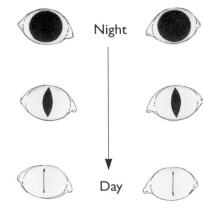

Night

Day

Closely set eyes

Cats and other hunting animals have eyes which point forwards. By superimposing the images from each eye, which overlap slightly, the brain provides the cat with a very accurate picture of the position of its prey.

Colour blindness

Distinguishing features amongst an array of different coloured dots is a good test for colour blindness.

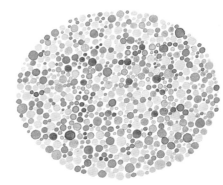

Letting light in

The shape of cats' pupils varies, depending on whether it is sunny or dark. At night the pupils are fully opened, to capture as much light as possible. In bright sunlight they constrict to slit-like openings.

Seeing at night and in colour

The retina, at the back of the eye, contains special cells called rods and cones. While cones are needed for colour vision, animals that hunt at night have more rods in their retinas, because these cells work better when the light is poor. Cats can see objects quite clearly in the dark which would not be visible to us. Not everyone can see individual colours easily. About one in thirty people, mostly men, are unable to distinguish between the colours red and green.

EARS

Our ears are important to us not just for hearing, but also for balance. This is the function of the semi-circular canals in our ears.

How we hear

The ear consists of the outer ear, the middle ear and the inner ear. A sound passes into the outer ear, and reaches the eardrum, causing a vibration which passes into the middle ear. This continues, like an echo, through the ear ossicle bones. The vibrations cause movement in the fluid in the cochlea, in the inner ear. This is then picked up by the auditory nerve, and the sound is carried to the brain.

Ears vary throughout the animal kingdom. Fish do not have ears, but instead, have lateral lines along their bodies to detect sound waves. Birds also have no earflaps but have ear holes, usually hidden by feathers. Marine mammals, like whales and seals, also lack earflaps.

Ear ossicles
There are three bones: the malleus, incus and stapes.

Auditory canal

Semi-circular canals

Inside an ear

Cochlea
Filled with fluid which vibrates in response to sound waves.

Eardrum

Earflap

Hearing ranges
High-pitched sounds made by some animals, like mice, are outside our hearing range. But they can be heard clearly by other animals, for example, cats.

Eustachian tube
Connects the middle ear to the throat.

Earflaps

The main purpose of earflaps is to trap sound waves and channel them down into the middle ear. In some mammals, such as the African elephant, the earflaps are very large. An elephant flaps its ears to help it to stay cool.

A DESERT FOX
In the desert, sounds travel a long way because there is little other noise. Animals which hunt here, like this fennec fox, usually have very large ears. This helps them to trap sound waves and so track down food more easily.

NOSES

The insides of our nostrils are lined with hairs, which act as filters to keep out dust. There are also tiny **glands** in the lining of our nose which produce **mucus**. This traps smaller particles of dust, preventing them from entering our lungs, where they could cause irritation and coughing. Trapped dust particles can be removed by blowing our nose. Air is warmed as it passes up the nostrils, gaining heat from the many blood vessels here.

Cross section of our airways

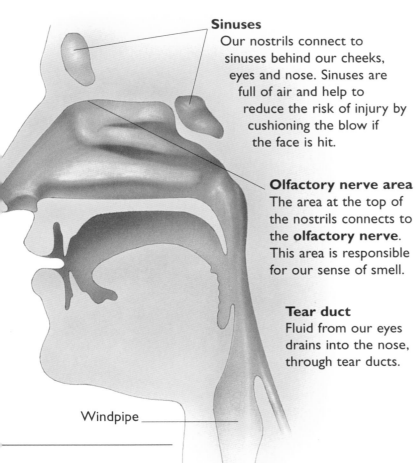

Sinuses
Our nostrils connect to sinuses behind our cheeks, eyes and nose. Sinuses are full of air and help to reduce the risk of injury by cushioning the blow if the face is hit.

Olfactory nerve area
The area at the top of the nostrils connects to the **olfactory nerve**. This area is responsible for our sense of smell.

Tear duct
Fluid from our eyes drains into the nose, through tear ducts.

Windpipe

Elephant's nose
An elephant's nose is joined with its upper lip, forming a trunk. An elephant sucks water up through its nose and squirts it into its mouth when drinking, or over its body if it is taking a shower. An elephant also uses its trunk to pull down branches to eat.

Ivory tusks are actually enlarged teeth.

Dog's nose
The shape of a dog's nose affects its ability to detect scents. Dogs with long, broad noses make the best trackers. Dogs' sense of smell is about one hundred times more sensitive than our own.

Nose looks shiny because it is moist.

Male mandrill
Some animals use their colourful noses to communicate with each other. The male mandrill uses his nose to act as a warning to other males, who might want a fight.

Only adult mandrills have scarlet noses.

BLOOD AND THE HEART

Our bodies contain about five litres of blood, which consists mainly of red and white blood cells in a fluid called plasma. Red blood cells carry oxygen from the lungs round the body, and bring carbon dioxide back to the lungs. This is made possible by a chemical called **haemoglobin**. Each red blood cell has a life of about three months.

Blood cells

Most blood cells are made in the bone marrow of our bodies. Some white blood cells are produced in the spleen and by lymph nodes round the body.

WILLIAM HARVEY (1578-1657)
In 1628 William Harvey proved that blood was circulated round the body, and that the heart was responsible for this movement.

Aorta

Arteries

Heart

Veins

The heart pumps blood round the body. The heart is made up of four chambers – two **atria** and two **ventricles** separated from each other by valves. As the heart contracts blood moves from the atria into the ventricles.

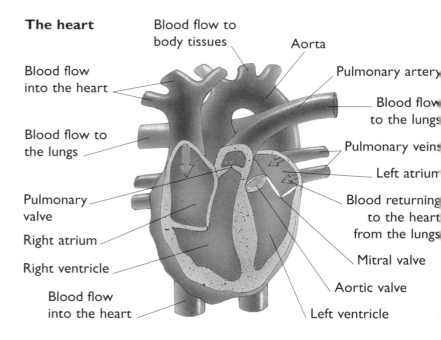

The heart

Blood flow to body tissues

Aorta

Blood flow into the heart

Pulmonary artery

Blood flow to the lungs

Blood flow to the lungs

Pulmonary veins

Left atrium

Pulmonary valve

Blood returning to the heart from the lungs

Right atrium

Mitral valve

Right ventricle

Aortic valve

Blood flow into the heart

Left ventricle

Your pulse

You can measure the rate of your heartbeat by taking your **pulse**. Press on the underside of your wrist. You should feel the movements in the artery wall there, caused by the pumping action of your heart. Count these for a minute, to find out your heart rate – how many times your heart beats per minute.

BREATHING

All living cells in our body need oxygen. This gas acts as a fuel, which allows food to be converted into energy. Air containing oxygen is taken into our body when we breathe in through our nose or mouth. The air passes down in a tube, called the windpipe, to the lungs in our chest.

How we breathe

As we inhale, our lungs expand with air. The air passages within the lungs are like a branching tree. Oxygen moves into the bloodstream from tiny branches called the **alveoli**, with carbon dioxide leaving the blood at the same time. When we exhale, the unwanted carbon dioxide passes out.

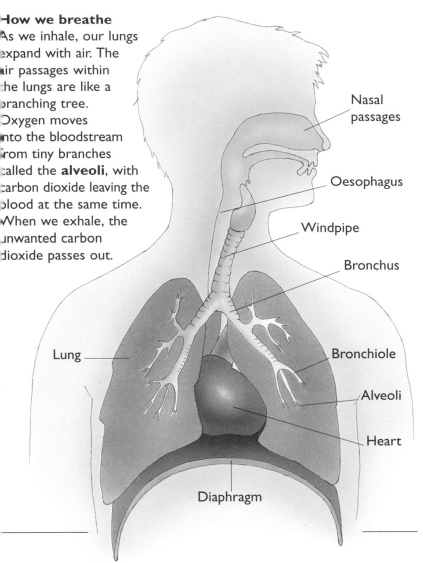

Nasal passages

Oesophagus

Windpipe

Bronchus

Bronchiole

Alveoli

Heart

Lung

Diaphragm

Where the air is thin

The higher up a mountain you climb, the less oxygen there will be in the air. This can make you feel sick and giddy. The body can adapt gradually to life at a high altitude. Mountain people have more red blood cells, which allow their bodies to take more oxygen from the air.

Pressure below the sea

If a diver returns to the surface quickly, nitrogen dissolves into the blood and forms gas bubbles in the bloodstream. These can block small blood vessels which can be fatal. This condition is known as the 'bends'.

BREATHING INTERMITTENTLY

Whales can live deep in the ocean, without suffering from the 'bends', but they return to the surface to breathe air. When whales come up for air, they breathe out through their nostrils, on top of their heads.

159

THE FEMALE BODY

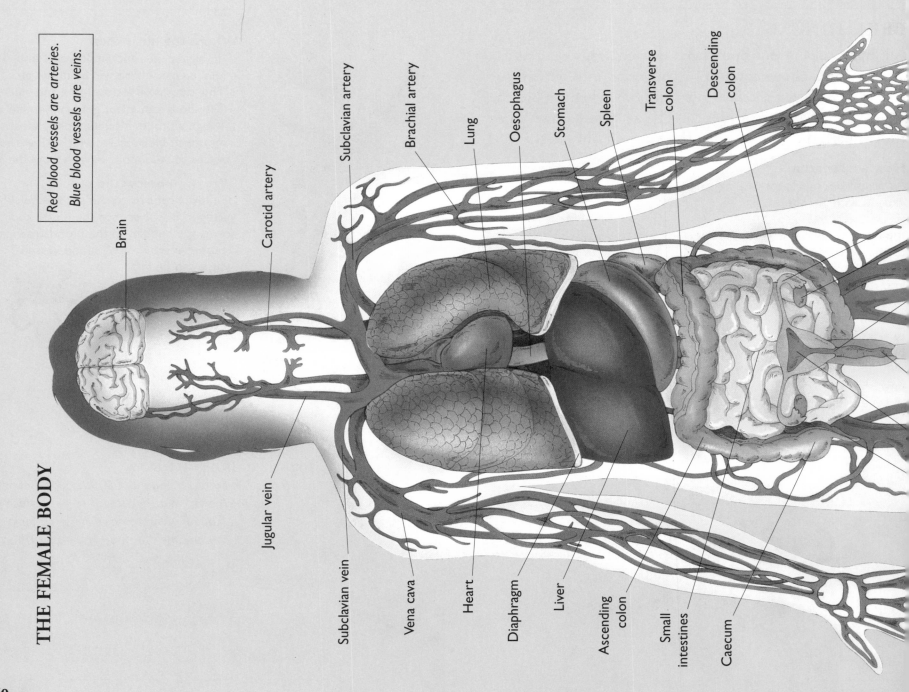

Red blood vessels are arteries.
Blue blood vessels are veins.

Brain

Carotid artery

Subclavian artery

Brachial artery

Lung

Oesophagus

Stomach

Spleen

Transverse colon

Descending colon

Jugular vein

Subclavian vein

Vena cava

Heart

Diaphragm

Liver

Ascending colon

Small intestines

Caecum

160

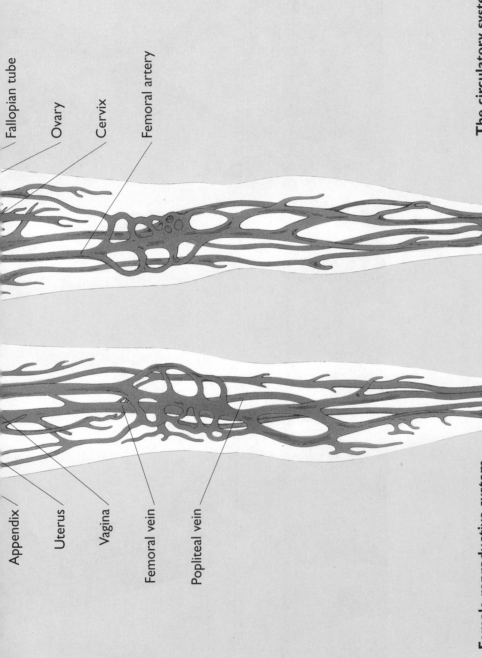

Fallopian tube

Ovary

Cervix

Femoral artery

Appendix

Uterus

Vagina

Femoral vein

Popliteal vein

Female reproductive system

The ovaries are at the start of the female reproductive system. A tiny egg released from here can develop into a baby, if it is fertilized. The egg travels down the Fallopian tube, towards the uterus. This is where the baby will develop and grow, connected to the wall of the uterus by the placenta. The baby has a separate blood supply from its mother. The baby's blood flows into the placenta via the umbilical cord and back again, absorbing oxygen from the placenta.

The circulatory system

Blood containing oxygen (oxygenated blood) travels from the lungs to the heart. From the heart, arteries carry blood all around the body. Arteries finally divide into tiny blood vessels, called capillaries. Oxygen leaves the blood in the capillaries and is replaced by carbon dioxide. Veins then take the blood containing carbon dioxide (deoxygenated blood) back to the heart. It is then pumped to the lungs to be oxygenated, ready for circulation.

161

ANIMAL BODIES

1 Black rhinoceros (Africa)

The pointed upper lip can be used rather like a hand, to pull vegetation. The horns are not made of bone, but keratin — the main component of our hair.

2 Duck-billed platypus (Australia)

This is one of only three living mammals which lay eggs. The duck-like beak helps the platypus to find food underwater, probing through mud for worms and other similar creatures hidden here.

3 Frilled lizard (Australia and Papua New Guinea)

Its bright collar of skin is raised to frighten predators.

4 White's tree frog (Australia and Papua New Guinea)

Sticky sucker pads on the toes of this frog help it to balance on lily leaves and climb trees.

5 Giant anteater (Central and South America)

The anteater's sharp claws help it to crack open the nests of ants and termites, so that its long tongue can probe inside to catch insects.

6 Greater flamingo (Caribbean and Galapagos Islands)

Its bill acts as a filter, sieving out the tiny water creatures which it eats. These creatures contain the coloured pigment which makes the flamingo's plumage pink.

7 Jacana (The Americas)

Very long toes mean this bird can walk easily on thin water lily pads, without sinking into the water.

8 Koala (Australia)

Sharp claws help the koala to climb without falling, and it spends most of its life in the treetops, feeding on eucalyptus leaves.

9 Scarlet-tufted malachite sunbird (Africa)

A long narrow bill allows this bird to probe flowers and find sweet nectar. The sunbird also pollinates flowers when feeding.

10 Tree kangaroo (Australia)

A tree kangaroo has special feet to help it climb and its tail provides balance in the trees where it lives.

11 Pond terrapin (The Americas)

Terrapins live mainly in water. Their shells are flatter in shape than those of tortoises, which helps them to swim fast.

12 White-spotted gecko (Middle East and North Africa)

The large, flat tips of this lizard's toes allow it to run straight up walls, without sliding off. Its colouration can change, to match its background.

Animals have bodies that are specially adapted to how they live.

FINGERS AND TOES

We use our fingers to do all kinds of things, from hanging onto a ladder to picking up delicate objects. This is made possible because of the muscles in our hands. These muscles are linked to **tendons** which control the movements of the joints in our fingers. All our muscles are controlled by nerves.

Gripping
Muscles have to exert exactly the right amount of pressure.

Sensitive muscles
If you grip an egg too tightly it will crack. But, if you don't hold it firmly enough, the egg will drop and break.

Fingerprints
The surface of the skin on our fingers is covered with ridges. These are known as fingerprint patterns. Each person has his or her own unique set of fingerprints.

DEW CLAWS

Dew claws

Dogs walk on four toes, with the fifth toe, the dew claw, held off the ground. The Norwegian puffin dog has two dew claws on each front foot, which help it to climb cliffs.

163

TONGUE AND TASTE

Our tongue lies at the bottom of our mouth, and while we can move the front very easily, it is firmly anchored at the back by muscles. Glands in our mouth produce saliva, which keeps our mouth moist. When we eat, more saliva is produced which helps us to soften and swallow our food.

Papillae
These are raised areas on the surface of the tongue, making it feel rough.

Taste buds
These are found in the papillae. There are more than 10,000 taste buds on the human tongue.

Soft palate

Uvula

Bitter tastes detected here.

Salty tastes are sensed here, on both sides.

Sweet items register here, at the tip of the tongue.

Sour tastes are picked up on both sides of our tongue, behind the salt tasting receptors.

A useful tongue
Cats use their tongues like a ladle, expanding them at the tip to lap up drinks easily. Cats also use their tongues for grooming. Cats' tongues have a rough surface that helps remove dead hairs.

A deceptive tongue
Some animals use their tongues for hunting. The alligator snapping turtle from North America waits for fish to swim into its mouth and then closes its jaws. The fish are lured by the shape of the turtle's tongue, mistaking it for a worm.

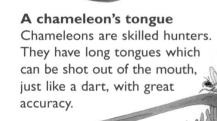

A chameleon's tongue
Chameleons are skilled hunters. They have long tongues which can be shot out of the mouth, just like a dart, with great accuracy.

The chameleon's prey sticks to the tip of the tongue, which is then pulled back into its mouth. This all happens so quickly, in just a fraction of a second, that it is hard to see except in slow motion. The muscles in the tongue and a bone at the back of the mouth propel the tongue out of the chameleon's mouth at high speed.

THE DIGESTIVE SYSTEM

We use our teeth to chew food before we swallow it. The narrow incisor and canine teeth at the front of our mouth allow us to bite chunks of food, which are ground down by the molar teeth at the back of our mouth.

The digestive process

Food passes down the **oesophagus** into the stomach, where it is mixed with digestive juices and ends up as a thickish liquid called chyme. This then passes through the small intestine. Enzymes, which are chemicals that break down food into simple substances, are released from the pancreas into the small intestine. Bile from the gall bladder, which is attached to the liver, helps to break down fatty foods.

Hormones

Hormones are chemical messengers that help the body to function. One of the most important hormones is insulin, which is produced in the pancreas and regulates the body's sugar level.

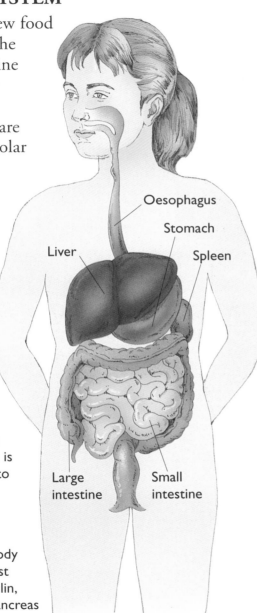

Oesophagus

Stomach

Liver

Spleen

Large intestine

Small intestine

Our intestines

The small intestine is lined with minute finger-like projections called **villi**, through which most of the basic ingredients in food are taken up into the body. After leaving the small intestine, the remains of the food enters the large intestine. Here, water is taken into the body, along with some vitamins.

Four stomachs in one

Cows have a four chambered stomach to help them digest the plants and grasses which they eat. Bacteria help digestion.

Bacteria and tiny organisms called protozoa live in two of a cow's stomach chambers – the rumen and reticulum. When cows are resting, food is regurgitated up into the mouth, chewed and swallowed again.

Rumen   Reticulum

At the next stage of a cow's digestive process, food passes into another stomach chamber, the omasum. Here, water is absorbed, and food carries on through the abomasum and intestines, to complete the digestive process.

Omasum   Abomasum

THE URINARY SYSTEM

Our bodies need to remove waste substances. This process is known as excretion. The lungs exhale carbon dioxide, while solid waste is passed out of the intestines. The kidneys have the task of filtering out unwanted nitrogen and other substances from the blood, as well as any excess water. They also help to balance the level of salt in our body.

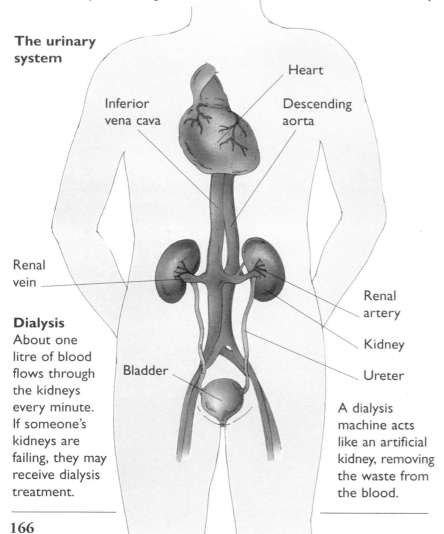

The urinary system

Inferior vena cava

Heart

Descending aorta

Renal vein

Renal artery

Kidney

Ureter

Bladder

Dialysis
About one litre of blood flows through the kidneys every minute. If someone's kidneys are failing, they may receive dialysis treatment.

A dialysis machine acts like an artificial kidney, removing the waste from the blood.

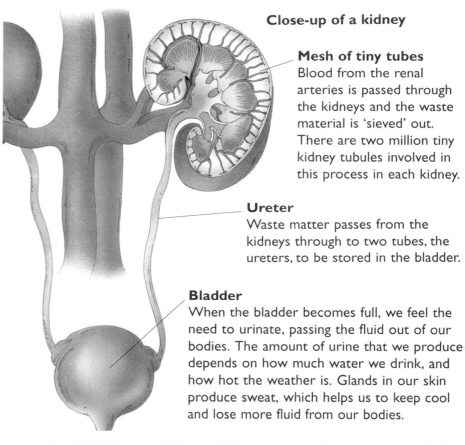

Close-up of a kidney

Mesh of tiny tubes
Blood from the renal arteries is passed through the kidneys and the waste material is 'sieved' out. There are two million tiny kidney tubules involved in this process in each kidney.

Ureter
Waste matter passes from the kidneys through to two tubes, the ureters, to be stored in the bladder.

Bladder
When the bladder becomes full, we feel the need to urinate, passing the fluid out of our bodies. The amount of urine that we produce depends on how much water we drink, and how hot the weather is. Glands in our skin produce sweat, which helps us to keep cool and lose more fluid from our bodies.

LIVING IN THE DESERT
Desert animals, such as gerbils, have very efficient kidneys and only produce a small amount of urine. This means that gerbils do not need to drink very often which helps them to survive in the desert where water is hard to find.

REPRODUCTION

The mating process results in sperm from the male fertilizing the female's eggs. This is known as reproduction. Whereas birds lay hard-shelled eggs in nests, almost all mammals give birth to live young. Their eggs develop in the part of the female's body called the uterus or womb. The length of time it takes for the young to grow here, up to the stage of being born, is called the **gestation period**.

Hereditary features

Babies often have features of both their parents. Eye and hair colour are two **traits** that are passed on through **genes**.

Gestation periods

The female Indian elephant has the longest gestation period of all animals – over two years. Baby elephants are about 90 centimetres tall at birth. A human baby takes nine months to grow inside its mother's body. But we then spend longer caring for our young than any other animal.

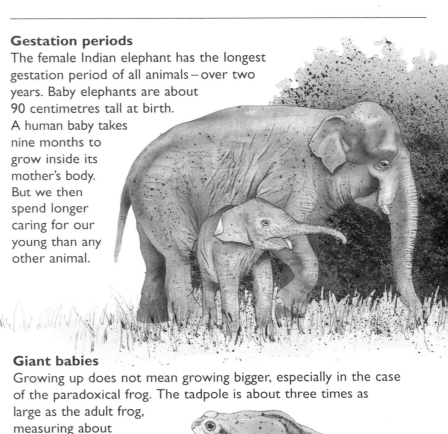

Giant babies

Growing up does not mean growing bigger, especially in the case of the paradoxical frog. The tadpole is about three times as large as the adult frog, measuring about twenty centimetres. These frogs are found in northern South America.

AMAZING BODY FACTS

- **Body cells** Cells lining the intestine last just three days, but brain cells can survive throughout our lives.

- **Eyesight** There are over 100 million cells at the back of each eyeball, which enable us to see.

- **Heart power** The heart has the strength to pump a jet of blood two metres high up into the air.

- **Strong creature** The rhinoceros beetle can lift objects that are 850 times its own weight. We can lift objects that are equal to seventeen times our own body weight.

- **Loudest sound** The call of the blue whale can be heard by another whale over 850 kilometres away on the other side of the ocean. Human voices can rarely be heard clearly more than 180 metres away.

- **Muscle power** There are a total of 639 muscles in the human body. These make up about half of our total body weight.

- **Nail growth** Fingernails grow about one millimetre each month, which is four times faster than toenails.

- **Hair** We have about 120,000 hairs on our head. Our hair grows at a rate of about one-and-a-quarter centimetres a month. Hair has been known to grow to almost four metres in length.

- **Sneezing** This can cause particles to be blown out of our nose at a speed of 167 kilometres per hour, which is much faster than the top speed of most cars.

GLOSSARY

Alveoli The smallest airways in the lungs, where oxygen passes into the blood and carbon dioxide leaves it.

Atria The chambers in the heart where blood returns from the body or the lungs.

Axon The connecting nerve fibre running from a nerve cell to a nerve ending.

Conscious Something which we are aware of, or an action which we can control, such as standing up.

Gene Part of the blueprint in our bodies that determines how we look and how our bodies function.

Gestation period The time taken for young mammals to develop in their mothers' bodies, before being born.

Gland An organ in the body, such as the pancreas, which releases chemicals.

Haemoglobin The colour pigment in our blood that makes it appear red, and carries oxygen from the lungs.

Joint The place where two bones join together and movement can take place.

Mucus A substance that keeps surfaces in the body moist, preventing infection or injury.

Oesophagus The tube that connects the mouth to the stomach.

Olfactory nerve The nerve carrying a scent to the brain.

Pulse The movement produced in the arteries by the heart beating.

Skeletal muscles Those muscles in our bodies which allow our skeleton to move.

Synapse The gap between the nerve fibre and the muscle.

Tendon A tough fibrous link which binds skeletal muscles onto bones.

Trait Characteristic, such as hair or eye colour, which is passed from parents to their offspring, through genes.

Ventricles The chambers in the heart which contract to drive blood out into the lungs or the body.

Villi Projections in the small intestine through which nutrients pass into the body.

SKELETONS

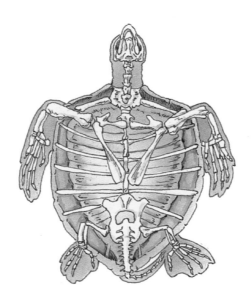

CONTENTS

WHAT IS A SKELETON?

A skeleton is the framework of an animal. It supports the body and holds it in shape. It also protects parts of the body from injury and helps its owner to move. In some animals the skeleton is inside the body, in others it is on the outside, and some animals have no skeleton at all.

Internal skeletons
We have a skeleton inside our bodies. This kind of skeleton supports our bodies in the same way as steel girders support a skyscraper. An internal skeletal frame holds a body or building up, and supports its weight.

Framework of a skyscraper

A human skeleton

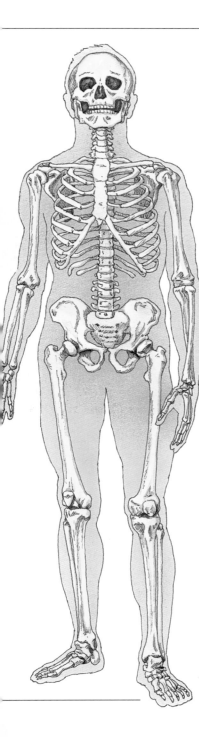

HUMAN SKELETONS

In some parts of your body, your bones are closer to the surface than in others. If you press the sides of your wrists or ankles, you will be able to feel the hard bones under the skin. Other bones are buried too deeply under big muscles to be felt easily.

Where bones touch each other, there is often an extra support, provided by **ligaments**. These act like tight tape, helping to bind your bones together and reinforce them. Your muscles are fixed to bones by **tendons**.

Staying upright
Your skeleton does the same job as the poles in a tent. It stops you from collapsing into a heap.

ANIMAL SKELETONS

Animals with backbones, or spines, are called **vertebrates.** They all have a skull, which protects the brain, at the top of the spine. Vertebrates have ribs at the sides of their bodies, and limbs, wings or fins supported by bones. All skeletons are adapted to an individual animal's lifestyle. For example, our skeleton is adapted for walking on two legs.

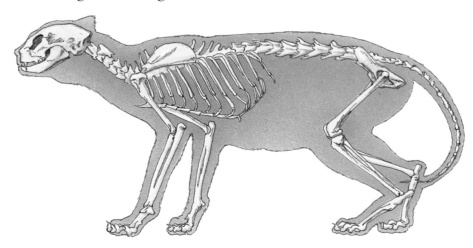

A cat's skeleton
Some animal skeletons, like a cat's, include a long tail. This helps the animal to jump and keep its balance.

A cat is a successful hunter and its skeleton is specially adapted for this activity – four long legs help a cat to run fast.

Fish bones
Fish use their bony fins, flat tail and muscular bodies for swimming.

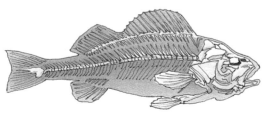

INSIDE BONES

Skeletons are made of bones that have to be light and strong. A bone has a thick, outer wall of compact bone and a softer part inside, called spongy bone.

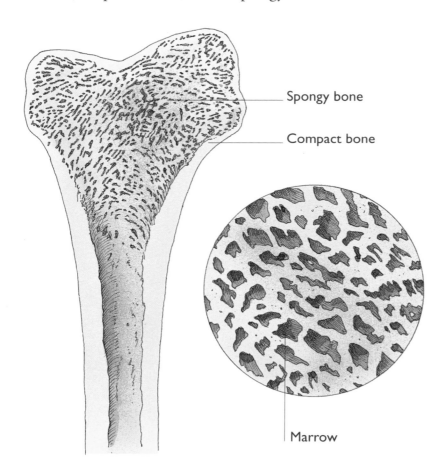

Spongy bone

Compact bone

Marrow

Healthy bones
Minerals, mainly calcium, vitamins and water help keep bones healthy and in tip-top condition.

Magnified spongy bone
The honeycomb-like holes are filled with **marrow**, which makes **red blood cells**.

BREAKING BONES

If you break a bone, it will slowly mend itself. It may need the help of a plaster cast to hold it straight while the fractured parts repair themselves. Doctors use X-rays to look at **fractures** and to check that bones are healing.

Seeing bones with X-rays

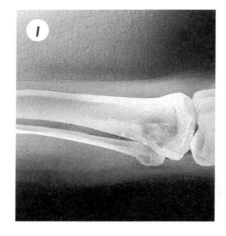

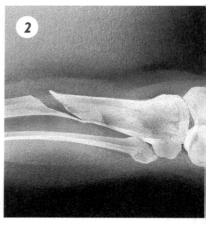

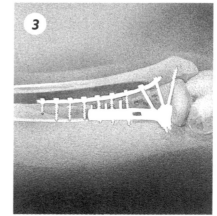

REVEALING BROKEN BONES

1 An X-ray of a normal, healthy bone.
2 An X-ray of a broken bone.
3 If a bone is badly broken, a surgeon may need to attach a metal plate to keep the fractured parts in place, as seen in this X-ray.

SHELLS AND EXOSKELETONS

Animals that do not have backbones are called **invertebrates**. Many animals, such as crabs or insects, have hard, outer casings called **exoskeletons**. Other animals, such as mussels or snails, are protected by shells, which are also exoskeletons. Exoskeletons cannot expand, so creatures such as the crab must shed their old shell before they can make a new, larger one.

Borrowing a skeleton

1 The hermit crab does not have an exoskeleton of its own and has to find an abandoned shell.

2 When the hermit crab grows bigger, it crawls out of its old shell.

2

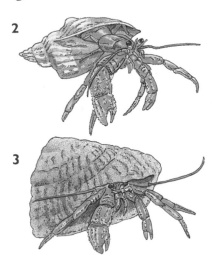

1

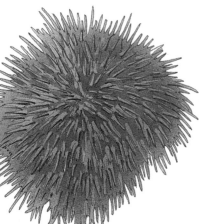

3

3 The hermit crab finds a larger shell to move into and so its soft body is protected.

Poisonous exoskeleton

The sea urchin has a hard, ball-shaped exoskeleton covered in sharp, poisonous spines. These spines may stick and break off into any animal which touches the sea urchin. This does not hurt the sea urchin.

ARMOUR FOR PROTECTION

Exoskeletons do the same job as bony skeletons, giving animals shape, support and protection. Some exoskeletons have flexible joints, like hinges in armour, that allow the animal to move.

Protecting a delicate body

The giant clam has a huge shell made up of two halves that fit together perfectly when they close.

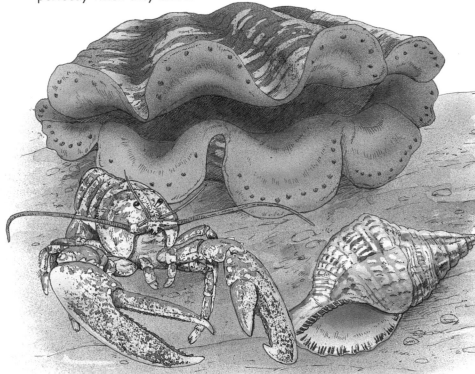

Large-clawed lobster

A lobster's pincers are strong enough to crush your finger.

Conch shell

Shells grow by adding extra spirals to the original shell.

HEADS AND SKULLS

A skull is a bony case which protects the brain. A baby's skull is very soft. This allows the skull to change shape and helps the baby to squeeze out of the mother's body at birth.

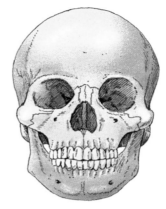

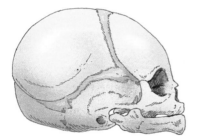

Fontanelle

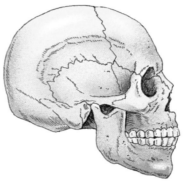

Top of a baby's skull
There is a soft central part of a baby's skull, called the fontanelle. It is usually filled with bone by the time the baby is one year old.

Why we don't all look the same
Although everyone has a similar basic skeleton, the shape of your skull is unique. It directly affects the appearance of your face. Experts can now reconstruct the faces of dead people from their skulls. This has shown how ancient Egyptian Pharaohs might once have looked.

Suture

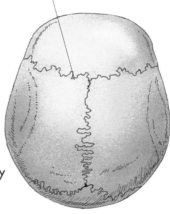

A hole for your nose
There is a hole in the skull where your nose should be. You can bend your nose because it is made of gristly **cartilage**, not bone.

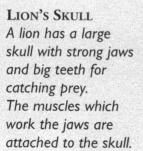

LION'S SKULL
A lion has a large skull with strong jaws and big teeth for catching prey. The muscles which work the jaws are attached to the skull.

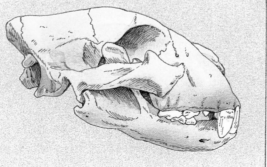

CROCODILE'S SKULL
A crocodile's eyes are set high on the head and its nostrils at the tip of the snout. This helps a crocodile see and breathe while submerged in water.

BACKBONES

Running down the middle of your back is a long chain of bones called your spine or backbone. It is made up of twenty-six **vertebrae**, linked together so that you can twist and bend. The bones also help to protect the **spinal cord**, a delicate bundle of nerves that runs between your brain and body.

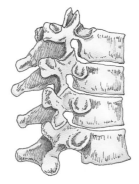

Your vertebrae

Your vertebrae are separate bones. You can feel each bone as a knobbly bump along your back. Imagine how difficult life would be if your back was a solid rod of inflexible bone!

Supporting your head

The top two vertebrae, called the atlas and axis, support your skull. The atlas allows you to nod your head up and down, and the axis enables you to shake your head from side-to-side.

Atlas

Axis

A tail bone

The lowest four bones of the spine are fused together. In some animals there may be more of these bones, forming a tail.

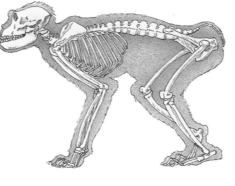

Using four legs

A monkey's skeleton looks similar to a human one, but the spine and **pelvis** are not strong enough to allow the monkey to walk upright on two legs. Monkeys can sometimes stand up on their hind legs, just to look around.

The giraffe

Despite being the tallest animal in the world, a giraffe's neck has the same number of bones as our neck has. Both have seven altogether.

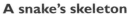

A snake's skeleton

A snake has a very small skull and a long spine, with as many as 400 vertebrae.

PROTECTING YOUR HEART

Your ribs branch off the upper part of your spine and curve round to form a strong cage around the chest. This helps to protect your heart and lungs. The rib cage is flexible and can move up and down to let you breathe in and out.

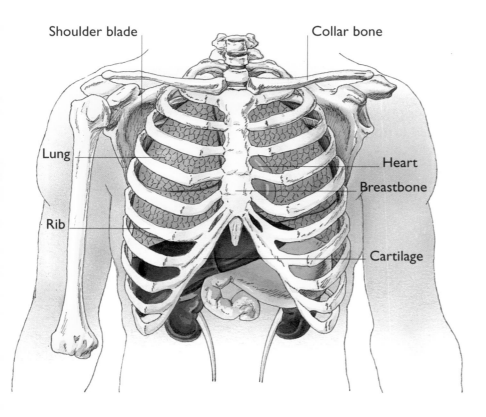

Shoulder blade

Collar bone

Lung

Heart

Breastbone

Rib

Cartilage

Your rib cage
Most people have twelve pairs of ribs. Very few people have eleven or thirteen pairs. The two bottom pairs of ribs, called **floating ribs**, are not attached to the breastbone.

HANDS AND FEET

The digits on our hands and feet are formed from fourteen bones. Fingers and toes are each made up of three bones, apart from our big toes, which are supported by two bones. Thumbs also have two bones in them. The way we move our hands and feet is controlled by muscles and joints.

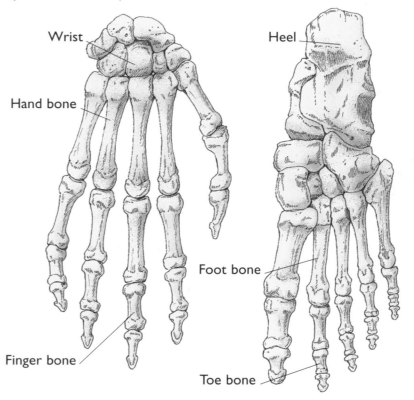

Wrist

Heel

Hand bone

Foot bone

Finger bone

Toe bone

The hand
The five hand bones attach to the eight wrist bones. These form the wrist and allow us to rotate our hands.

The foot
Our toe bones are wider and flatter than those in the fingers. These help to support the weight of our bodies.

ARMS, LEGS, HANDS AND FEET

Over half the bones in your body are in your arms and hands, legs and feet. They are specially designed to do a variety of jobs. Your arms and hands are built for precision and your legs and feet are built for balance, strength and movement.

Leg bones
The bones and muscles in your legs are longer and stronger than those in your arms, because your legs need to support your whole body.

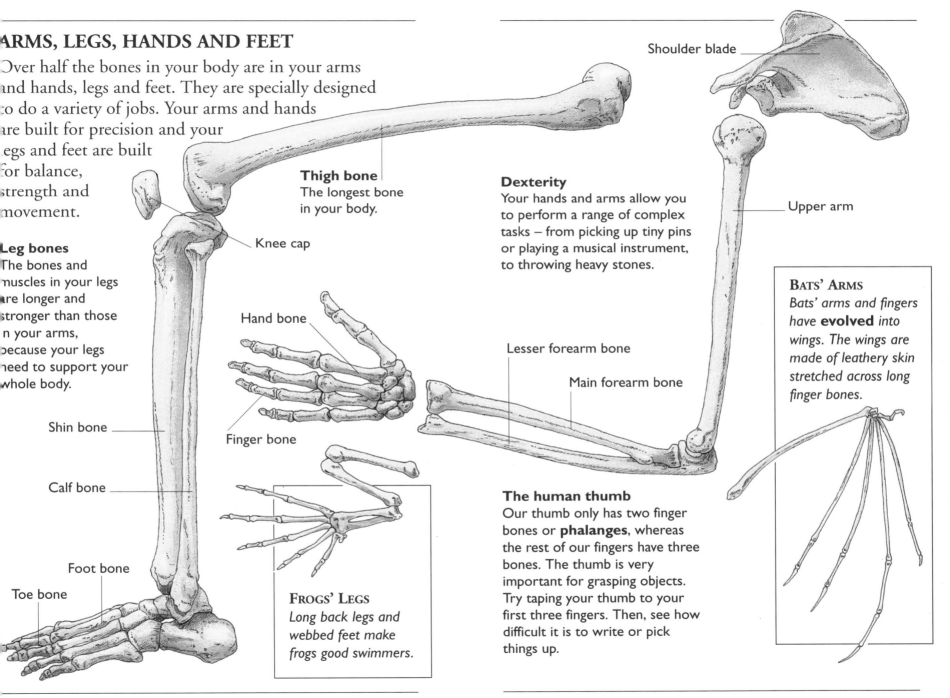

Shoulder blade

Thigh bone
The longest bone in your body.

Knee cap

Upper arm

Dexterity
Your hands and arms allow you to perform a range of complex tasks – from picking up tiny pins or playing a musical instrument, to throwing heavy stones.

Hand bone

Shin bone

Finger bone

Calf bone

Foot bone

Toe bone

Lesser forearm bone

Main forearm bone

FROGS' LEGS
Long back legs and webbed feet make frogs good swimmers.

The human thumb
Our thumb only has two finger bones or **phalanges**, whereas the rest of our fingers have three bones. The thumb is very important for grasping objects. Try taping your thumb to your first three fingers. Then, see how difficult it is to write or pick things up.

BATS' ARMS
*Bats' arms and fingers have **evolved** into wings. The wings are made of leathery skin stretched across long finger bones.*

177

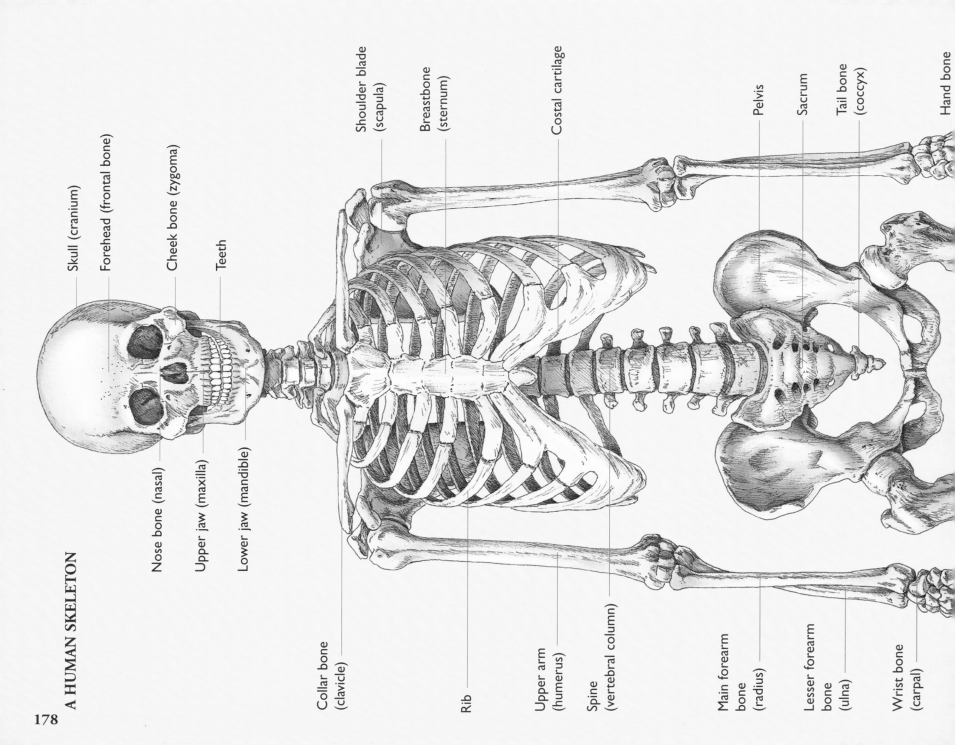

A HUMAN SKELETON

Skull (cranium)

Forehead (frontal bone)

Cheek bone (zygoma)

Teeth

Nose bone (nasal)

Upper jaw (maxilla)

Lower jaw (mandible)

Shoulder blade (scapula)

Breastbone (sternum)

Costal cartilage

Pelvis

Sacrum

Tail bone (coccyx)

Hand bone

Collar bone (clavicle)

Rib

Upper arm (humerus)

Spine (vertebral column)

Main forearm bone (radius)

Lesser forearm bone (ulna)

Wrist bone (carpal)

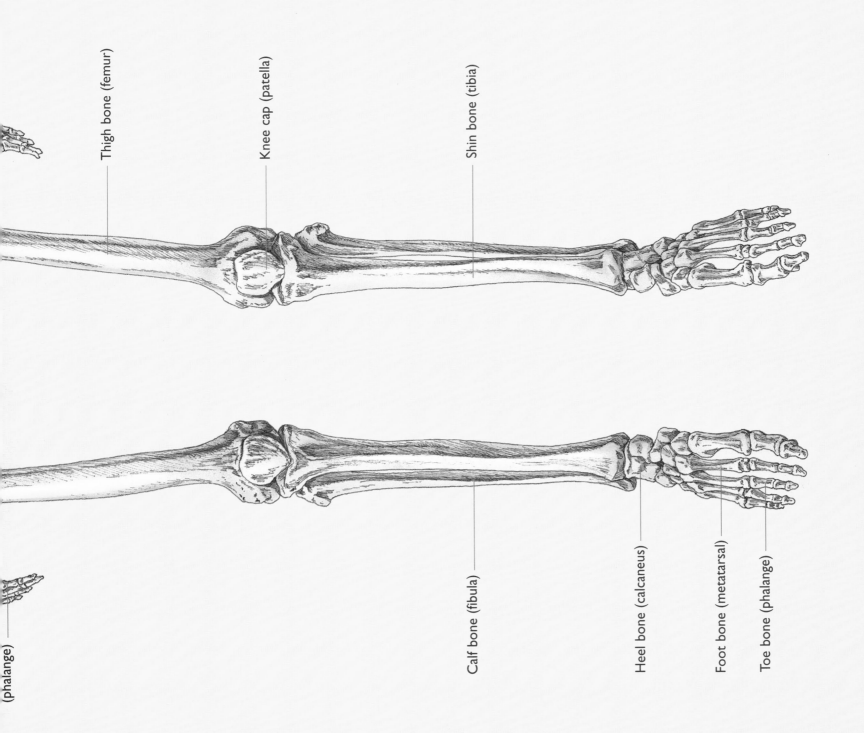

Thigh bone (femur)

Knee cap (patella)

Shin bone (tibia)

Calf bone (fibula)

Heel bone (calcaneus)

Foot bone (metatarsal)

Toe bone (phalange)

(phalange)

179

MOVING PARTS

Your skeleton helps you to move. There are **skeletal muscles** all over your body. Many are attached to bones. Muscles pull on the bones to move different parts of your body, such as your arms and legs. Bones and muscles work together and allow you to run, jump, pick things up and even breathe. Joints are places where two bones meet. They allow you to bend, turn or twist. There are joints all over your body – in your knees, ankles, elbows, shoulders, neck, back and even in your head.

JOINTS AND HOW THEY WORK

HINGE JOINTS
The elbow and knee joints work like hinges. They allow movement back and forth.

SLIDING JOINTS
Between the bones in your back are sliding joints. These enable each vertebra to rotate and slide over one another.

BALL AND SOCKET JOINTS
The shoulder and hip joints work like a ball bearing. This allows movement in several different directions.

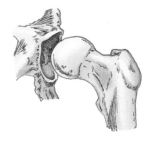

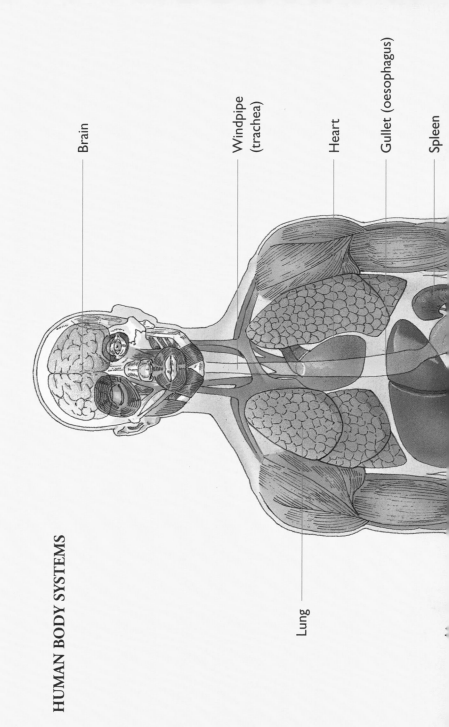

Brain

Windpipe (trachea)

Heart

Gullet (oesophagus)

Spleen

Lung

HUMAN BODY SYSTEMS

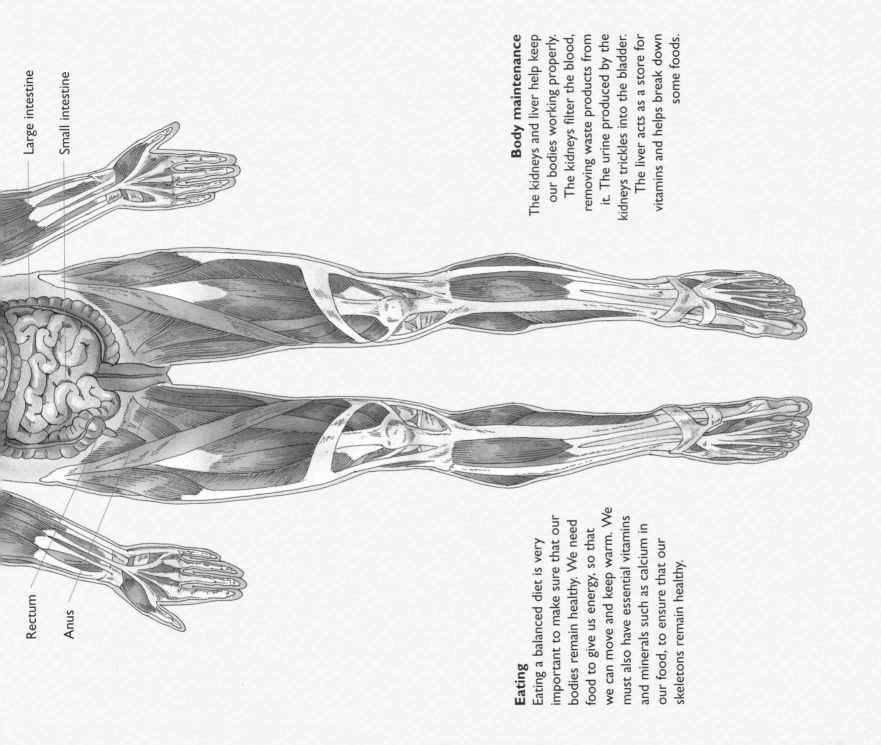

Large intestine

Small intestine

Rectum

Anus

Body maintenance

The kidneys and liver help keep our bodies working properly. The kidneys filter the blood, removing waste products from it. The urine produced by the kidneys trickles into the bladder. The liver acts as a store for vitamins and helps break down some foods.

Eating

Eating a balanced diet is very important to make sure that our bodies remain healthy. We need food to give us energy, so that we can move and keep warm. We must also have essential vitamins and minerals such as calcium in our food, to ensure that our skeletons remain healthy.

181

BIRDS' BONES

Birds' bodies are streamlined and lightweight, especially for flying. Most birds have light, hollow bones. The bones are light because they have lots of air spaces and are strong because they are strengthened by an internal intricate honeycomb frame of stiff, supporting struts.

Birds' front limbs have developed into wings. All birds have wings, but some do not use their wings for flying. Penguins, for example, use their wings as flippers, so they can swim fast underwater. Ostriches use their wings to help them run faster.

A falcon's skeleton

Beak

Neck vertebra

Rib

Toe

Tail vertebra

Breastbone

Thigh bone

Heel

A falcon's wing

Upper arm

Finger

Main forearm bone

Lesser forearm bone

Breastbone

Air spaces

Cross-section of a bird's bone

Skulls, teeth and toes
Birds have light skulls with no teeth in their mouths. A bird uses its beak to pick up food.

Most birds have four toes on each foot. One or two toes point backwards to help birds grip.

Flying
Birds' bones consist of bone tissue and large air spaces. This honeycombed structure makes the bones strong and light.

Powerful flight muscles are attached to a large breastbone. These muscles enable birds to flap their wings.

SEA CREATURES

Animals that live in the sea, for example fish, have skeletons specially adapted for swimming. Instead of limbs, fish have fins to help them move through the water and control their speed and direction. Mammals such as whales and dolphins, which also spend their whole lives in the sea, have flippers, rather than hands and feet. As a result, whales and dolphins can swim very fast. Seals also have flippers. Seals use their flippers to move on land, too.

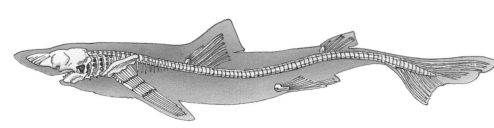

A shark's skeleton
A shark has no bones at all. Its skeleton is made of cartilage. Calcium is present in a shark's backbone, just as it is in ours. A shark's skeleton feels flexible, like our ears.

A fish's skeleton
Muscles attached to the fish's spine produce a side-to-side movement as the fish swims through water.

Fins
Fins are different for each kind of fish. Flatfish, such as plaice, swim using fins which run around the side of the fish's body.

A turtle's two skeletons
A turtle has a bony skeleton inside its body as well as a hard shell, or exoskeleton, on the outside. It can pull its head and flippers inside its shell, for protection.

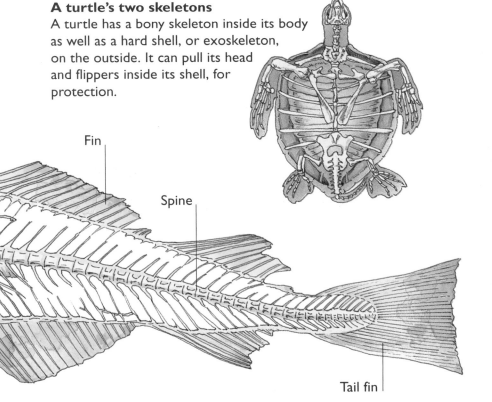

Eye socket

Skull

Fin

Spine

Fin

Tail fin

BODIES WITHOUT BONES

Some animals have neither a bony skeleton inside their body nor an exoskeleton around them. However, these animals, called invertebrates, have other ways of protecting and looking after themselves.

1 Starfish
A starfish moves along the seabed using tiny tubed feet with suckers at the ends. It feeds on shellfish, prising the shells open with its 'arms'.

2 Earthworm
An earthworm moves through the soil by bunching up and stretching out its body. Slime helps it move and rows of bristly hairs on its body help it to grip.

3 Jellyfish
A jellyfish moves through the sea by pumping water in and out of its body. Long tentacles, trailing underneath, are covered in tiny stinging cells and are poisonous enough to harm small fish.

5 Spanish dancer sea slug
The sea slug protects itself by producing a horrible-tasting substance from its skin. Its bright colour acts as a warning.

4 Sea fan
A sea fan may look like a plant but it is in fact an animal. Sea fans are covered in thousands of minute tubes that they use to trap food as it moves past in the water.

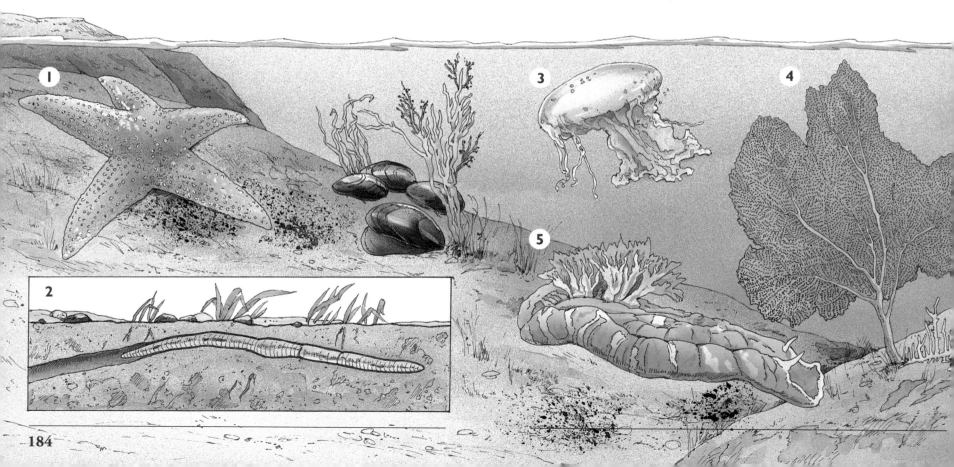

FOSSILS

Bones and shells are hard and long lasting. They remain intact in the ground for millions of years and are gradually turned into stone, and preserved as **fossils**. Most of what we know about **prehistoric** animals, like dinosaurs and early humans, comes from fossil evidence.

Formation of a fossil

Fossil hunting
Fossils can be deeply embedded in rock. Fossil hunters, or **palaeontologists**, carefully chip away at rocks around a bone, using implements like small hammers and saws. It can take years to piece together a whole dinosaur from the jigsaw of fossil bones.

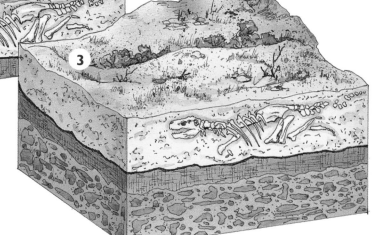

1 A dry, sandy or muddy place is ideal for the formation of fossils. When an animal dies, its soft parts rot away, leaving only the bones. This is why it is rare to find signs of skin on fossils, but in desert areas, the body may simply dry out, leaving the skin. Traces of fossilized dinosaur skin have been found in the Gobi desert in China.
2 Sand or mud builds up over the remains of an animal that has died and over millions of years the remains of the body are slowly transformed into rock. Eggs may also be turned into fossils. From these, we know that some dinosaurs laid eggs, rather than giving birth to live babies.
3 A fossil shows the size and shape of an animal and can also reveal skin markings.

AMAZING SKELETON FACTS

- **Our bones** The body of a human baby is made up of about 300 bones. Some of these gradually join together, so that the skeleton of an adult consists of 206 bones.

- **Hands and feet** Half of our bones are in our arms, hands, legs and feet.

- **Strength** Bone has the same strength as a hardwood timber such as mahogany.

- **Animal bones** In Asia, the ground down bones of tigers, bears and other large animals are believed to have medicinal powers. Already the tiger is on the edge of extinction, having been illegally hunted for its skeleton.

- **Protection** Seahorses cannot swim fast because their body is encased in bony plates. Their body armour deters other animals from attacking them.

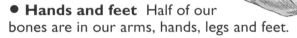

- **Blue whales** Blue whales have the largest skeleton of any animal. They can grow to a length of 35 metres, which is longer than an average swimming pool.

- **Horns and tusks** Both rhinoceros horns and elephant tusks are strong, and resemble bone. But in fact, elephant tusks are modified teeth, and rhino horn is made up of keratin—the same substance that makes our fingernails strong.

- **Giraffe** The world's tallest giraffe measured nearly six metres, taller than a double-decker bus.

GLOSSARY

Cartilage A firm, but flexible substance that may turn into bone.

Evolve To develop naturally over the years.

Exoskeleton A skeleton or shell outside an animal's body.

Floating ribs The bottom two pairs of ribs that are not attached to the breastbone.

Fontanelle The soft part on the top of a baby's skull.

Fossil The remains of a plant or animal that have been turned slowly into rock.

Fracture A break or splinter that occurs when a bone is broken.

Invertebrate An animal without a backbone.

Ligament A fibrous cord which binds bones and joints, and holds organs in place.

Marrow A substance found in spongy bone that makes red blood cells.

Palaeontologist A scientist who uses fossils to learn about previous forms of life.

Pelvis The large bone formation at the base of the spine that supports the back legs of humans and animals.

Phalange A bone in our toes and fingers, and also in the equivalent limbs of other vertebrates.

Prehistoric Something that lived or happened many years ago, before people began writing about events.

Red blood cell A microscopic cell that carries oxygen to parts of the body.

Skeletal muscle A fleshy part of the body that is made of many cells. When these cells change in shape, the muscle moves. This in turn causes the attached bone to move with the muscle.

Spinal cord A delicate bundle of nerves that runs from the brain to the base of the spine, through the backbone, controlling movements and reactions.

Suture A thin, wavy line on the skull that marks where the bones join together.

Tendon A tough, fibrous cord which connects a muscle to a bone.

Vertebra One of the bones that make up the backbone.

Vertebrate An animal that has a backbone.

THE SEA

CONTENTS

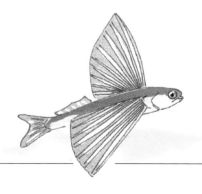

SEAS AND OCEANS

Nearly three-quarters of the Earth's surface is covered by oceans. These were first formed millions of years ago, as volcanoes produced steam, which cooled and became water. The salty taste of the sea comes from some of the **minerals**, especially sodium, which have dissolved into the water from the land.

What is a sea?

The world's oceans are divided into seven smaller areas, called seas. Some inland lakes are also known as seas, especially if they are very large and contain salty water.

CURRENTS, WAVES AND TIDES

The movement of water in the world's oceans is caused by currents. These follow set patterns, triggered by winds. Currents circulate the water, and help to even out the temperature in the entire ocean. Cold water from the **Poles** is forced towards the **Equator**, and so becomes warmer as a result. Other currents from the Equator then move water back towards the Poles.

Currents also occur close to land. Here they can be very dangerous, sweeping swimmers unexpectedly away from the shore.

The fastest current in the world is the Agulhas Current which flows along the east coast of Africa. It moves at a speed of about eight kilometres per hour.

Waves
Wind blowing on the surface of the sea causes **waves**. As the wind speed increases, so white tops appear on waves. The stronger the wind, the bigger the waves. When a wave hits a beach, it finally breaks up, and water drains back into the sea.

Tides
The way in which the sea moves up-and-down the beach each day depends on the **tides**. You can often spot the high tide mark, especially after a storm. This is where seaweed and other debris from the sea is left in a rough line, high up on the beach.

The daily effect of the orbit of the Moon around the Earth.

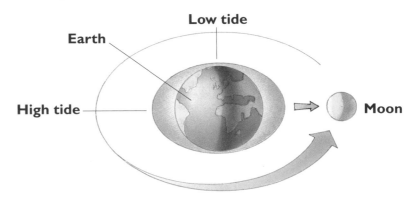

Low tide

Earth

High tide

Moon

Tides are the result of the daily pull of the Moon's **gravity** on the sea. Tide levels vary each day and in different parts of the world. When the Moon and Sun are aligned with the Earth, the gravitational pull becomes stronger, which causes higher tides. This happens about once every two weeks. At other times, neap tides occur. There is then less difference between high and low tides. The biggest tides occur in eastern Canada.

ALONG THE SEASHORE

A seashore can be pebbly or sandy. Beach sand is made up from rocks and seashells, which have been broken up by the sea into very fine particles. The origins of the sand affect its colour. Coral will give sand a whitish appearance, while yellow sand contains quartz, and black sand has either coal or volcanic rock in it.

In some areas, cliffs may make it impossible to reach the seashore. Waves crash directly against the cliff face, wearing it away and carving out caves and arches.

Seashore life

Animals that live along the seashore and in rock pools have to cope with the daily rise and fall of tides. Limpets cling tightly to the rocks so that they are not swept out to sea. Seaweeds have root-like anchors to hold on to rocks. Seaweeds are also coated in slime to stop them drying up when the tide is out.

Birds
At low tide, wading birds wander through **rock pools**.

Curlews
These birds use their long, pointed beaks to probe through sand in search of worms.

Barnacle

Mussel

Sea anemone

Starfish

Limpet

Shrimp

Bladder wrack

Crab

UNDERSEA LANDSCAPES

Around the edges of the land the seabed slopes before dropping down quite steeply into water, which may be four kilometres deep. The bottom of the sea is just as varied as dry land. Deep valleys, high mountain ranges, volcanoes and great plains stretch over this vast, submerged area of our planet.

Deep sea trenches

There are deep troughs in the seabed, called **trenches**. The Marianas Trench in the Pacific Ocean is over eleven kilometres deep. This is the deepest point in all the oceans.

DEEP SEA MOUNTAINS
The longest mountain range in the world is the Mid-Atlantic Ridge, which lies mainly under the sea.

Abyssal plains
Deep below the surface of the sea are flat areas called **abyssal plains**. These plains make up about half the ocean floor.

Seamounts
Isolated underwater mountains rise up from the ocean floor. One of the biggest **seamounts** is the Great Meteor Seamount in the Atlantic Ocean.

191

OCEAN FISH

Fish can be found throughout the world's oceans. Few creatures are as adaptable as fish. In the Antarctic Ocean, for example, ice fish have developed special chemicals in their blood to help them stay warm.

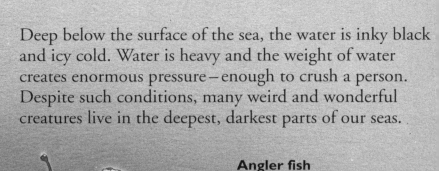

Flying fish
These swim near the surface and leap out of the water if in danger.

COD
*Cod live in **shoals** close to the ocean surface. When breeding, cod scatter their eggs in the sea.*

Sharks
These are the most feared fish in the sea. But not all sharks are dangerous. Nor are they all large.

FLATFISH
*When they first hatch, **flatfish** are shaped like normal fish. But as a flatfish grows older, one of its eyes gradually moves round to the upper side of its body. It then starts to swim using the fins around the edge of its body.*

Deep below the surface of the sea, the water is inky black and icy cold. Water is heavy and the weight of water creates enormous pressure – enough to crush a person. Despite such conditions, many weird and wonderful creatures live in the deepest, darkest parts of our seas.

Angler fish
Many deep sea creatures, such as angler fish, can make their own light. They use light to attract prey or to signal to one another.

Gulper eels
The huge mouth and stretchy stomach that these eels have helps them to swallow as much food as possible.

Tripod fish
Looking like a camera on a tripod, these fish balance above the seabed, supported on three thin fins. When prey passes by, tripod fish quickly pounce.

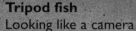

MARINE REPTILES

Marine reptiles live mainly in the tropical seas, where the water is warm. This allows them to maintain their body temperatures, whereas in colder waters they would become less active. There are fewer than sixty species of marine reptile alive today, but the world's oceans used to be home to many more different types, which are now known only as **fossils**.

Leatherback turtle
The leatherback turtle is the largest of the world's seven varieties of sea turtle. This turtle swims throughout the world's oceans.

Sea snake
There are about fifty different types of sea snake. They can be brightly coloured, and they are all highly poisonous. Sea snakes feed mainly on fish.

SEA CROCODILE
Some crocodiles can live in both fresh and salty water. Crocodiles of the Indian and Pacific Oceans are the biggest and most dangerous types of crocodile. At sea, crocodiles often drift with the currents.

SEA BIRDS

Many birds live close to the coast, coming inland when the weather is bad. Others use cliff faces as secure nesting sites, where they breed in huge colonies. A few birds, such as albatrosses, spend long periods gliding over the oceans, far away from land. They drop down to scoop up fish from the sea.

Frigate bird
This 'pirate of the skies' steals its food from other sea birds. It forces them to drop their catch and then grabs the food before it falls into the sea.

Pelican
The huge, expandable pouch under a pelican's beak acts like a fishing net. A pelican catches fish by trawling with its mouth open under the water. It then sieves the water, so it can swallow its catch.

Oystercatcher
This is one of a group of wading birds, which lives along the shoreline. The oystercatcher uses its blunt beak like a chisel to knock shellfish off the rocks.

PREHISTORIC SEA CREATURES

The first animals with backbones which evolved in the seas were fish. Their fossils have been traced back nearly 500 million years. Early fish were very different in appearance from those which live in the oceans today, but they did have gills. This meant that they could obtain oxygen from the water without coming up to the surface to breathe air.

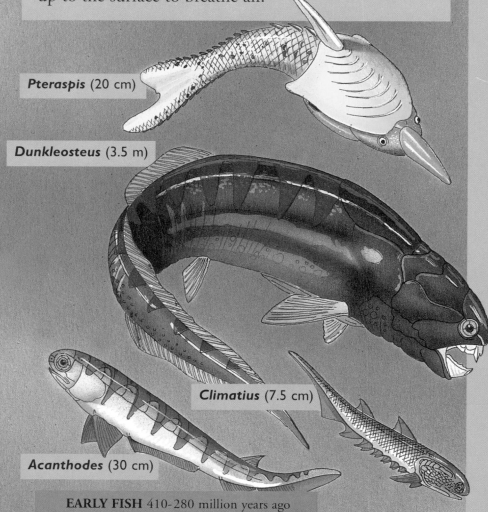

Pteraspis (20 cm)

Dunkleosteus (3.5 m)

Climatius (7.5 cm)

Acanthodes (30 cm)

EARLY FISH 410-280 million years ago

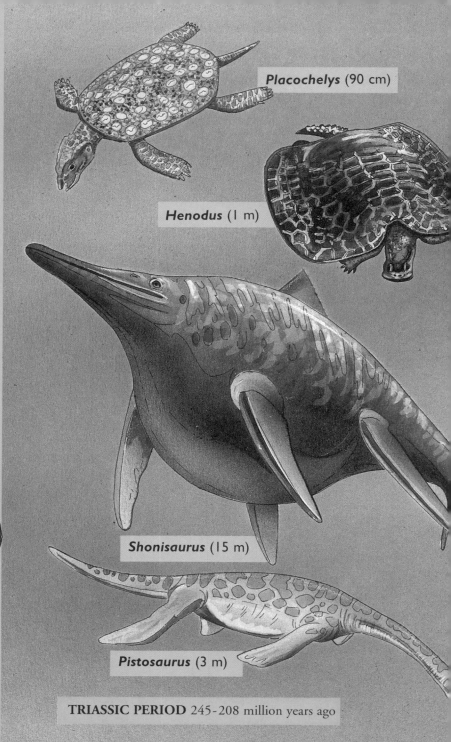

Placochelys (90 cm)

Henodus (1 m)

Shonisaurus (15 m)

Pistosaurus (3 m)

TRIASSIC PERIOD 245-208 million years ago

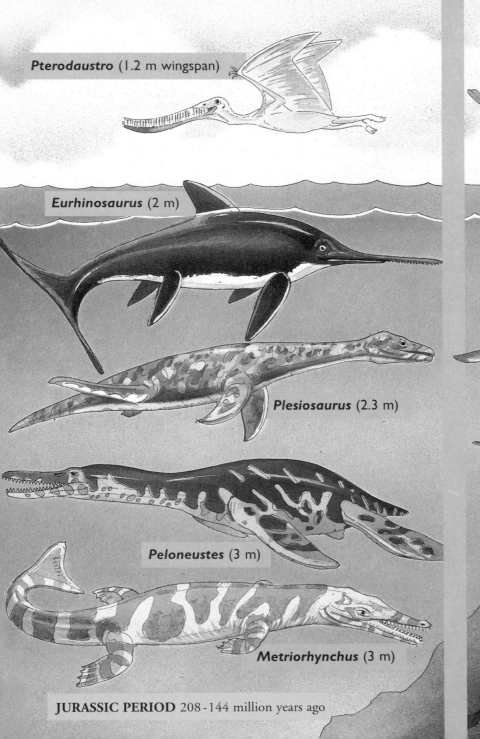

Pterodaustro (1.2 m wingspan)

Eurhinosaurus (2 m)

Plesiosaurus (2.3 m)

Peloneustes (3 m)

Metriorhynchus (3 m)

JURASSIC PERIOD 208-144 million years ago

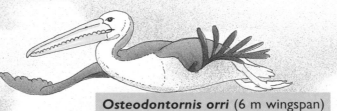

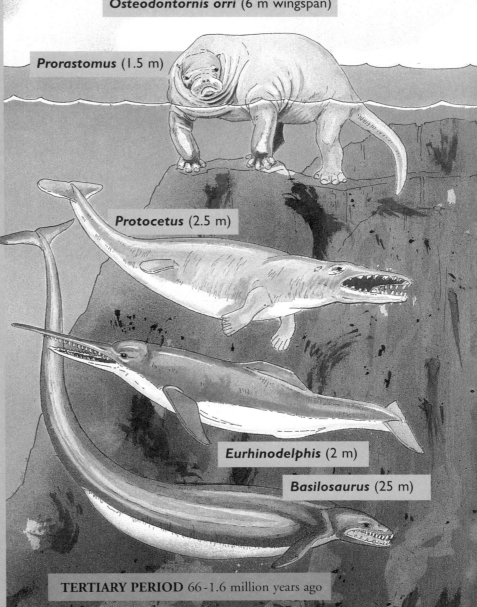

Osteodontornis orri (6 m wingspan)

Prorastomus (1.5 m)

Protocetus (2.5 m)

Eurhinodelphis (2 m)

Basilosaurus (25 m)

TERTIARY PERIOD 66-1.6 million years ago

PRESENT-DAY SEA CREATURES

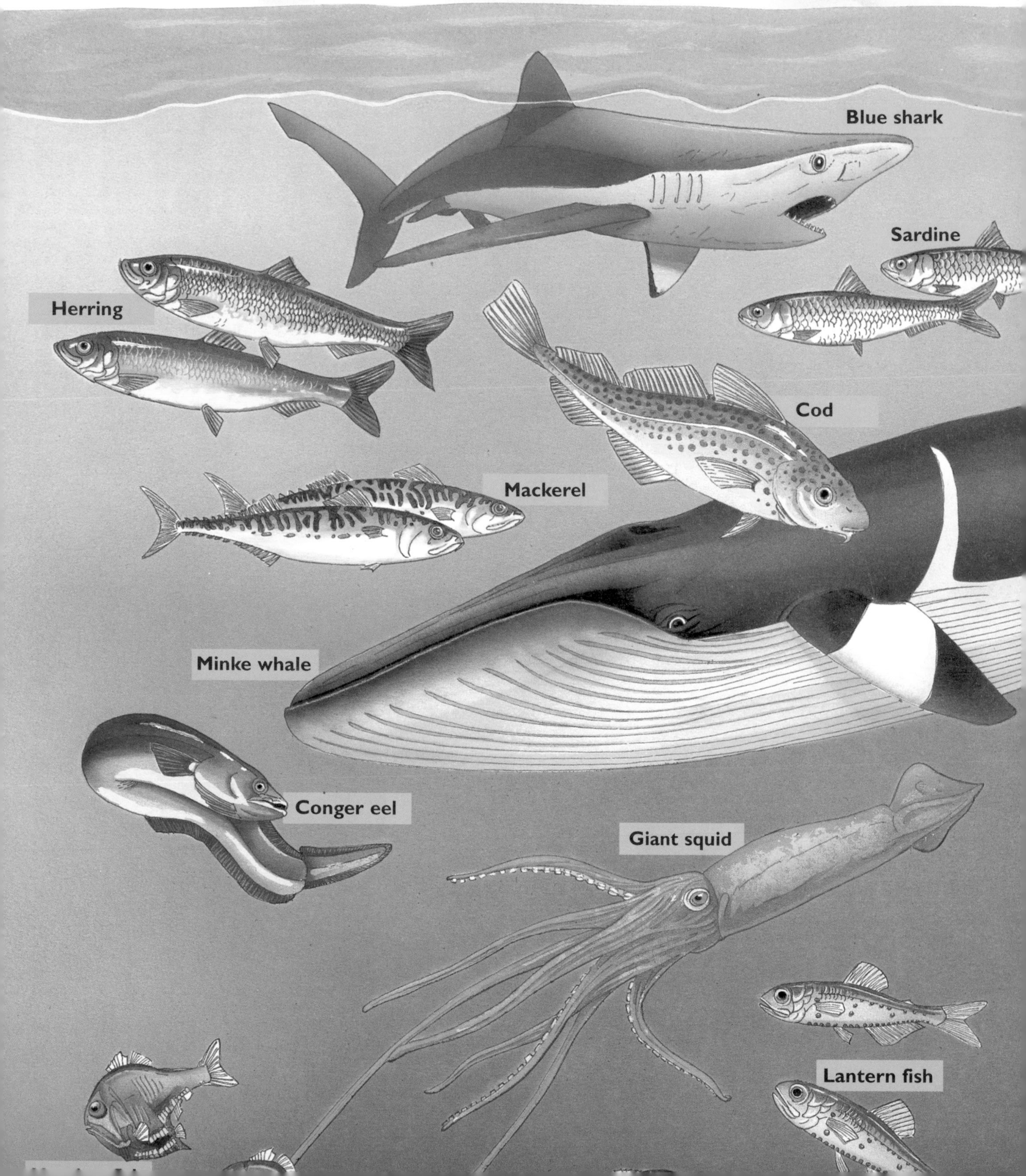
Blue shark
Sardine
Herring
Cod
Mackerel
Minke whale
Conger eel
Giant squid
Lantern fish

Viper

Angler fish

Gulper eel

THE DISCOVERY OF THE COELACANTH

In 1938, a fishing boat caught a strange fish which the crewmen did not recognise. Back in port, they asked an expert from the local museum to identify the fish for them. It turned out to be a coelacanth. Previously, these fish had only been known as fossils and they were thought to have been extinct for more than sixty million years. The coelacanth is now a protected fish.

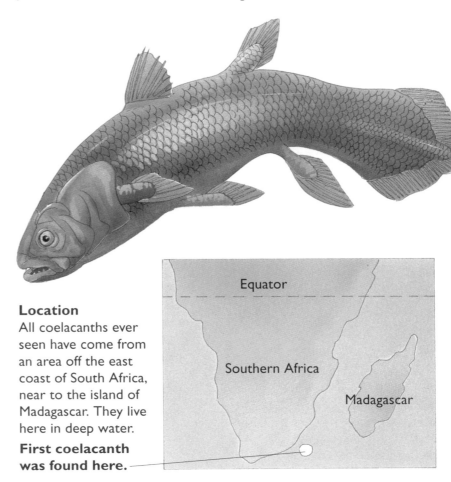

Equator

Location
All coelacanths ever seen have come from an area off the east coast of South Africa, near to the island of Madagascar. They live here in deep water.

Southern Africa

Madagascar

First coelacanth was found here.

SEA MAMMALS

All sea mammals are excellent swimmers. They have flippers, which help them to swim. Some sea mammals, such as whales and dolphins, spend their whole lives in the water and others, such as seals and walruses, divide their time between land and sea.

Sea otter
This sea mammal cleverly winds strands of seaweed around itself to stop it drifting away with the tide while it is sleeping. Sea otters place their front paws over their eyes when asleep.

Sea lion
Sea lions can swim faster than all other seals. They may reach a speed of 40 kilometres per hour for short distances.

Whale
All mammals need air to breathe. Whales can hold their breath for several hours underwater, but sooner or later, they have to come up for air.

DANGER AND ESCAPING DANGER

Octopus
If threatened, an octopus squirts a cloud of dark 'ink' to confuse its predator.

Sea cucumber
To escape from an attacker, the sea cucumber shoots out strings of sticky, spaghetti-like threads. The attacker is then too busy trying to disentangle itself to bother with the sea cucumber.

Stonefish
The stonefish is perfectly **camouflaged**. It looks just like a harmless stone on the seabed, but it is covered with deadly poisonous spines. The sting of this fish can kill people.

LIFE ON A CORAL REEF

Coral reefs grow in warm, shallow water in tropical seas. The coral is made up of millions of tiny sea creatures called coral **polyps**. The polyps build stony cases around their soft bodies for protection. When they die, the hard cases remain and gradually build up into a reef. A third of all fish live amongst the world's coral reefs.

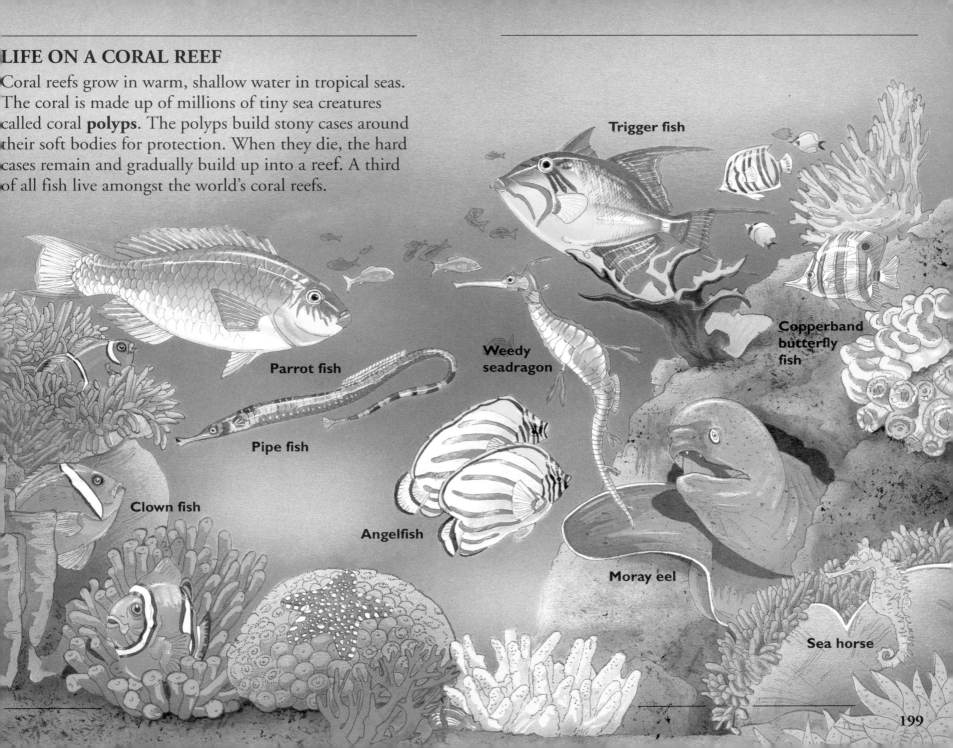

Trigger fish

Copperband butterfly fish

Weedy seadragon

Parrot fish

Pipe fish

Clown fish

Angelfish

Moray eel

Sea horse

SEA GIANTS AND DWARFS

Thousands of different kinds of animals and plants live in the sea. They come in a huge variety of shapes and sizes, from the gigantic blue whale to tiny plants that are smaller than pinheads.

Blue whale
The blue whale is the largest animal in the world. It is a mammal that lives in the sea.

Whale shark
The biggest fish in the sea, the whale shark, grows up to at least twelve metres in length, and weighs over fifteen tonnes. It feeds mainly on **phytoplankton** and is not dangerous.

Atlantic giant squid
This squid has the largest eyes of any known animal. The largest squid ever known was washed ashore in Newfoundland in 1878. Its tentacles were eleven metres in length.

Pacific giant kelp
A single strand of this seaweed can measure over 60 metres in length, which makes it the biggest sea plant. It also grows very fast.

DWARF GOBY
The smallest fish in the sea is the tiny dwarf goby, which lives in the Indian Ocean. Fully grown, it is less than one centimetre in length.

PHYTOPLANKTON
The smallest sea plants are phytoplankton. They drift on the surface, providing food for many sea animals, but they can only be seen under a microscope.

EXPLORING THE SEA

For thousands of years, people have sailed the seas. Their boats ranged in style from simple dug-out canoes to huge oil tankers. The earliest ocean journeys were voyages of exploration. Sailors relied on the Sun, Moon and stars to help **navigate**. Later, merchants searched for trade routes around the world.

A Polynesian raft

The Polynesian people built canoes from hollowed out tree trunks. Two canoes could be fixed together to make a raft. The Polynesian sailors used both sails and paddles to propel the boat. They strung seashells onto sticks, to make maps of the many islands in the South Pacific Ocean.

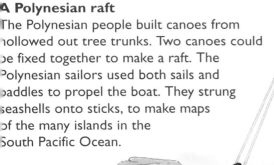

Exploring the oceans

Ferdinand Magellan left Spain with five ships and 260 men in 1519, in search of a westerly route to the Spice Islands, west of Papua New Guinea. Although the expedition eventually succeeded, Magellan was killed, and only one of the ships and eighteen men survived. It was the first round the world voyage.

Diving

Early diving suits had air piped to them through a hose from the surface. Divers today carry their own oxygen supply in tanks on their backs. This means they can explore underwater independently. Divers wear flippers and move their legs in an up and down motion to help them swim through the water.

Deep sea exploration

The deepest sea exploratory venture ever made was by the **bathyscaphe** *Trieste* in 1960. It dived to nearly eleven kilometres, almost to the bottom of the Marianas Trench.

TREASURES OF THE SEA

The sea is a vast treasure trove of useful and valuable things. Scientists analyse seabed rocks in search of oil or gas. Wells are drilled into the seabed and oil or gas is pumped up. Fish and other sea creatures are caught as food, and even seaweed is useful. It may be eaten, or used as a fertilizer.

Finding treasure

Underwater archaeologists study historical records of ships which sank. Archaeologists plan their search carefully on land, trying to locate where the ship was lost. Only then does diving start.

Treasure, ranging from gold bars and jewellery to ancient cargoes of porcelain, still lies undiscovered in sunken shipwrecks all over the world's seabeds.

An oil rig

Drilling for oil and gas in the sea is expensive and often dangerous. People live and work on the oil rig, usually for two weeks at a time. They are flown on and off the rig by helicopter.

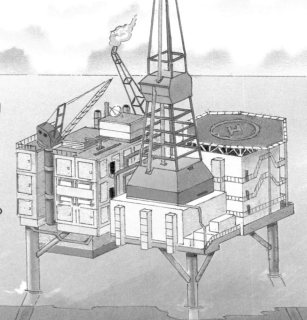

Underwater exploration

In deep water, submersible craft can be used to find wrecks, photograph them and even help to retrieve ancient artefacts.

TREASURE IN A SHELL

A pearl is formed if an oyster or clam shell has a speck of sand inside its shell. The oyster covers the speck with layers of a chemical called calcium carbonate. This builds up into a pearl.

SAVING THE SEAS

Pollution is a major threat to sea life. Steps are being taken to protect our marine environment. More than 300 areas round the world are now protected, and many governments have introduced laws that deter companies from polluting the seas.

Danger from sewage
Releasing raw **sewage** into the sea is dangerous because harmful bacteria can survive in water.

Hazards from ships
Oil spillages from damaged tankers kill large numbers of sea birds and other marine life.

Recently, overfishing has led to a decline in the numbers of popular food fish, such as tuna and shark. Controls are now being imposed to prevent fish from becoming **endangered**. Another environmental concern is the dumping of barrels of **toxic waste** into the sea. Toxic waste could eventually leak out of the barrels into the sea.

Fishing
Modern fishing methods result in high catches.

Barrels of toxic waste

Waste
Rubbish thrown from ships can be very dangerous to wildlife.

AMAZING SEA FACTS

- **Deepest living fish**
Brotulid fish have been found in the Puerto Rico Trench, 8,366 metres below the surface of the Atlantic Ocean.

- **Diving birds** The emperor penguin may dive to a depth of 250 metres below the surface of the sea.

- **Largest sea** The South China Sea, off the coast of Asia, is the largest sea in the world. It contains many small islands and has valuable stores of both gas and oil under its seabed.

- **Clearest water** It is possible to see an object which is 30 centimetres across, down to a depth of 80 metres below the surface, in the Weddell Sea, close to Antarctica.

- **Greatest number of eggs** The female ocean sunfish may lay as many as 30 million eggs at one time.

- **Sea bird droppings** Huge pillars of bird droppings, some more than 90 metres tall, have built up over thousands of years from colonies of sea birds nesting on islands off the coast of Peru, South America. In the 1800s, many columns were destroyed when it was realised they could be sold as a fertilizer, called guano.

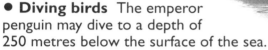

- **Largest ocean** The Pacific is the largest ocean in the world. Excluding the seas surrounding it, the Pacific represents nearly 50 per cent of the world's oceans.

- **Gold mine** More than 60,000 tonnes of gold have been found in the sea. All of the chemical elements exist in the world's oceans.

GLOSSARY

Abyssal plain A flat area occurring below the surface of the sea, sometimes in the deepest part of the oceans.

Bathyscaphe An underwater craft, used for exploring the deepest parts of the sea.

Camouflage The way in which a creature hides itself, using its body shape or colour to blend into the background.

Endangered When a species is in danger of dying out altogether and disappearing from the Earth.

Equator An imaginary line that runs round the middle of the Earth.

Flatfish A fish such as a plaice or a flounder, which has a flattened body shape.

Fossil The remains or impression of an animal or plant that have been preserved in the Earth.

Gravity The force that pulls the sea towards the Moon, creating tides.

Mineral A chemical that is present on land and may dissolve in water.

Navigate To direct or steer the course of a ship on a journey.

Phytoplankton Microscopic plants present in the oceans, which are a vital source of food for many sea creatures.

Poles The most northern and southerly parts of the Earth.

Pollution Damaging the environment with chemicals and waste materials.

Polyps Minute creatures whose remains gradually build up into a coral reef.

Rock pool The rocky area that still contains water when the tide goes out.

Seamount An underwater mountain that can rise from the seabed to a height of 4,000 metres.

Sewage Waste material.

Shoal A group of the same fish swimming together.

Tide The regular, daily movement of the sea up and down the beach.

Toxic waste Poisonous waste material.

Trench Crack in the seabed, which forms the deepest part of the oceans.

Wave The surface movement of the sea, caused by winds.

VOLCANOES
AND EARTHQUAKES

VOLCANOES
AND EARTHQUAKES

CONTENTS

INSIDE THE EARTH

The Earth is made up of a number of layers. Like an apple, it has a skin called the crust, a flesh called the **mantle** and a core.

Cross section of the Earth

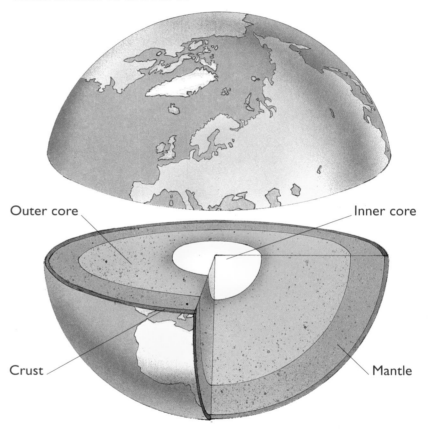

Outer core

Inner core

Crust

Mantle

The Earth's layers

The crust, made of solid rock, has two parts – continental crust and oceanic crust. Beneath the crust is the mantle, made from a layer of hot melted rock, called **magma**. The outer core is mainly made of nickel and iron and the inner core is mainly iron.

THE EARTH'S PLATES

The Earth's crust is in huge pieces called **plates**, which fit together like an enormous jigsaw puzzle. These plates are not still but are constantly moving about, extremely slowly. They may push together, pull apart, or slide past or under each other. Earthquakes and volcanoes are most likely to occur at the plate boundaries. Mountains and trenches also occur where plates meet.

Moving continents

The continents float on the plates and so when the plates move, the continents move too. About 500 million years ago, most of the southern continents were part of one big landmass, called Gondwanaland.

New land and sea

Very gradually, the landmasses drifted apart and came together again. About 175 million years ago, they formed a new continent called Pangaea and a new sea, called Tethys.

Break up of Pangaea

The large landmass of Pangaea began to break up. Over the past 175 million years, very gradually, the continents have drifted apart to where they are now. The continents are still drifting. This makes the Earth 'alive', unlike our Moon, which is said to be dead.

PLATES MOVING APART

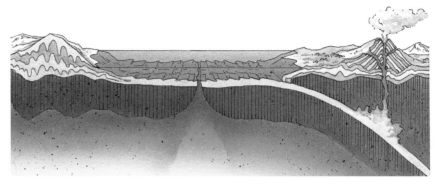

Currents of magma

Molten rock from the mantle pushes up through cracks at plate boundaries in the Earth's crust.

The Earth divided into plates

The plates move extremely slowly each year – about the rate that your fingernails grow.

Satellite pictures show that the Atlantic is growing wider whilst the Pacific is becoming narrower.

207

WHAT ARE VOLCANOES?

Volcanoes are formed when magma, a mixture of gases, ash and hot melted rock, gushes up from inside the Earth and breaks through a crack or weak spot in the Earth's crust. The magma lies in a **chamber** far below a volcano's **vent**. Pressure builds up, forcing the magma to escape through the vent. Once the magma reaches the surface it is called **lava**.

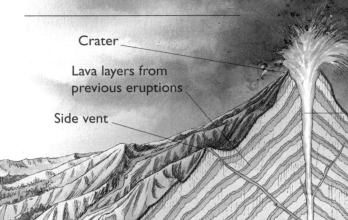

Crater

Lava layers from previous eruptions

Side vent

Ash cloud

Main vent

Magma chamber

Lava

Lava is red when hot, turning grey or even black as it cools and hardens on the Earth's surface.

Kinds of volcanoes

Dormant, active and extinct
Around the world, some 800 volcanoes regularly erupt. These are the **active** ones. Others seem to be quietly sleeping or **dormant**. (This comes from the Latin word *dorm*, meaning sleep). A dormant volcano is sometimes mistakenly thought to be **extinct**.

Basaltic volcanoes
These are wide and low, shaped like a shield, and so they are sometimes called shield volcanoes. Dark, runny lava, **basalt**, flows out of basaltic volcanoes, which occur where the Earth's crust is thin, especially at the bottom of the ocean.

Kinds of eruptions

Hawaiian hotspot
Runny lava gently pours out from a volcano with a very wide base.

Vesuvian
Cone-shaped volcanoes that erupt explosively, like Vesuvius in Italy.

Strombolian
Volcanoes that produce huge amounts of volcanic ash and **viscous** lava.

VOLCANOES UNDER THE SEA

More volcanoes are found under the sea than on land because the oceanic crust is thinner than the continental crust. Volcanoes usually occur along the edges of the plates, but some are found in places where the mantle is so hot that it melts a hole in the thin crust above. These are called hotspots. Some of the islands in Hawaii, in the Pacific Ocean, were made by volcanoes forming over a hotspot and erupting under the sea.

The new island of Surtsey

In the 1960s a new volcanic island gradually formed off the coast of Iceland. It took about four years for the volcanic rock to pile up above the sea. The new island was named Surtsey after Surt, the Nordic god of fire.

Iceland: land of fire and ice

Most underwater volcanoes cannot be seen, but sometimes layers of **pillow lava** build up into slopes. Eventually the volcanic slopes may grow high enough to emerge above the surface of the sea.

Hawaii: a chain of volcanoes

As the Pacific plate moves, it carries the volcano formed directly above the hotspot away. This volcano becomes extinct. In this way, a chain of volcanic islands – the Hawaiian islands – is created. An active volcano lies directly above the hotspot and extinct volcanoes beyond it.

New, active volcano forming over hotspot

Mauna Kea

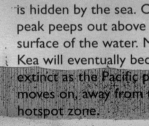

Most of this dormant volcano is hidden by the sea. Only its peak peeps out above the surface of the water. Mauna Kea will eventually become extinct as the Pacific plate moves on, away from the hotspot zone.

Plate boundary

VOLCANOES AROUND THE WORLD

Many dramatic and destructive volcanoes have erupted throughout history. Today there are more than 800 active volcanoes on Earth. About 300 of these are in the 'Ring of Fire', around the Pacific Ocean.

Covering of ash
When Mount St Helens, in America, erupted on 18 May 1980, a layer of hot ash covered the surrounding land.

Destroyed civilisation
In 1628 BC the volcano on the island of Santorini erupted, destroying an early civilisation that was flourishing there.

Big tidal wave
When the volcano erupted on the island of Krakatoa, the island was almost destroyed. The land shook so violently that it caused a gigantic tidal wave.

Changed climate
When Pinatubo, in the Philippines, erupted in 1991, gigantic clouds of dust and gases polluted the air. These drifted around the world, blocking the Sun's heat.

Famous eruptions

1 Santorini, Greece, 1628 BC
2 Vesuvius, Italy, AD 79
3 Mount Fuji, Japan, 1707
4 Mayon, Philippines, 1814
5 Tambora, Indonesia, 1815
6 Krakatoa, Indonesia, 1883
7 Mount Pelée, West Indies, 1902

Famous eruptions

8   Stromboli, Italy, 1921
9   Mauna Loa, Hawaii, 1950
10 Surtsey, Iceland, 1963
11 Kilauea, Hawaii, 1971
12 Mount St Helens, America, 1980
13 Etna, Sicily, 1986
14 Mount Pinatubo, Philippines, 1991

VOLCANOES ON OTHER PLANETS

Volcanoes do not just happen on Earth. The biggest volcano in the Solar System is on Mars and is called Mount Olympus. Venus too, has giant volcanoes, created by hotspots deep below the Venusian surface. Maxwell, the tallest Venusian volcano, is nearly two kilometres higher than Mount Everest – our highest continental mountain. Some volcanoes on Venus erupt continuously, pouring out clouds of gas into the flame-coloured sky.

Volcanoes on Io

Sulphur plumes rise from volcanoes on Io, one of Jupiter's moons. A *Voyager* spacecraft found that Io has at least six vents, where gas spurts hundreds of kilometres into space, in shapes that resemble huge umbrellas. Some plumes of gas rise 150 kilometres into the loan sky.

Martian volcanoes
Mount Olympus on Mars is the largest volcano in the Solar System. It is nearly three times as high as Mount Everest.

VOLCANIC ROCKS

When magma from within the Earth pours out of volcanoes – either on land or on the sea floor – as lava, it cools and hardens. Once the lava reaches the surface, it cools quickly and turns into a hard, dark rock, called basalt. As **minerals** in the lava cool, they form tiny crystals. You can see the crystals in basaltic rocks, especially if you use a magnifying glass.

Volcanologists
Studying and measuring volcanoes in action is very exciting and very dangerous. **Volcanologists** wear heatproof suits. Even so, several eminent volcanologists have been killed unexpectedly, due to an unpredictable eruption.

Rivers of rock
Some molten lava is like a red hot river of rock, setting fire to everything in its path. The lava and ash from volcanoes eventually breaks down and turns into a rich soil, on which plants and trees thrive.

Volcanic islands are usually lush and green with plenty of plant life.

POMPEII

Pompeii was a rich, beautiful and busy city, built in Roman times, on the slope of a mountain called Vesuvius, in Italy. Vesuvius was a volcano that had been dormant for so long that no one thought it would ever erupt again. Crops grew well in the volcanic soil around Vesuvius so the Romans built many villas, farms and grand houses with wonderful views overlooking the sea, on the side of the volcano.

Vesuvius was not as peaceful as everyone thought. It was still active, but a lump of solid rock was blocking its central vent.

The eruption
On 24 August AD 79 Vesuvius began to erupt with terrible force. Hot poisonous gases gushed up, blasting the rock that had been plugging the vent, high into the air. Pompeii was instantly buried under five metres of rock and ash.

The buried city of Herculaneum
When Vesuvius erupted, steam rising from the volcano turned into water, mixed with the volcanic ash and made a sticky mixture like hot, muddy cement. This rolled down one side of Vesuvius, completely burying the town of Herculaneum.

213

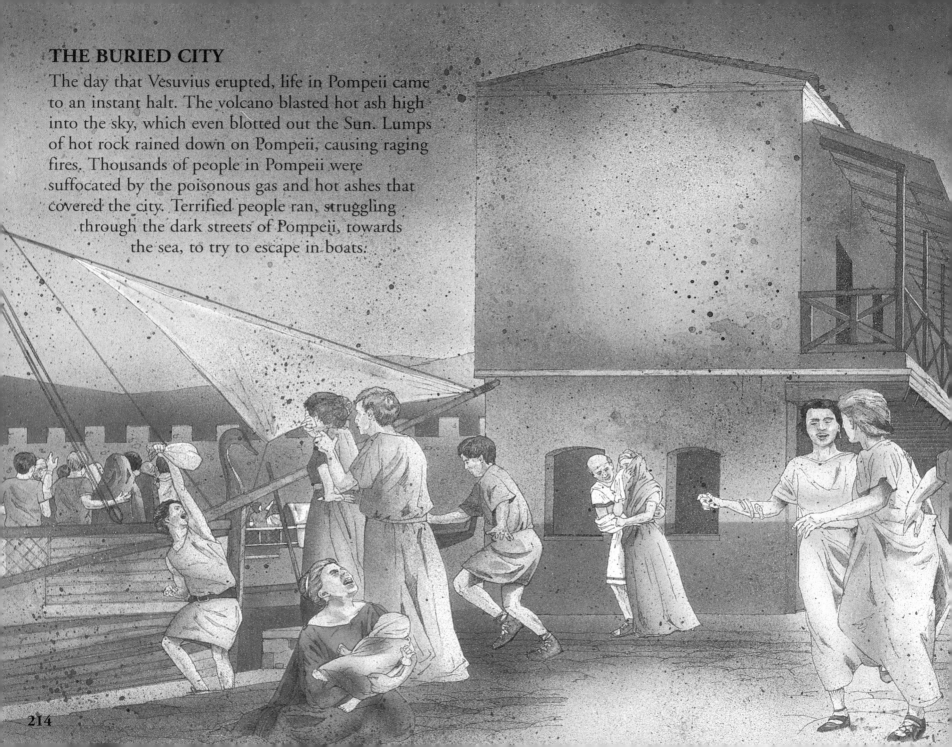

THE BURIED CITY

The day that Vesuvius erupted, life in Pompeii came to an instant halt. The volcano blasted hot ash high into the sky, which even blotted out the Sun. Lumps of hot rock rained down on Pompeii, causing raging fires. Thousands of people in Pompeii were suffocated by the poisonous gas and hot ashes that covered the city. Terrified people ran, struggling through the dark streets of Pompeii, towards the sea, to try to escape in boats.

214

POMPEII AND HERCULANEUM TODAY

The two towns of Pompeii and Herculaneum lay hidden and almost forgotten under a deep blanket of volcanic ash for 1,700 years. Earth, grass and vineyards covered the land where the cities had once stood. In the 18th century, scholars began to excavate the area. They were amazed to find two lost Roman cities.

Excavations
Centuries after Vesuvius suddenly erupted, archaeologists found the remains of Herculaneum and Pompeii, perfectly preserved under a layer of mud and volcanic ash.

Exhibition
A special museum was built in Italy, where many of the remains of the two cities are exhibited.

The ruins of Pompeii
Most of the ruins of Pompeii can still be seen. There is a town called Resina built on the site where Herculaneum once stood.

BURIED VOLCANIC ROCKS

Sometimes, magma never reaches the surface of the Earth as lava. Instead, it remains deep down in the Earth, as a magma chamber. Here, the magma cools slowly. Over millions of years the surface rocks are eroded to expose volcanic rock. This kind of volcanic rock is called **granite**. The crystals in granite are large because they had plenty of time to grow.

Pumice
Lava cools to form a very light, frothy rock, with air bubbles trapped in it.

Basalt
Basalt is a dark rock with tiny crystals. It is formed from solidified lava flows.

Granite
Granite is a volcanic rock which has large crystals of feldspar, quartz and mica.

Hidden features
When a very thin slice of rock is looked at under the microscope, in **polarised** light, the shapes and colours of the crystals in the rock are revealed.

A magnified thin section of granite

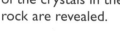

Feldspar crystal

Quartz crystal

Pyroxene crystal

Olivine crystal

WHY EARTHQUAKES HAPPEN

Most earthquakes occur along great cracks in the Earth called **fault lines**. These are found where one of the Earth's plates is moving against another and building up so much tension that the rock cracks. The sudden crack and movement of the rock sends out shock waves, making the ground shake violently. Every year there are more than one million tiny earthquakes around the world, which cause very little damage. About once every seven years, however there is a huge earthquake.

Cross section of an earthquake

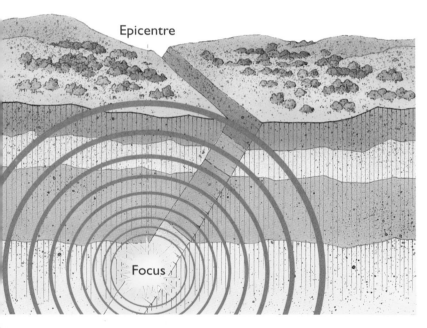

Epicentre

Focus

The focus and epicentre

The point within the Earth where the earthquake originates is called the focus. The place on the surface of the Earth, immediately above the focus, which vibrates, is called the epicentre.

THE SAN ANDREAS FAULT

Many earthquakes happen around the edges of the plate under the Pacific Ocean. The most famous earthquake zone is called the San Andreas fault. It is the most active fault line on Earth. The cities of San Francisco and Los Angeles in California, America, are built near the fault line. Terrible earthquakes have happened in both cities. An earthquake that hit Los Angeles on 17 January 1994 killed fifty-four people and caused chaos.

WHAT TO DO IN AN EARTHQUAKE

1 Put out any fires
Fires can be more dangerous than the earthquake itself.
2 Don't run about outside
Roof tiles, broken glass or concrete blocks might be falling from buildings.
3 Protect your head
If you can, find a soft pillow or cushion to protect yourself with. The safest place to crouch during an earthquake is inside a door frame.

An early earthquake detector
The earliest known **seismometer** was designed by Chang Heng, in China, in AD 132. It was built around a heavy pendulum, attached to dragon's heads, each of which held a metal ball. At the onset of an earthquake, the pendulum would swing, causing a ball to drop down into a frog. This frog pointed towards the earthquake.

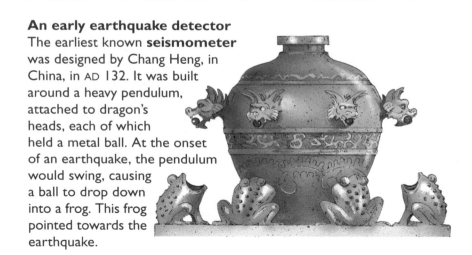

PREDICTING EARTHQUAKES

It is impossible to prevent earthquakes from happening, but scientists, called seismologists, can sometimes predict when and where an earthquake might occur. They use creepmeters, **laser beams** and magnetometers to monitor fault lines that are known to be active, where the Earth's plates are touching or sliding past one another.

A laser beam
Seismologists use laser beams to identify rock movements before an earthquake.

Sensitive animals
Some animals can detect vibrations or changes in the ground, moments before an earthquake happens, giving a warning signal.

Chinese snakes
Prior to the earthquake in Haicheng, China, in 1975, snakes left their burrows.

Japanese catfish
Before the earthquake in Tokyo, Japan, in 1923, catfish jumped out of their ponds.

MEASURING EARTHQUAKES

Instruments called seismometers measure the size of an earthquake. The relative force of each earthquake is recorded on a Richter scale. Most of the one million tremors that occur every year only reach 2 on the Richter scale. But the earthquakes that reach 8 on the scale are powerful enough to flatten cities.

A Richter scale recording

The Mercalli scale
The intensity of an earthquake can also be measured in terms of damage caused and the amount of shaking that happens.

SHOCK WAVES

During an earthquake, shock waves of pent-up energy are sent round the Earth. Some shock waves travel through all the layers of the Earth. These waves can be picked up on a seismometer anywhere in the world. They travel like sound waves, in the same way as you push and pull a toy train, to make it move. In an earthquake, the ground ripples up and down like water. This is caused by shock waves that only travel along the surface of the Earth, through solid rock. These waves make the ground rise and fall, like when you pump a wave through a rope.

QUAKEPROOF BUILDINGS

The extent of earthquake damage depends on where the earthquake strikes, the number of people living in the area and the types of buildings found there. Nothing can be done to prevent earthquakes happening, but with careful planning, the amount of damage can be reduced. Buildings in areas known to have earthquakes are specially designed to allow them to sway instead of collapsing. Steel cables or 'jackets' are used to strengthen buildings. Special foundations help to absorb ground movement and reduce shaking.

FAMOUS EARTHQUAKES

LISBON, PORTUGAL 1755

Tens of thousands of people died in this earthquake. Some people were killed when the shaking earth made the buildings collapse. Many more were killed when huge fires then broke out, destroying what was left of the city.

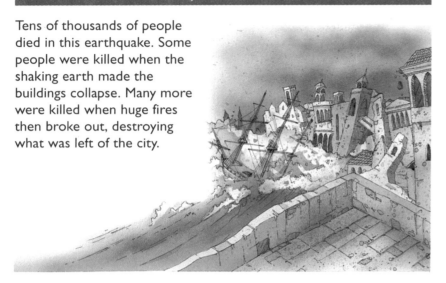

TOKYO, JAPAN 1923

Tokyo, the capital of Japan, is built on a fault line. In 1923, while families were cooking their mid-day meal, an unpredicted earthquake suddenly struck. Wooden houses collapsed without hurting many people. But, a whirlwind of fire followed the earthquake, killing thousands.

TANGSHAN, CHINA 1976

On 28 July 1976 there was an earthquake in Tangshan in China that was one of the greatest natural disasters in history. The city had been built over a gigantic coalmine, with many coal tunnels under the city. When the earthquake struck, all the tunnels collapsed and Tangshan was destroyed. Almost 650,000 people were killed.

ARMENIA 1988

In 1988 an earthquake hit the small country of Armenia. An international rescue effort helped the victims. Specially-trained dogs were used to find people trapped under the rubble. Also, infra-red cameras, that can detect body heat, were used to find people surviving under the rubble of fallen buildings.

TSUNAMIS

Earthquakes and volcanoes under the sea can sometimes cause a giant wave called a tsunami. A tsunami can be 50 metres tall and destroy everything in its path. They most often happen around the Pacific Ocean, and a warning system has been set up in this area, to predict a tsunami and tell people of the oncoming danger. A tsunami travels at speeds of up to 800 kilometres per hour. This is faster than a jet plane.

Formation of a tsunami

Drop a stone in a river and watch the ripples. The effect is similar to the pattern created by a tsunami and a **seismic wave**. As the sea becomes shallower near the coast, the waves become taller and build up into enormous heights – into waves as tall as tower blocks.

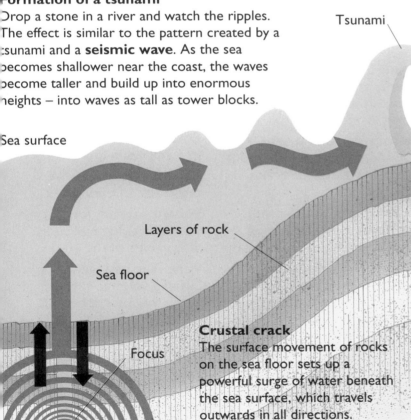

Tsunami

Sea surface

Layers of rock

Sea floor

Focus

Crustal crack
The surface movement of rocks on the sea floor sets up a powerful surge of water beneath the sea surface, which travels outwards in all directions.

HOT ROCKS

Volcanoes and earthquakes sometimes leave small holes or vents in the Earth. Gases from inside the Earth escape through these vents, called **fumaroles**. Hot volcanic rocks can heat water under the ground. The water becomes so hot that it turns into steam and gushes up out of the Earth in a boiling fountain. This is called a **geyser**. Sometimes the heated water bubbles through cracks in the ground and forms hot springs.

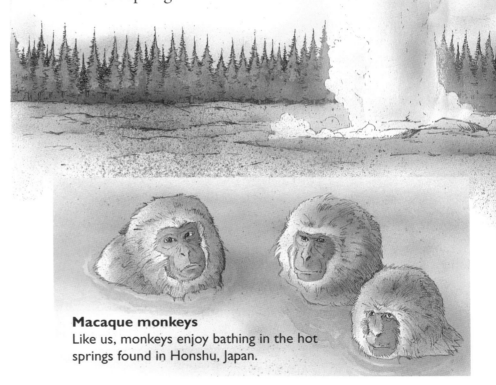

Macaque monkeys
Like us, monkeys enjoy bathing in the hot springs found in Honshu, Japan.

AMAZING VOLCANO & EARTHQUAKE FACTS

- **Tsunami** The highest tsunami ever recorded happened off the coast of southern Japan in April 1971. The wave created a great wall of water, 85 metres high.

- **Atlantis** In 1628 BC the volcanic island of Thera (now called Santorini), in Greece, erupted. All life on the island was completely destroyed. People believe that the story of the lost continent of Atlantis, the legendary island in the Atlantic Ocean, developed from stories of the terrible disaster on Santorini.

- **Krakatoa** When Krakatoa erupted, the noise made by the explosion was so loud that it was heard by people living in Australia, more than 7,500 kilometres away. It made the loudest noise ever recorded.

- **Detecting volcanoes** There are likely to be one million detectable signs of volcanic activity each year. Out of these, only about 1,000 eruptions cause any serious damage.

- **Geyser** The tallest geyser ever recorded was the Waimangu geyser, near Rotorua, in New Zealand. In 1903, it spouted up to a height of 460 metres.

- **Fire Dragons** People used to believe that fire-breathing dragons lived inside volcanoes and caused volcanoes to erupt.

GLOSSARY

Active A volcano which has erupted at least once in the past 10,000 years.

Basalt A volcanic rock that is dark and hard and is composed of tiny crystals.

Chamber The area deep within a volcano where hot, molten rock is found.

Dormant A volcano which has not erupted recently.

Extinct A volcano which is thought to be dead.

Fault line A crack in the Earth's surface, which may result in valleys or mountains being formed.

Fumarole A vent in a volcano through which steam and other gases are released.

Geyser A spring of hot water, heated in the depths of the Earth, which spurts up at regular intervals, like a fountain.

Granite A volcanic rock, with large crystals, that has cooled deep in the Earth.

Laser beam Straight line of light, which can be used to measure distances accurately.

Lava The very hot, melted rock ejected from a volcano.

Magma Molten rock in the Earth, which is ejected to form lava.

Mantle The area of the Earth separating the outer crust and the inner core.

Mineral A crystal which makes up rocks. A mineral is formed naturally in the Earth.

Pillow lava Pattern of lava produced by underwater volcanoes.

Plate A part of the outer layer of the Earth which moves very slowly. There are eight major plates, and other minor ones.

Polarise Light waves being transmitted in one direction

Seismic wave A wave caused by an earthquake.

Seismometer An instrument that measures movements of the ground.

Vent The passageway up and out of a volcano, through which the magma erupts.

Viscous Lava that does not flow freely.

Volcanologist A scientist who specifically studies and measures the Earth's volcanic activity.

THUNDER
AND LIGHTNING

CONTENTS

IN THE BEGINNING

Storms can be very frightening and destructive, but they may also be the reason that life exists on Earth. There have almost certainly been thunderstorms here since the planet was formed. There is evidence of storms which happened more than 200 million years ago, from changes in the soil caused by ancient lightning strikes.

The intense heat of lightning causes the oxygen and nitrogen gases in the air to combine together to form **nitrate**. This could have been used as food by the first tiny forms of life.

WINDY WEATHER

Wind is moving air. When air is heated, it becomes lighter and then rises. Cooler air from surrounding areas moves in to take the place of the rising air. This air movement forms wind. When wind blows, it brings different types of weather with it.

Heat from the Sun

The Sun's rays heat the Earth's surface. But, dust in the Earth's **atmosphere** from pollution and volcanic eruptions can reduce the amount of heat reaching the Earth. The dust acts like a barrier, reflecting heat back into space.

Warm air rises

Air rising in one place may form winds far away.

Cooler air moves in, forming a wind.

The strength of a wind depends on how fast the heated air rises. When air rises quickly, surrounding air rushes in to take its place. This forms strong, blustery winds. Light, gentle breezes happen when heated air rises slowly.

About 10,000 metres high in the atmosphere, there are areas of strong winds called jet streams. Jet streams help to move hot air from the Equator towards the poles, keeping the Earth at a more even temperature.

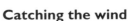

TRADE WINDS
In the past, sailing ships relied on winds to travel between continents. These winds, known as **trade winds**, *always blow in a constant direction.*

Arctic Circle

Equator

Antarctic Circle

Catching the wind

In parts of the sea close to the Equator, there is sometimes hardly any wind. Sailing ships can be dangerously becalmed in these areas of no wind, which are known as the **doldrums**.

225

CLOUDS AND RAIN

When water in rivers, lakes and seas is heated by the Sun, some of the water **evaporates** to form **water vapour**. As air rises, the water vapour cools and **condenses** onto pieces of dust in the air, forming tiny droplets of water that accumulate into clouds. When these drops of water fall from the cloud, it rains.

Clouds
Clouds are made up of millions of tiny water droplets.

A rain droplet
Water droplets in a cloud are thrown around by air currents. The droplets bump into each other, and grow bigger and bigger.

Rainfall
When water droplets in a cloud become too heavy, they fall as rain.

Clouds vary in size and shape, and they form layers in the sky. Cirrus and cirro-type clouds occur at altitudes above 7,500 metres. Alto-type clouds form lower down at heights of about 3,000 metres. Clouds can help to forecast the weather. For example, the appearance of cumulonimbus clouds indicates the approach of a storm.

Kinds of clouds

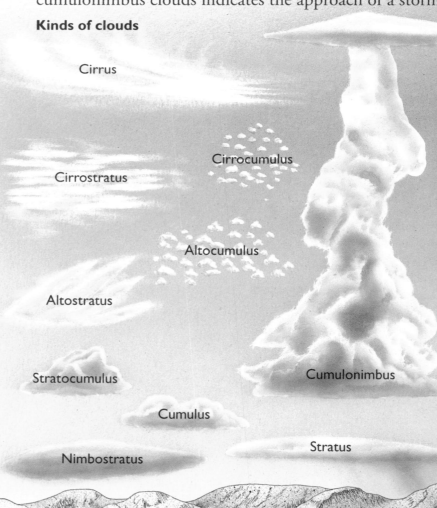

Cirrus

Cirrocumulus

Cirrostratus

Altocumulus

Altostratus

Stratocumulus

Cumulonimbus

Cumulus

Stratus

Nimbostratus

HEATING THE EARTH

The Earth is surrounded by a mixture of gases which form our atmosphere. The atmosphere is made up of several layers. The lowest layer is called the **troposphere** and contains the air that surrounds us. Movement of air within this layer brings different weather conditions. The ozone layer, which helps to protect us against harmful radiation from the Sun, occurs above the troposphere.

The Sun gives out huge amounts of energy, called **solar radiation**, which is made up of different types of rays. About 30 per cent of solar radiation is reflected straight back into space. The remaining 70 per cent warms the air, powers the weather systems on Earth and is used by plants to create energy for photosynthesis.

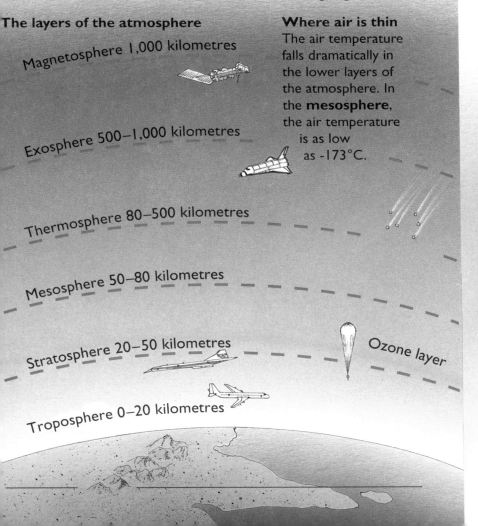

The layers of the atmosphere

Magnetosphere 1,000 kilometres

Exosphere 500–1,000 kilometres

Thermosphere 80–500 kilometres

Mesosphere 50–80 kilometres

Stratosphere 20–50 kilometres

Ozone layer

Troposphere 0–20 kilometres

Where air is thin
The air temperature falls dramatically in the lower layers of the atmosphere. In the **mesosphere**, the air temperature is as low as -173°C.

Our Sun
Temperatures on the surface of the Sun may be as high as 6,000°C.

Reflection
Clouds reflect some of the Sun's rays back into space.

Increasing storms
A global temperature rise of one degree Celsius could mean that there will be five times as many thunderstorms than there are now.

The greenhouse effect
A build up of gases, such as carbon dioxide, from Earth is occurring in the atmosphere. Although the Sun's rays can reach the Earth, the gases are forming a barrier to prevent heat escaping, acting like the glass in a greenhouse. This effect creates **global warming**.

SOLAR SYSTEM STORMS

The Earth is not the only planet where there is thunder and lightning. Storms may occur on some of the other planets in the Solar System. Signs of thunderstorms have been seen on photographs relayed back through space to Earth by satellites and spacecraft.

There is no lightning on Mercury or on our Moon, because they have no atmosphere. Nobody knows for sure whether there are thunderstorms on the outer planets – Uranus, Neptune and Pluto.

Jupiter
The *Voyager* spaceprobes flew past Jupiter in 1979 and detected huge lightning flashes and storms in Jupiter's atmosphere. The *Great Red Spot* may itself be a storm so big that it could swallow three planets the size of the Earth.

Mars
Lightning is generated in dust storms on Mars. It forms in the same way as it does in sandstorms on Earth – by particles of sand rubbing together.

Neptune
Winds on Neptune blow ten times faster than hurricane force winds on Earth, making Neptune the windiest place in the Solar System.

Pluto

Uranus

Mercury

Earth

Sun

Venus
In 1978, *Pioneer* spaceprobes found thick clouds of sulphuric acid droplets floating 50 kilometres high in a thick Venusian atmosphere. Beneath the clouds, there is gloomy darkness lit only by flashes of great thunder and lightning storms.

Saturn
Saturn is like Jupiter, but smaller and less active. It also has thunderstorms.

Storms on the Sun
Storms do occur on the Sun. They consist of ultra-hot gas that sweeps outwards in a powerful wind that affects the whole family of planets.

SPARKS OF LIGHTNING

Water droplets are changed into small ice particles as they are blown upwards in the sky and become frozen. Within a storm cloud, there is a layer of heavy ice balls through which smaller particles of ice are blown. As the particles hit the ice balls, there is a separation of electrical charge into positive and negative particles. This builds up and causes sheet lightning in the cloud.

———— Sprite

A storm cloud

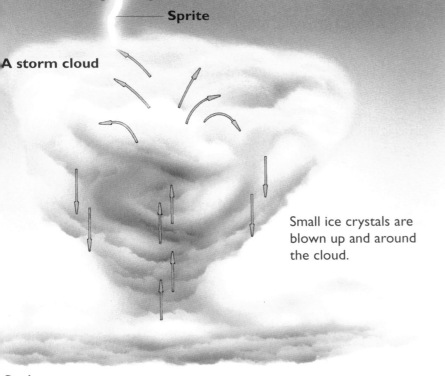

Small ice crystals are blown up and around the cloud.

Sprites
Brief flashes of light, known as **sprites**, have been seen above storm clouds. We do not know what causes a sprite.

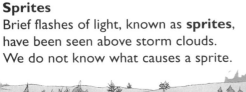

Lightning begins as a small spark in a thundercloud. As it travels towards Earth, the spark connects up with an object here. When this link is made, the effect is similar to turning on a light switch. The lightning strikes the ground and can pass down through it. The light actually moves upwards from the ground, towards the sky.

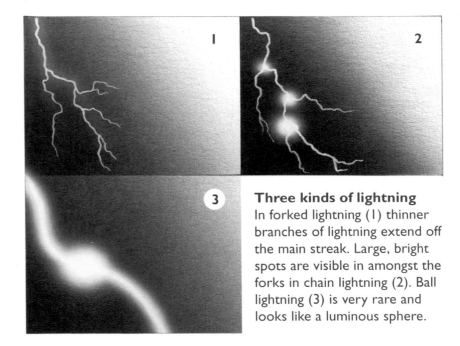

Three kinds of lightning
In forked lightning (1) thinner branches of lightning extend off the main streak. Large, bright spots are visible in amongst the forks in chain lightning (2). Ball lightning (3) is very rare and looks like a luminous sphere.

WHAT IS LIGHTNING?

Thunder and lightning both happen at the same time, but you see lightning before you hear thunder because light travels much faster than sound.

Today, many high buildings are protected from being struck by lightning by metal rods called **conductors**. The lightning is channelled along the rod and through a cable so that it drains away safely into the ground, rather than damaging the building.

A shocking experience
Benjamin Franklin, an American statesman and scientist, was the first person to prove that lightning was a form of electricity, by a dangerous experiment. He flew a kite, made from a silk handkerchief, in a storm and saw how the sparks flew from the string to the metal key attached to it, and then on to his hand. His research led to the development of the first lightning conductor, in 1753.

An electrical spark
Lightning is simply a gigantic electrical spark. Sparks may occur in the clouds, producing sheet lightning, or they may move from a cloud to the ground, causing forked lightning.

THE SOUND OF THUNDER

Thunder is caused by lightning and is really hot air exploding. A flash of lightning is extremely hot and as it travels, it makes the air around it expand and contract very quickly, causing the loud rumbling crash or crack of thunder.

Thunderbird
North American Indians believed thunder was caused by huge thunderbirds, which rose up in the sky and caused the noise by flapping their wings.

Thor
In Scandinavia, the Norse god Thor was said to cause thunder with his hammer, battling with giants in the skies.

Measuring a storm
You can measure how far away a storm is by counting the seconds between the flash of lightning and the sound of thunder. Dividing the number of seconds by three will then tell you how near or how far away the storm is, in kilometres.

HURRICANES, TYPHOONS AND CYCLONES

In tropical areas where the air is hot and moist, thunderstorms over the warm sea sometimes develop into violent, whirling storms called hurricanes. In the North Pacific Ocean and the China Sea they are called **typhoons**, and elsewhere they are known as **cyclones**. When a hurricane is forecast, people living in coastal areas often evacuate their houses and go inland. Hurricanes usually die out soon after hitting land.

In the eye of a storm

In the centre of the storm is a calm, quiet area called the eye.

Cross section of a hurricane

Strong howling winds rush in and spiral upwards forming massive clouds.

Flashes of lightning often occur.

Torrential rain falls.

Air rises very quickly above a warm sea.

Hurricane winds can reach speeds of 300 kilometres per hour.

HURRICANE DAMAGE

Hurricanes cause a great deal of damage. They occur in warm, tropical areas (1). Heavy rain and huge waves can flood the land near coasts (2). Fierce winds batter and destroy buildings and trees (3).

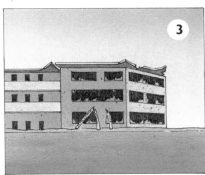

STAYING SAFE IN A STORM

One of the safest places to be in a thunderstorm is in a car. Metal has a low resistance to electricity, so the electricity will flow through the metal rather than passing inside the car and hurting the people inside.

AVOIDING DANGER

If you find yourself out in a thunderstorm and you cannot get inside a vehicle, crouch down with your legs together. This should help to protect you, as lightning usually strikes the tallest object around. People can survive being hit by lightning, provided that it misses both the heart and the central nervous system.

FLYING IN A STORM

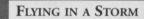

Pilots try to avoid thunderstorms but sometimes it is impossible to fly around a storm. On average, every airliner will be struck about once a year. In almost all cases, a plane acts like a metal case and the lightning passes safely through it.

It is always a good idea not to be trapped outdoors in a storm. Lightning kills about 400 people every year in America alone. Storms bring other dangers, such as falling trees, floods and high seas.

STAYING SAFE INSIDE

Speaking on the telephone with a storm overhead can be dangerous because lightning may pass down the line to the metal earpiece.

It is wise to disconnect the television aerial because if this is struck by lightning, it may blow up your television set and cause a fire.

Fishing is dangerous

Stop fishing when there is a thunderstorm. Simply holding the fishing rod up can attract a lightning strike, and act as a conductor, passing the electricity through your body.

Staying out in the open playing golf during a thunderstorm is exceedingly risky. But you should also avoid taking shelter under a tree. Lightning may strike the tree, and the shock can travel a long way across the ground.

There is also the possibility that the tree will explode. This happens because the liquid sap inside the tree boils as a result of the heat of the lightning.

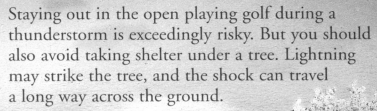

BENEFITS OF A NATURAL STORM

Lightning strikes will ignite dry vegetation, and cause fires. This is most common in tropical parts of the world, such as the grasslands of Africa. Here, plants and animals have adapted to survive these fires.

As the fire spreads, it catches the dry grass and burns very quickly, moving on, often being driven by strong winds. The direction of the fire may change as a result of the prevailing winds.

Some animals can escape more easily from lightning fires than others. Most birds can fly away, but some birds, such as storks, stay around the edges of the flames. Here, they can catch small animals like lizards trying to run to safety.

Slow moving tortoises cannot outrun the fire, so they retreat into their shells when the flames reach them. Tortoises are unlikely to be harmed because they are protected by their shells and the thick scales on their feet mean they can walk safely on the cooling embers.

When the rains come after the storm, the burnt grassland starts to be transformed. The fire cleared the ground of dead vegetation, and seeds in the soil now sprout into life. *Banksia* seeds actually need to be burnt out of their seed capsules before they will start to grow in the fresh soil.

The ash left by the fire acts as fertilizer for the young plants. Larger trees which may have been burnt by the fire now start to grow new shoots and leaves. The area becomes green and animals return here to feed on the fresh vegetation. Soon however, the ground dries out, as the dry season begins again.

FORECASTING A STORM

Helium-filled balloons are used to lift instruments high into the atmosphere. These instruments gather information, such as the size of water droplets in clouds. They help to detect atmospheric changes which indicate an oncoming storm.

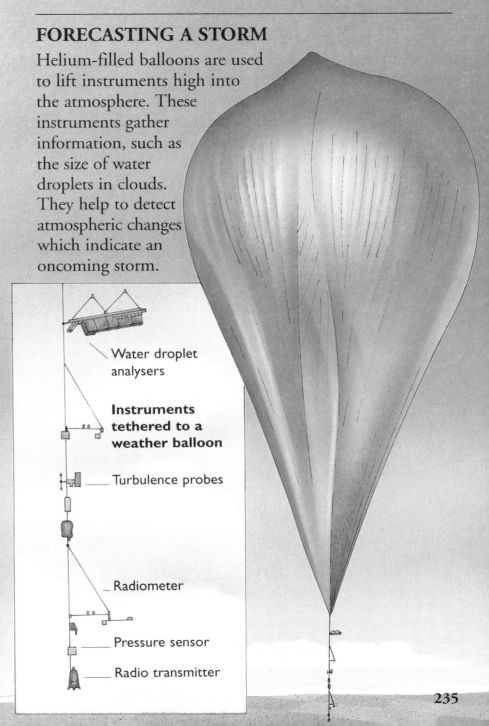

Water droplet analysers

Instruments tethered to a weather balloon

Turbulence probes

Radiometer

Pressure sensor

Radio transmitter

235

FROST AND SNOW

On clear nights, as the air cools, droplets of water called **dew** form on leaves and grass. But on very cold, cloudless nights the ground temperature falls below freezing. Then the water vapour in the air freezes as it condenses onto cold surfaces, covering everything with a layer of thick, sparkling frost.

Snowflakes are formed from ice crystals that join together in very cold clouds. If the air is warm, these snowflakes will melt into rain, but if the air is cold, they will stay as snow. Scientists believe that different weather conditions produce different shaped ice crystals.

Frost
Patterns of frost appear on cold surfaces such as windows, as the droplets of water on the glass turn into ice.

Snowflakes
All snowflakes are different. Most are like six-pronged stars, but some are pointed, like needles, or flat like plates.

Needles	Stars	Plates

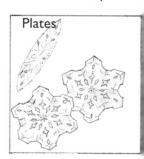

TORNADOES

Very dangerous whirlwinds, known as tornadoes or twisters, can cause terrible damage when they strike. Powerful tornadoes have been known to lift cars, destroy buildings and overturn trains. Tornadoes can vary in size from just a few metres to 500 metres across.

Tornadoes often occur in the mid-western states of America on hot **humid** days where warm, moist air is blowing from different directions. A tornado begins as a funnel-shaped cloud, which stretches down from the base of a huge thundercloud and rotates violently. It soon reaches the ground where there is a deafening roar of upsurging winds.

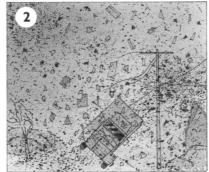

Tornado damage
People who live in areas prone to tornadoes are warned of oncoming damage (1) and take cover in a tornado cellar.

The rapid fall of pressure as a tornado sucks air in causes buildings to explode (2), leaving total devastation (3).

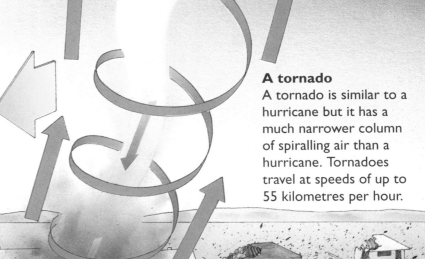

A tornado
A tornado is similar to a hurricane but it has a much narrower column of spiralling air than a hurricane. Tornadoes travel at speeds of up to 55 kilometres per hour.

FLOODS

Floods occur when very heavy rain falls, resulting in so much water that it cannot seep into the soil or flow away into rivers and lakes, or run away into drains. Floods can also happen when rivers swell and burst their banks, or coastal areas are hit by massive storm waves, or large amounts of snow melt quickly.

Many people still choose to live in areas at risk from floods. Often the soil near riverbanks is very rich and good for growing crops. Barriers can sometimes help to protect people against floods.

CHANGING CLIMATES

Long ago, the Earth's **climates** were different from those of today. There have been times, called ice ages, when it was much colder than it is now and huge ice sheets covered many countries. There have also been times when it was hotter and more humid than today, and the land was covered in forests.

Ice Ages
During the ice ages, much of the Earth was covered in ice and animals such as the woolly mammoth roamed the frozen land. Today, ice sheets are only found at the poles.

Woolly mammoth

The ozone layer
There is a layer of ozone found about 50 kilometres high in the atmosphere. Ozone is simply a form of oxygen and it protects us from some of the Sun's harmful rays. But pollution is destroying the ozone layer and its protective effects. The hole in the ozone layer is most prominent around the South Pole.

WEATHER WATCHING

In the past, before technology was used to monitor the weather accurately, people looked at the skies, watched how animals and plants behaved, and relied on signs and superstitions to forecast the weather. For example, some people still believe that when cows lie down or a cat sneezes, it is going to rain.

Seaweed
People used to keep seaweed to help forecast the weather. Seaweed feels damp and limp in wet weather, and crispy and dry in the Sun.

Pine cone
Pine cones predict the weather by closing up in the cold, and opening up when it is warmer to let the seeds fall out.

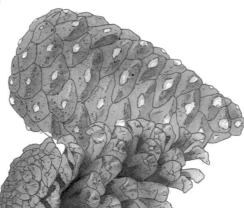

Spider's web
Spiders are said to start spinning their webs before windy weather.

Nowadays, scientists who study the weather, called meteorologists, use many different methods to make their forecasts. Satellites monitor our weather and send information to computers at special processing stations. On the ground, weather stations all over the world record wind speeds and directions, temperature, clouds and **air pressure**.

Satellites
Weather satellites record the Earth's atmosphere. They transmit photographs daily and are very useful in detecting hurricanes.

Radar
Radar stations on the ground pick up and transmit information round the world.

Balloons
Instruments aboard gas-filled balloons record weather conditions.

Stevenson's screen
This screen provides weather information at ground level.

USING COMPUTERS
People at weather stations record the temperature, humidity and pressure every few hours. Powerful computers analyse these recordings to forecast the weather.

AMAZING THUNDER & LIGHTNING FACTS

- **Fire in the sky** Fireballs are a rare form of lightning occasionally seen during thunderstorms on high trees or masts of ships. They are reddish in colour, range in size from an orange to a football and last less than a minute.

- **Power source** The power of a lightning flash is equivalent to 100 million volts, which is enough to light a small town for several weeks.

- **Greatest survivor** Park ranger Roy Sullivan, of Virginia, America, was first hit by lightning in 1942. He was then struck another six times up until 1977. He only had minor injuries – burnt eyebrows, hair and legs, and the loss of a toenail.

- **Heat generation** The heat generated by lightning may be five times hotter than the surface of the Sun.

- **Thunderstorms on Earth** Today on Earth, about 1,800 thunderstorms strike constantly at different points around the globe, every single second of every day. There are also about 6,000 lightning flashes every minute. There are more than 40 million lightning strikes in America alone every year.

- **Explosions in the air** Early airships built in the 1930s often exploded if hit by lightning. Just a tiny spark would ignite the highly inflammable hydrogen gas in the balloon.

- **Speed of lightning** Lightning travels at a speed close to 1,600 kilometres per second to Earth, and the flashes can be as long as 140 kilometres.

- **Stormy planet** The winds on the planet Neptune are so fast, they almost break the sound barrier.

GLOSSARY

Air pressure The weight of the atmosphere pushing down on the surface of the Earth.

Atmosphere The mixture of gases, made up of layers, which surround the Earth.

Climate The average weather conditions of a particular place.

Condense When a gas cools down to a certain temperature and becomes a liquid.

Conductor Materials like metal or water which allow electricity to flow through them.

Cyclone A tropical storm with very strong winds and heavy rain.

Dew Moisture which forms on the ground overnight, especially on grass, when the weather is clear and not windy.

Doldrums Region of sea close to the Equator with little or no wind.

Evaporation A process where water is heated and is transformed from a liquid into water vapour.

Global warming An increase in the temperature of the Earth's atmosphere.

Humid When the air is warm and full of moisture.

Mesosphere The part of the upper atmosphere, at heights of 50 to 80 kilometres, where meteors from outer space usually burn up before they reach the Earth.

Nitrate A combination of nitrogen and oxygen, which can be used as a fertilizer.

Solar radiation The heat and light that come from the Sun.

Sprite A brief spurt of light above a thundercloud, which was first seen by aircraft pilots.

Trade winds The constant winds blowing north and south towards the Equator.

Troposphere The layer of the atmosphere that surrounds us, up to a height of twenty kilometres. Storms and other weather changes take place in this layer.

Typhoon The name given to storms which occur off the coast of Asia, in the North Pacific Ocean and China Sea.

Water vapour An invisible gas which is formed when water is heated.

THREATENED
PLANET

CONTENTS

SPACESHIP EARTH

Billions of stars are scattered through the darkness of space. Some are seen at night as pinpricks of light. Many stars have planets, but only the Earth is known to have life. Stable temperatures, oxygen and plenty of water have brought millions of different animals and plants to life.

The Sun
The Sun is the closest star to Earth – about 150 million kilometres away. Without the Sun's energy there would be no life on Earth.

Stars
Stars are made from gases that produce tremendous heat and light. A large cluster of stars is called a galaxy. Light from some stars takes so long to reach the Earth that although the star appears to be shining in the sky, it may no longer exist.

LIFE ON EARTH

The Earth was formed about 4,000 million years ago. About 3,000 million years ago, the earliest forms of life appeared. The process of development which has continued since then is called **evolution**. This usually occurs slowly, taking place over millions of years. The Earth is probably home to about thirteen or fourteen million different **species** – no one knows the exact number.

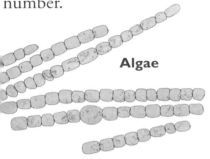

Algae

The first life
The first life forms were very simple. They were bacteria and very small algae, which can only be seen with a microscope.

Shelled sea animals
By about 600 million years ago, larger creatures had evolved in the seas. These were soft-bodied worms, jellyfish and animals with shells, like the trilobite. The first fish followed later.

Trilobite

Land animals
About 300 million years ago, animals with backbones first appeared on land. Millions of years later, they evolved into reptiles, like the eryops.

Eryops

Wild boar

Archaeopteryx

Mammals and birds
These groups have only developed over about the past 150 million years. The first bird, called *Archaeopteryx*, is thought to be related to the dinosaurs. The earliest **mammals** were tiny creatures, a bit like mice in appearance.

The first people
The first people are thought to have evolved from apes about three million years ago. They lived by hunting animals and gathering plants.

Much later on, people spread across the world and started to settle down. They built houses and made inventions that began to change the whole world.

People today
Today, people are the most widespread form of life. In just a few thousand years people have transformed from being hunter-gatherers to being inventors and users of complex machines like computers, aircraft and spaceships.

PEOPLE AND OUR PLANET

As the number of people on the Earth has grown, so has the need for vast amounts of fuel, food and **natural resources**. Finding and using these things can cause damage to the **environment**, threatening other life forms and even people themselves.

An oil rig

Fuel

Fuel is needed to power vehicles and factories and to heat homes. Most fuels come from the remains of dead plants, trapped millions of years ago in rocks. These are **fossil fuels** and include coal, oil and gas. Most oil and gas is drilled for by rigs and coal is mined on land. Sometimes, forests are cut down so that coal and metals can be mined from under the ground. This activity can change large areas of land.

Cities

Large cities contain millions of people. They all need huge quantities of clean water, food, petrol, electricity and paper. As people use up more and more natural materials, resources become depleted and the environment is more at risk.

Rain forests

Rain forest trees help to keep the balance of the Earth's environment by soaking up water from the soil and releasing it slowly into the atmosphere through their leaves. They also affect **carbon dioxide** levels in the air which, in turn, affects the Earth's climate. These forests stop the soil being washed away by heavy rain and provide homes for millions of different kinds of plants and animals.

Wood

People need wood for many things, such as building homes and making furniture. A lot of the wood we use comes from rain forests. But rain forest trees do not grow quickly enough to meet the demand for wood. Trees are often cut down just to clear the land for farming, but without the trees the soil is washed away and the forest is gone forever. This is known as **deforestation**.

PAPER

Newspapers, magazines and writing paper are all made from wood fibres. Huge numbers of trees are needed to provide the world's paper supply.

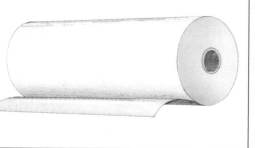

THE GREENHOUSE EFFECT

Most scientists now believe that **pollution** in the air is warming up the Earth's climate. Gases such as carbon dioxide act like a sheet of glass above the Earth trapping the Sun's heat and making the air warmer than usual. This is called the greenhouse effect.

A Greenhouse Round the Planet

*The Sun's heat passes through the Earth's atmosphere. Some of this heat is then reflected back into space. But now, gases such as carbon dioxide, methane and **chlorofluorocarbons** (CFCs) are building up in the atmosphere. They prevent the heat from escaping from the Earth, and so the temperature on Earth warms up, just like it does in a greenhouse.*

Fossil fuels

The main cause of the greenhouse effect is the release of extra carbon dioxide gas into the air. This gas comes mainly from the burning of fossil fuels like coal, oil and gas.

Power and energy

Fossil fuels are used in many ways. Coal is often burnt in power stations to make electricity. Oil is processed into petrol and diesel to power cars, buses and trains. And gas is piped to homes for cooking and heating.

Forests

Carbon dioxide is also released into the atmosphere when forests are cleared and burnt.

Hotting up

Scientists believe that the amount of carbon dioxide in the Earth's atmosphere has doubled in the last century. As a result of this, the Earth's average temperature is likely to increase by about 2°C. In fact, the four warmest years ever recorded on Earth have been between 1990 and 1994.

THE CHANGING CLIMATE

The greenhouse effect is changing the Earth's climate. Although the climate has changed many times since life first appeared, past changes were much slower than now. This gave plants and animals more time to adapt to new conditions. Rapid climate change, such as is happening now, could threaten many forms of animal and plant life.

Rising seas

As water warms, it expands. As the warming oceans expand, sea levels will rise. Helped by the melting ice, some low lying land will be flooded. No one knows exactly how fast the seas will rise.

The danger of flooding

Changes for wildlife

As the climate changes, the **habitats** of many animals and plants change too. Animals may have to move to other areas where they can live, but plants cannot move in the same way. They will have to adapt to the new conditions or they could die out.

Puffin

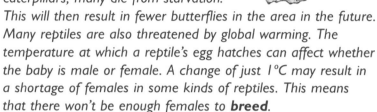

ANIMALS IN DANGER

The threat to animals and plants whose habitats change may not always be obvious. For instance, if there is not enough food for caterpillars, many die from starvation. This will then result in fewer butterflies in the area in the future. Many reptiles are also threatened by global warming. The temperature at which a reptile's egg hatches can affect whether the baby is male or female. A change of just 1°C may result in a shortage of females in some kinds of reptiles. This means that there won't be enough females to **breed**.

Food

The greenhouse effect is likely to affect the Earth's weather. Some areas will become warmer and drier, and there may be more storms. This could have serious effects on the world's food production. Areas that are now used for growing crops like rice or wheat might suffer from drought or flooding. They will become less suitable for farming and new areas will be needed.

THE OZONE LAYER

High up in the Earth's atmosphere is a layer of gas called **ozone**. Ozone protects life forms from harmful solar rays that cause cancer in people and damage plant growth. The protective ozone is disappearing because of pollution.

Antarctica

High level shield
Ozone envelops the Earth in a layer about 25 to 30 kilometres above the ground. New ozone is being made all the time.

Ozone destruction
The ozone layer is in a part of the upper atmosphere called the stratosphere. The ozone layer has been damaged because of chemical gases which have been released into the atmosphere.

Antarctic problem
Ozone loss is a worldwide problem, but it is most serious in Antarctica, where there is a hole in the ozone layer.

Stratosphere

Ozone layer

Chlorofluorocarbons (CFCs)
CFCs are one of the most damaging groups of gases to the ozone layer. They break down and release harmful chlorine into the atmosphere. CFC damage caused today can last for 100 years.

Fridges
Some fridges use CFCs to keep cool. If fridges are thrown away, CFCs can escape into the air.

Pesticides
Methyl bromide is a **pesticide** which destroys ozone 50 times faster than CFCs.

Fire extinguishers
Some types of fire extinguishers contain halon gases. These can be even more damaging than CFCs.

Aerosols
Aerosol sprays used to contain CFCs. Today, many countries do not allow CFCs in aerosols.

SEAFOOD
Because of the reduced ozone in Antarctica, rays from the Sun are entering the sea and slowing the growth of the tiny plants that shrimps and fish feed on. Animals that feed on fish, such as penguins, could suffer food shortages as a result.

MOVING AROUND

All over the world people rely on transport to help run their lives. They need to travel to work, visit friends and go shopping. They also need to move resources, for example, take coal from a mine to a power station. Traditionally, people have used either road vehicles, such as cars, buses and trucks or rail vehicles, like trains and trams. But pollution is produced by many forms of transport, from the fuel that is burnt in the engines.

Catalytic converter

The exhaust fumes from car engines contain many gases which pollute the atmosphere. In recent years, the catalytic converter has been developed. This is a device which is fitted to the exhausts of cars and reduces some types of the pollution that is produced. All new cars now have to be fitted with catalytic converters.

BIKES

Riding a bicycle helps to keep you fit and does not cause any pollution. Cycling on roads can be dangerous, because of the numbers of cars. It could be made safer by building more cycle lanes, where cars aren't allowed.

Trams

People in cities have made efforts to reduce the number of cars on the streets by introducing trams as an alternative way to travel. Trams run on electricity and do not give out as much pollution as cars do. They are also safer to other road users, such as cyclists, because trams run on rails and not all over the road.

Trains

Trains can transport large numbers of people in relation to the pollution they cause. If everyone travelling on a train used a car, the roads would be blocked and the polluting fumes would cause widespread damage to the environment.

WATER POLLUTION

People need water to drink, flush the lavatory and to wash dishes and clothes. Factories use lots of water in making all kinds of products from steel to plastics. But afterwards, unless this dirty water is treated it can make people ill and may kill wildlife.

Treating polluted water
Used water travels out of homes in pipes called sewers. It is cleaned in a sewage treatment works before flowing into a river or sea. Sometimes, untreated water goes back into the sea, causing pollution. Even cleaned water may still contain chemicals that are non-**biodegradable**, and can harm wildlife.

Factory pollution
Many countries have laws to protect water supplies from factory waste. But accidents still occur, and many fish and water animals die as a result.

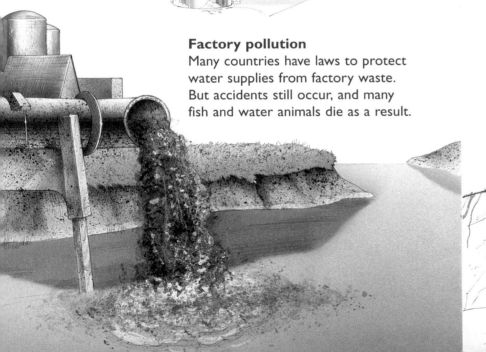

A LOAD OF RUBBISH

Millions of tonnes of rubbish are thrown away every year. It is very wasteful, particularly as much of this rubbish could be recycled and reused. Having to dispose of this rubbish by burying it in the ground or burning it can be harmful to the environment as well.

Waste
In some countries, people produce huge amounts of waste. Getting rid of it can cause serious problems, especially if the waste is poisonous. Burning waste can cause air pollution and dumping it in the sea could cause water pollution if the containers leak.

Up in smoke
Because there are fewer places to bury waste, more is being burned in **incinerators**. By using this method, toxic gases can be released into the air and the ash left behind can be poisonous too.

Buried rubbish
Millions of tonnes of rubbish is buried underground. This waste produces poisonous liquids which can enter underground water supplies, polluting people's drinking water.

SAVING OUR EARTH

Despite all the problems facing the Earth and its environment at the moment there are many things that we can all do to improve the quality of life. Using alternative sources of energy, setting up nature reserves and recycling resources are all practical and positive moves in saving our Earth.

Renewable energy
Natural energy from the Sun, wind and sea can be collected and turned into electricity. This is called renewable energy. It can be cheaper than other forms of energy, doesn't cause pollution and will last forever.

Recycling
When items made from paper, glass, plastic and some metals must be thrown away, recycling is the best way to help save resources, reduce waste and cut pollution. For example, kitchen and garden waste can be made into compost, which is used to improve soil and help plants grow better. Used motor oil from car engines, corks, old clothes and some batteries can all be recycled too.

Friends of the Earth
Friends of the Earth and *Greenpeace* are international organisations that work towards preventing the Earth's natural resources being wasted and the environment spoiled. They try to educate people about the problems facing the Earth today and in the future, and how some of the problems can be avoided. Campaigners spread their ideas using television, newspapers and radio.

Endangered animals
By breeding animals in zoos and then releasing them into the wild, a few endangered creatures might be saved from **extinction**. For example, the European bison became extinct in the wild because of hunting and habitat loss. Bison that had been bred in zoos were released in 1919 and can now be found in a few places in the wild.

Rescued animals
Some birds of prey were wiped out from many areas because of poisonous chemicals sprayed on crops. In the places that the chemicals have been banned, the birds have come back.

251

THREATENED EARTH

Today the Earth is under threat because we are using its resources too quickly and we do not do enough to prevent pollution of the air, water and land. The growth of industry and transport has brought many benefits but it has also led to a large increase in the levels of pollution.

Traffic

The world's vehicles are a major source of pollution. As the number of vehicles increases, more roads are built to make room for them. Some of these roads cut through countryside or woodland and the wildlife there might be wiped out.

Nuclear pollution

Nuclear power stations make electricity without burning fossil fuels. But radioactive waste is produced which is very dangerous if exposed to humans and wildlife. It must be stored properly, in secure containers. Sometimes nuclear waste leaks from containers, causing major environmental problems.

Industrial pollution

Every year, factories all over the world release millions of tonnes of chemicals into the air which can harm the environment. Some chemicals travel in air and water to cause damage hundreds of kilometres away from where they were released.

ACID RAIN

Harmful gases such as sulphur dioxide are produced by cars, factory chimneys and oil or coal power stations. In the atmosphere, these gases combine with water, to form 'acid rain'. When this falls on the land, trees and other vegetation may be killed, while in ponds and lakes, fish and other aquatic creatures are likely to die. Acid rain may also damage buildings.

Disasters at sea

Large quantities of oil are transported in huge ships called supertankers. Sometimes, during heavy storms these ships crash into rocks on the coastline. If the ship breaks up on the rocks, thousands of tonnes of oil are spilled out into the sea. Because oil floats on water it forms a slick which can be many kilometres wide. Hundreds of birds, fish and other animals die by suffocating or drowning as a result of these oil spills. It can take weeks for the affected area to be cleaned up and much longer for the dead wildlife to be replaced.

THE RICH, THE POOR AND THE WORLD

Many of the world's most serious environmental problems are caused by people in the **developed world**. Although only 20 per cent of the world's people live in this part of the world, they use 80 per cent of the world's energy and raw materials. Many people believe that sharing the world's resources more fairly between people is necessary to solve environmental problems.

In this way, the rich would use up less and the poor would be able to meet their needs without destroying valuable local resources.

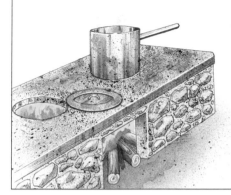

COOKING
People in poor countries use lots of wood to cook their food. To find this wood, they must chop down local trees. If they had more efficient cookers they could use less wood and areas of forest would be saved.

The risk of starvation
If the world's climate changes, people in poorer countries who depend on the land will suffer most. If it does not rain, for example, their crops will not grow, their animals will die through lack of water and the people are likely to starve.

A different world
It is common for people in the developed world to use water whenever they want to, and they often throw it away when it could be used again.

But one billion of the world's people do not have supplies of clean water. Millions of children become ill and die as a result of this.

RENEWABLE ENERGY

We can help protect the environment by using less of the Earth's resources. There are ways of producing energy such as electricity other than by burning fuel in power stations.

Solar power

Light and heat from the Sun can be trapped by **solar panels** on house roofs and turned into electricity.

WIND POWER
Windmills can be used to capture energy from the wind and turn it into electricity. Wind farms can be noisy but there are no fuel costs and no pollution.

Bright idea

Energy efficient light bulbs have been developed that use far less electricity than traditional ones. They cost more but save money in the long term because they last much longer.

DESTROYING HOMELANDS

Many important wildlife areas are under constant threat of destruction. Forests, ponds and heathlands are all home to a great variety of plants and animals. If these areas are destroyed some plants and animals may die out.

Farming

Modern intensive farming helps to produce the food needed to feed the world's growing population but it can affect the environment. Pesticides can kill wild animals, and natural woodlands are cleared to make way for fields of crops. Millions of tonnes of oil are needed to power farm machines like combine harvesters.

Ploughing

Wild grasslands are wonderful places for different kinds of flowers, insects and birds to live. All over the world areas like this are being ploughed up to provide land for growing crops.

Drainage

Swamps, bogs and other watery places are called wetlands. They are home to a rich variety of wildlife. Most wetlands have been drained to make way for farms, hotels, factories and houses. The wildlife that lived there has gone.

SAVING RESOURCES

Everyone can help the environment by making things last longer. This saves resources, cuts pollution and reduces waste. It can save money and provide people with new jobs too.

Wood
Beautiful wood is often thrown away or burnt, even when it can be used again. By using wood to make something else we can stop more trees being cut down.

Bags
Baskets are best as they can be used many times before being replaced. Paper bags are thrown away after one use, and plastic bags can be used a few times, but are not biodegradable.

Paper
Using both sides of a sheet of paper is a small but useful way of saving resources.

RECYCLING

Recycling saves natural resources by making new products from old ones. Materials such as paper, glass and metal can all be recycled and made into packaging and containers that are every bit as good as the original.

Recycling centre
In many towns there are now special containers where people can leave bottles and other items for recycling. Lorries then collect this waste and take it to factories.

Home collection
In some towns people don't even need to take their rubbish to recycling centres. Paper, glass and cans simply have to be put outside in boxes for collection.

Glass

Glass can be melted down and made into new bottles and jars.

Cans
Cans are crushed and recycled so the metal can be used again.

Paper

Waste paper can be recycled four or five times before it has to be thrown away.

NATURE RESERVES

Nature reserves are areas of land or water set aside to protect wildlife. Some are very large, covering tens of thousands of square kilometres. These reserves can help prevent rare animals and plants from becoming extinct.

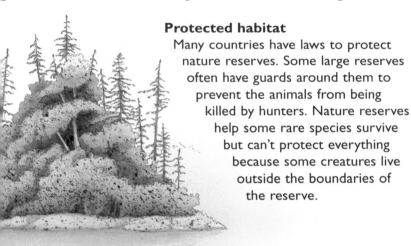

Protected habitat

Many countries have laws to protect nature reserves. Some large reserves often have guards around them to prevent the animals from being killed by hunters. Nature reserves help some rare species survive but can't protect everything because some creatures live outside the boundaries of the reserve.

City wildlife

Nature reserves can be set up in towns and cities too. They are usually quite small but can be ideal places to see many wild animals and plants without travelling to the countryside. City nature reserves can give people a chance to see species that are quite rare in the wild.

FUTURE FORESTS

Forests are vital to us, not just as a source of wood, but also because they affect the world's climate. Many areas of forest are now carefully managed to make sure new trees are planted every time old trees are cut down.

Good wood

Wood from managed or **sustainable forests** sometimes carries a label to say this. If we only buy wood that has these labels we can help forests and their wildlife survive.

AMAZING THREATENED PLANET FACTS

- **Forest destruction** About half of the world's tropical rainforests have been cut down since the 1940s. Every year another 160,000 square kilometres of tropical forest is cleared. This area is larger than England and Wales put together.

- **Today's technology** The light bulbs that were used in the 1920s used 100 times more electricity than the energy efficient bulbs that are in use today.

- **Who uses what?** In India, each person uses an average of 300 litres of petrol per year. In America, each person uses up 7,600 litres. That's about 25 times as much.

- **Oil boom** In the 1990s, the world used about fifteen times more oil every year than was used at the end of the 1940s. Present oil consumption is taking place one million times faster than new oil is being made.

- **Can savings** Aluminium made from recycled cans uses only one twentieth of the energy needed to make new aluminium.

- **Waste production** Industrial activity in America produces about 250 million tonnes of poisonous waste every year. That's equivalent to one tonne of toxic waste for every person who lives there.

- **Species loss** Up to 75 species of animal and plant are becoming extinct every day. That adds up to over 27,000 every year. The main reason for these extinctions is tropical forest destruction.

- **People all over the world** In 1950 there were about two and a half billion people in the world. By 2025 it is estimated that there will be about eight and a half billion.

GLOSSARY

Biodegradable Able to be broken down into tiny harmless products by decay.

Breed To produce offspring.

Carbon dioxide A gas in the air that is very important to the environment.

Chlorofluorocarbons A group of gases that damage the ozone layer.

Deforestation The removal of trees causing the disappearance of an area of forest.

Developed world The name given to countries which are wealthy and where most people have comfortable lives.

Environment Air, water, soils and the animals and plants in one place.

Evolution The gradual change of animals and plants, often as a result of changes in their environment.

Extinct When an animal or plant species has died out forever.

Fossil fuels Fuels such as coal, oil or gas that are burnt to make energy.

Habitat The preferred home of particular animals and plants.

Incinerator A container that burns waste.

Mammal A warm-blooded animal with body hair.

Natural resources Materials which occur naturally in the world, such as wood, oil and water.

Ozone A layer of gas in the atmosphere which protects the Earth from the Sun's rays.

Pesticide A chemical used to kill animals and plants that cause damage to plants and crops.

Pollution Harmful substances released into the environment.

Solar panel A panel that can trap the energy from sunlight and convert it into electrical energy.

Species A group of animals or plants that look similar and which normally will only breed with each other.

Sustainable forest A type of forest where new trees are planted when the old ones are cut down.

PLANETS

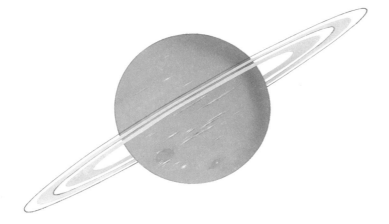

CONTENTS

THE SUN'S FAMILY

Our home in space, the Earth, is one of nine planets that circle the Sun. Millions of asteroids and comets also belong to the Sun's family, the **Solar System**. The Sun is a star, far bigger than everything else in the Solar System put together. Its powerful **gravitational pull** keeps the planets, asteroids and comets in **orbit**, and also provides them with light and heat.

The Solar System
The planets form a very mixed family. Some are made of rocks, like the Earth, while others are nearly all gas. Pluto is extremely cold, while cloud-wrapped Venus is too hot for anyone to live there. Some planets have rings and over a dozen moons.

BIRTH OF THE SOLAR SYSTEM

The planets and the Sun were born together, from a vast cloud of gas and tiny specks of rock and ice (called 'dust'). As gravity pulled this cloud together, most of the matter fell to the centre, making the Sun, while matter further out **condensed** into the planets.

Some of the rubble from this **celestial** building site was left over, including the rocky asteroids and the icy comets. By studying meteorites – small pieces of asteroids that fall to Earth – scientists have deduced that the Solar System was formed about 4,600 million years ago.

BETA PICTORIS
Here, planets are forming round another star, Beta Pictoris (hidden behind the black circle). We see its surrounding disc of gas and dust edge-on, as red and yellow 'wings'.

The formation of the Solar System

1 A huge, dark cloud of gas and dust in space began to shrink under its own gravitational pull. As it shrank, it swirled around and flattened out into a spinning disc. A sphere of denser gas grew at the centre.

2 The sphere at the centre shrank to become the Sun. At the same time, the **microscopic** particles of dust in the surrounding disc stuck together, forming solid blocks, each several kilometres across.

3 The solid blocks condensed to form the planets. Four rocky worlds formed near to the Sun. Four icy worlds formed further out: they snatched gas from the remains of the disc to build up into huge planets. Pluto, the outermost planet, is probably an icy block left over from the birth of the Solar System.

261

MERCURY – CLOSEST TO THE SUN

Mercury is a small, barren world, pocked with craters and almost airless. As the nearest planet to the Sun, it is generally very hot, though some permanently shaded craters at its poles are so cold they contain patches of ice. Astronomers think Mercury was originally bigger, but a small planet smashed into it, blasting away much of Mercury's outer layers.

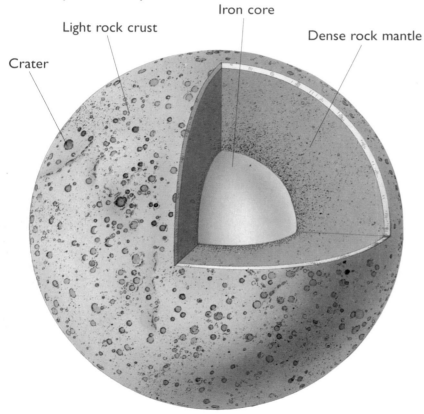

Crater

Light rock crust

Iron core

Dense rock mantle

Composition

The large core, made of iron, generates a **magnetic field**. The **mantle** consists of denser rock than the thin crust. The surface has a few small plains between the many craters.

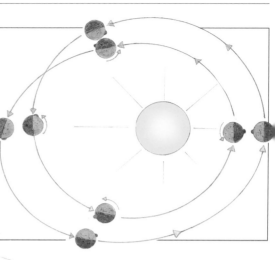

THE LONG DAY
Between one sunrise and the next, Mercury travels twice round the Sun, completing two Mercury years. So a Mercury-dweller would celebrate his or her birthday twice every day!

Mariner 10

The American probe, *Mariner 10*, is the only spacecraft that has visited Mercury. During 1974-75 it flew past Mercury three times, and sent back detailed pictures from its two cameras.

Iron core

As Mercury cools down, its iron core gradually shrinks. The crust above has to buckle up, like the wrinkles on an old apple. These wrinkles show up as long narrow ridges that run round and between the craters: some are 3,000 metres high and 500 kilometres long.

VENUS – HELL-PLANET

Venus is Earth's twin in size – yet no twins could be more different. Venus is covered in clouds of concentrated sulphuric acid. Its 'air' presses down with 90 times the pressure of Earth's atmosphere, and is made of unbreathable carbon dioxide. This gas traps the Sun's heat and raises the temperature to 465°C. Stepping onto Venus, you would be **corroded**, crushed, suffocated and baked all at the same time!

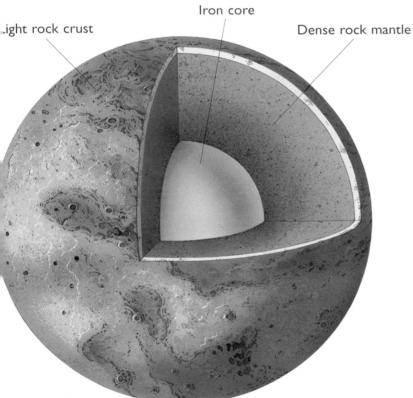

Light rock crust

Iron core

Dense rock mantle

Composition

Because Venus rotates very slowly, its iron core generates no detectable magnetism.

Hot molten rock rises from the mantle and punches through the crust to form volcanoes.

Volcanoes

Venus is a volcanic hell, dotted with lava lakes and studded with 100,000 volcanoes, some almost as high as Mount Everest. Radar equipment that can 'see through' Venus's clouds has revealed this volcanic crater, Sacajawea, which is 200 kilometres wide.

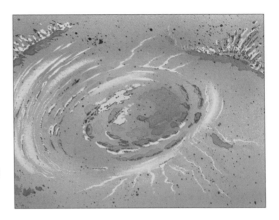

The surface of Venus

The heavily protected Russian spacecraft *Venera 13* landed on Venus in 1982. Before succumbing to heat and pressure, it sent back **panoramic** views of a rocky volcanic slope under dull, orange clouds. Volcanic eruptions are constantly covering the surface rocks with fresh lava.

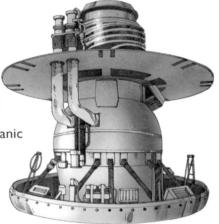

EARTH AND MOON – THE HOME WORLDS

If you were an alien visiting the Solar System, one planet would stand out as being very odd. The third planet from the Sun looks like a double planet: it has a companion world fully one-quarter its own size. The bigger of the two – the Earth – has a strange blue tinge, because it is one of the few planets in the Solar System with water. It is the only planet with much oxygen, and the only place where life is found in the Solar System. Its companion, the Moon, is dry, airless and barren.

Earth
Our planet has just the right temperature for water to be liquid. As a result, life could begin in the oceans long ago.

Moon
The Moon's weak gravity cannot hold on to any atmosphere. So all its air and water have long since escaped to space. There is no life on the Moon.

CONTINENTAL DRIFT
Over hundreds of millions of years, the continents drift round the Earth. Where they collide, vast mountain ranges are pushed up, like the Himalayas.

Astronauts on the Moon
Between 1969 and 1972, twelve American astronauts walked on the Moon. They brought back a third of a tonne of moonrock.

Origins of the Moon
The Moon might have been made soon after the Earth was born, when another planet hurtled into it and splashed off a spray of molten rock. These drops cooled to form a ring of fragments, which **coalesced** to form the Moon.

MARS – FIT FOR LIFE?

Of all the other planets, Mars looks most like the Earth. It has a day about the same length, it has air, it has frozen polar caps, and it has deserts with dark markings. But the first spacecraft to visit Mars warned scientists not to be too optimistic about finding any kind of life there. The choking carbon dioxide 'air' is much thinner than Earth's, and the temperature rarely rises above freezing, even at the Equator.

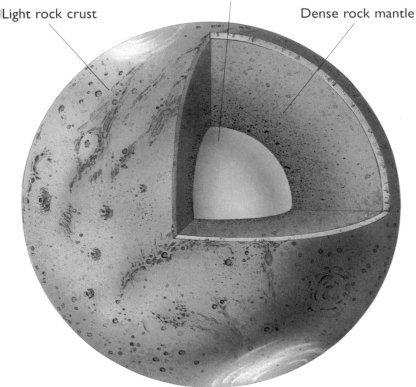

Light rock crust

Iron core

Dense rock mantle

Composition

Mars has only a small iron core, producing no detectable magnetism. Molten rocks have welled up from the mantle to build giant volcanoes and split the crust with deep canyons.

Olympus Mons

Although Mars is only half the diameter of Earth, it has some impressive features, including many **extinct** volcanoes, like Olympus Mons. It is three times the height of Mount Everest and wide enough to cover Spain. It far overshadows the Earth's biggest volcano, Mauna Kea on the Pacific island of Hawaii.

Olympus Mons

Mauna Kea

Valles Marineris

This canyon on Mars is so vast you could hide the whole of the Alps inside. The *Mariner* spacecraft first photographed it in 1971. Running into Valles Marineris are dried-up river beds, showing that Mars was once much wetter and warmer than it is now.

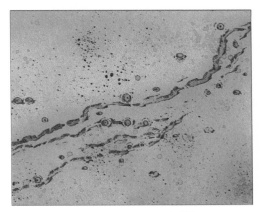

Viking lander

Long ago, when Mars was warmer, tiny cells may have formed and then **hibernated** as the climate became colder. In 1976, two *Viking* spacecraft landed on Mars and warmed up samples of soil and added **nutrients** to wake up the cells. But no life was found on Mars.

JUPITER – GIANT PLANET

Jupiter is the king of the planets. It is so big you could fit all the other planets inside, and its gravity controls sixteen moons. This 'gas giant' has no solid surface. It is made almost entirely of hydrogen gas, becoming denser and hotter towards the centre. Among the bands of clouds in Jupiter's atmosphere is the Great Red Spot, a storm three times the size of Earth.

SHOEMAKER-LEVY 9
This was a comet that smashed into Jupiter in 1994. The enormous explosions showered the planet with black patches the size of Earth.

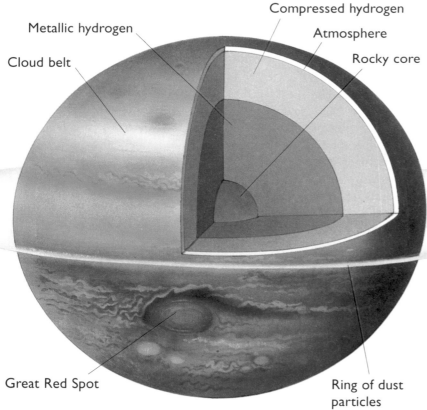

Metallic hydrogen

Cloud belt

Compressed hydrogen

Atmosphere

Rocky core

Great Red Spot

Ring of dust particles

Composition
Surrounding a core of molten rock, hydrogen is so compressed that it conducts electricity, like a metal. Above the sea of compressed hydrogen is a thin **methane** atmosphere.

Moons
Four of Jupiter's moons are bigger than Pluto, including the largest moon in the Solar System, Ganymede. It is covered by a network of cracks. Dark Callisto is peppered with craters, and a layer of ice on Europa conceals oceans where alien fish may live.

Io
Io is the weirdest of Jupiter's family. Looking at first glance like a giant pizza, it is covered with volcanoes erupting yellow and red sulphur **compounds**.

The spacecraft *Galileo* is monitoring Io's eruptions as it orbits Jupiter at a safe distance. *Galileo* has also dropped a probe into Jupiter's stormy atmosphere.

ASTEROIDS AND METEORITES

Between the orbits of Mars and Jupiter lies the rubbish dump of the Solar System – the asteroid belt. Astronomers have already found 6,000 small rocky worlds here, and the total probably runs to 100,000. The biggest of these asteroids is less than 1,000 kilometres across, and the smallest just a few kilometres in diameter. They are the building blocks of the Solar System, left over from the birth of the other planets. The gravity of nearby Jupiter prevented them from assembling into a planet.

Gaspra

From Earth, all asteroids are so tiny that they look like points of light ('asteroid' means 'looking like a star'). The first close up view of one came in 1991 when the *Galileo* spaceprobe, on its way to Jupiter, took a snapshot of Gaspra. Only sixteen kilometres across, this rocky world is shaped like a potato.

METEORITES

Small bits of asteroids collide with Earth all the time, and many fall to the ground as meteorites (particles that burn up in the atmosphere are called meteors). Fragments from an asteroid's core land as iron meteorites while its outer layers fall to Earth as stony meteorites.

Meteor Crater

Large chunks of asteroids can blast out craters when they hit the Earth. Meteor Crater in Arizona, North America, is one kilometre across. It was created by a million-tonne lump of iron that crashed there 50,000 years ago. Older craters on Earth have largely been eroded away by rain, wind and frost.

Killing dinosaurs

The dinosaurs may have been wiped out by a large asteroid that hit Mexico 66 million years ago. The impact disrupted the climate and in turn affected plant life, which was the main source of food for many dinosaurs.

THE PROPERTIES OF THE PLANETS

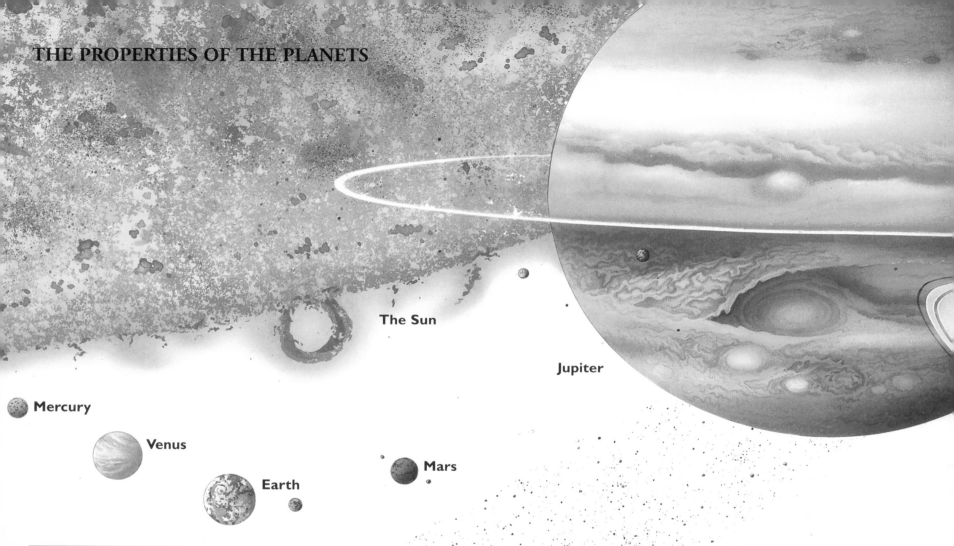

The Sun

Jupiter

Mercury

Venus

Mars

Earth

Planet	Diameter at Equator (kilometres)	Average temperature (°Celsius)	Period of rotation	Number of known moons	Planet	Diameter at Equator (kilometres)	Average temperature (°Celsius)	Period of rotation	Number of known moons	Planet	Diameter at Equator (kilometres)	Average temperature (°Celsius)
MERCURY	4,878	350	59 Earth days	0	MARS	6,786	-23	24hrs 37mins	2	URANUS	51,120	-210
VENUS	12,103	465	243 Earth days	0	JUPITER	142,080	-150	9hrs 55mins	16	NEPTUNE	49,530	-220
EARTH	12,756	15	24 hours	1	SATURN	120,540	-180	10hrs 39mins	18	PLUTO	2,280	-220

Pluto

Uranus

Neptune

Saturn

eriod of otation	Number of known moons
rs 14 mins	15
hrs 7 mins	8
ays 9 hrs	1

THE ORBITS OF THE PLANETS

Planet	Average distance from Sun in millions of kilometres	Time taken to orbit the Sun	Planet	Average distance from Sun in millions of kilometres	Time taken to orbit the Sun
MERCURY	57.9	88 days	SATURN	1,427	29.5 years
VENUS	108.2	225 days	URANUS	2,871	84 years
EARTH	149.6	365 days	NEPTUNE	4,497	165 years
MARS	227.9	687 days	PLUTO	5,914	248 years
JUPITER	778.3	11.9 years			

Jupiter

Aster

Pluto

Uranus

Neptune

Saturn

Venus

Sun

Earth

Mercury

Mars

COMETS

A bright comet is a spectacular sight, with a long tail stretching across the sky. It is caused by a tiny **nucleus**, only a few kilometres across. Billions of icy **nuclei** orbit in a huge cloud beyond the planets. Occasionally, one drops towards the centre of the Solar System. There the Sun's heat boils away its ice, to create its huge glowing head and tail.

Orbits
Comets follow long looping orbits, often tilted up compared to the orbits of the planets.

Orbit of a comet

Sun

Orbit of Jupiter

Orbit of Earth

ANATOMY OF A COMET
A comet is made of four parts: a gas head around a solid nucleus, a gas tail and a dust tail.

Giotto
In 1986, the *Giotto* spacecraft sped through Halley's Comet and photographed jets of gas spouting from the black surface of its nucleus.

271

SATURN – RINGWORLD

Saturn, with its beautiful rings, is the most glorious planet. This gas giant is second in size only to Jupiter. Saturn is so low in **density** that it would float in water – if you could find an ocean big enough! The famous rings are so wide that they would stretch almost from Earth to the Moon, yet they are only one kilometre thick. Saturn also has the largest family of any planet, with at least eighteen moons.

Weather systems

The cloud patterns are quite dull, but once every 30 years a huge storm breaks through, giving Saturn a Great White Spot.

Saturn's rings

The rings are made of billions of tiny chunks of ice, ranging in size from a snowball to an iceberg. As each chunk follows its own orbit round Saturn, some are 'herded' by small moons acting like sheepdogs.

Mimas

Saturn's moon, Mimas, looks like a giant eyeball. Long ago, an asteroid or comet blasted out a huge crater on its surface. Mimas was lucky to survive the impact.

Titan

The largest of Saturn's family, Titan is the only moon in the Solar System with a thick atmosphere, denser than Earth's air. Titan is shrouded with orange clouds made of tiny **organic** droplets, rather like grease. This moon is so cold that water would be frozen there, but its surface may have lakes filled with liquefied gas.

Voyager 1

Voyager 1 sent back the first detailed pictures of Saturn as it sped past in 1980. It found several small moons and discovered that the rings are split into millions of narrow 'ringlets'.

Tethys

The tortured surface of Tethys is cracked and cratered. Like Saturn's other moons, Tethys contains very little rock – it is made almost entirely of ice.

An Earth in deep-freeze

If we could visit Earth soon after it was born, it would look like Titan today. On the early Earth, rain washed any organic droplets into the oceans, where they built up into the first life. Titan is too cold for rain, so its **'primeval soup'** has been preserved.

URANUS – TIPPED-OVER PLANET

Uranus is so far away and faint that you need a telescope to see it. This planet is tipped up on its side, probably because it was knocked over long ago by a smaller, wayward planet. Sometimes its North Pole points towards the Sun, and sometimes its South Pole: the seasons on Uranus are very extreme!

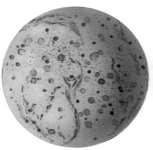

Atmosphere

Water

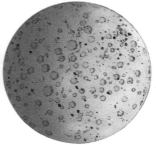

Rocky core

Composition
Composed largely of water, Uranus has no solid surface. In the centre is a core of molten rock. The deep green atmosphere, made up mainly of hydrogen and methane, has few clouds.

Rings
Uranus has a set of very narrow, dark rings, tipped up like the planet itself. Astronomers only had hints of these rings until 1986, when the spaceprobe *Voyager 2* flew past Uranus and sent back detailed pictures. The eleven rings are made of tiny blackened pieces of rock and ice, as dark as coal, orbiting Uranus like miniature moons.

Rings

Uranus's family of fifteen moons is made of a mixture of rock and ice. The five biggest are visible with a powerful telescope, and *Voyager 2* discovered ten more tiny moons. While most moons are named after characters from Greek mythology, the moons of Uranus bear names from English literature, especially the plays of Shakespeare, for example, Titania, Oberon, Miranda and Puck.

Ariel
Huge cracks run round Ariel's equator between bright and dark patches of cratering. Ariel may have cracked open when water inside froze solid and then expanded.

Umbriel
A thin, black layer coats the icy interior of Umbriel, darkest of the moons. It has only one bright crater, called Wunda.

Miranda
A patchwork world, with enormous cliffs and markings that resemble a racetrack, Miranda may have been broken up and then reassembled.

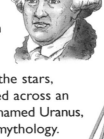

William Herschel
Herschel was a German astronomer, working in England. He built telescopes and studied the stars, and in 1781, he stumbled across an unknown planet. It was named Uranus, after Saturn's father in mythology.

NEPTUNE – WATERWORLD

Uranus's twin in size, Neptune lies so far away it was not discovered until 1846. Astronomers tracked it down because Neptune's gravity was pulling Uranus off course. It was named after the Roman god of the oceans – which is very appropriate, as we now know Neptune is made mainly of water. Most of our knowledge of Neptune has come from *Voyager 2* as it swept past the planet in 1989.

A family of eight moons orbits Neptune. Triton is as big as the planet Pluto, and it orbits Neptune in the opposite direction to the planet's own rotation – the only large moon in the Solar System to do this. Little Nereid follow an elongated orbit round Neptune, and can be seen from Earth, using large telescopes. The other six small moons were found by *Voyager 2*.

Composition
The interior of Neptune is very like Uranus, although its atmosphere is much cloudier. It too is surrounded by a set of dark rings.

Triton
Triton is the coldest world in the Solar System. It has a very **tenuous** atmosphere, made up largely of nitrogen. Frozen methane ('natural gas') forms pink, icy caps at its poles.

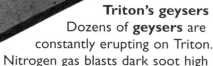

Direction of winds

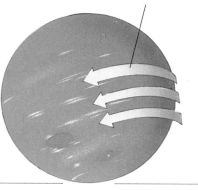

Hurricane winds
Voyager 2 discovered a storm larger than the Earth, Neptune's Great Dark Spot, and many white clouds, propelled by the strongest winds in the Solar System. One white cloud was nicknamed *The Scooter*, as it races round the planet so fast.

Triton's geysers
Dozens of **geysers** are constantly erupting on Triton. Nitrogen gas blasts dark soot high into the atmosphere. The wind blows it sideways for hundreds of kilometres, smearing a dark streak across the surface.

Voyager 2
Between 1979 and 1989, this record-breaking spacecraft visited four different planets – Jupiter, Saturn, Uranus and Neptune.

PLUTO – FRONTIER PLANET

Tiny, frozen Pluto is the smallest of the planets; it was found as recently as 1930. Although Pluto is usually the most distant planet, its elongated orbit crosses Neptune's path, and sometimes (as in the years 1979-99) it is closer to the Sun than Neptune. Pluto's moon is fully half the planet's own size, and many astronomers regard it as a 'double planet'.

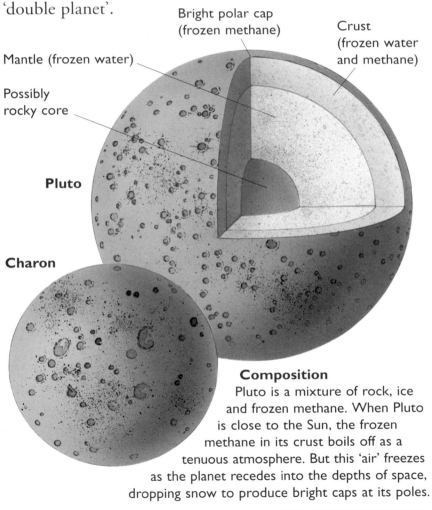

Bright polar cap (frozen methane)

Crust (frozen water and methane)

Mantle (frozen water)

Possibly rocky core

Pluto

Charon

Composition
Pluto is a mixture of rock, ice and frozen methane. When Pluto is close to the Sun, the frozen methane in its crust boils off as a tenuous atmosphere. But this 'air' freezes as the planet recedes into the depths of space, dropping snow to produce bright caps at its poles.

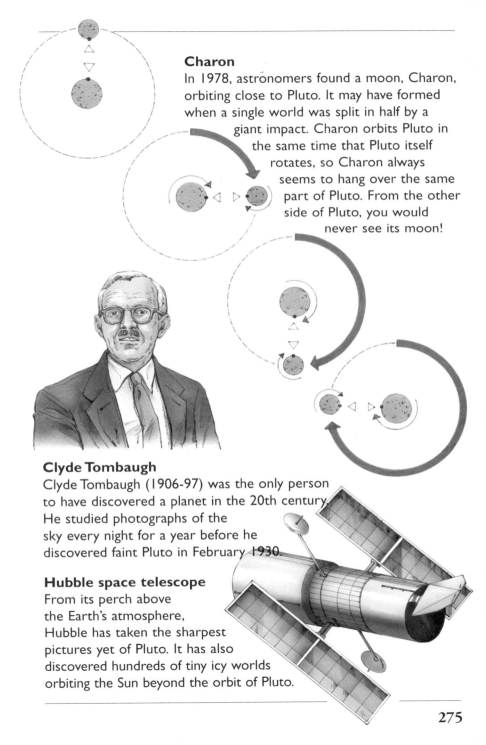

Charon
In 1978, astronomers found a moon, Charon, orbiting close to Pluto. It may have formed when a single world was split in half by a giant impact. Charon orbits Pluto in the same time that Pluto itself rotates, so Charon always seems to hang over the same part of Pluto. From the other side of Pluto, you would never see its moon!

Clyde Tombaugh
Clyde Tombaugh (1906-97) was the only person to have discovered a planet in the 20th century. He studied photographs of the sky every night for a year before he discovered faint Pluto in February 1930.

Hubble space telescope
From its perch above the Earth's atmosphere, Hubble has taken the sharpest pictures yet of Pluto. It has also discovered hundreds of tiny icy worlds orbiting the Sun beyond the orbit of Pluto.

AMAZING PLANET FACTS

- **Planet or not?** Pluto is so small that some astronomers see it as the largest of thousands of 'ice dwarfs' orbiting the Sun beyond Neptune, and not a planet at all.

- **Fast and slow** Mercury orbits the Sun 1,028 times in the time it takes Pluto to complete just one orbit.

- **Back to front** Although Earth – and most of the planets – rotate from west to east, Venus spins east to west.

- **Hottest world** Venus is the hottest world, though it's not the closest to the Sun, with a temperature of 465°C. The coldest is Neptune's moon, with a temperature of -235°C.

- **Magnetic fields** A magnetic compass needle would not be much use on other planets: Venus and Mars have no magnetism, and on most of the others the 'north' end of the needle would point south because their magnetic fields are the opposite to the Earth's.

- **Fastest winds** Neptune has the fastest winds in the Solar System, blowing at 2,000 kilometres per hour – ten times hurricane force on Earth.

- **Annual shrinking** Jupiter is shrinking, at the rate of one millimetre per year. This compression heats up the interior of the giant planet, generating **infrared** radiation that astronomers can measure from Earth.

- **Shooting stars** These are really specks of dust from a comet, burning up in Earth's atmosphere.

- **Biggest planet** Jupiter is the biggest planet, but it spins more rapidly than any other, with a 'day' – from sunrise to sunrise – that is less than ten hours long.

GLOSSARY

Celestial An object that is found within the sky.

Coalesce Merge together to form a new object.

Compound A substance formed from two or more separate elements: water is a compound of hydrogen and oxygen.

Condense Reduce a collection of matter to a more compact form.

Corrode To destroy, usually slowly, by chemical action.

Density The extent to which an atmosphere is packed with gases.

Extinct Something that has died out and no longer exists.

Geyser A spring that throws up jets of hot water and steam.

Gravitational pull The force exerted by a large body such as Earth to attract things through space towards it.

Hibernate To go into a long sleep during the winter.

Infrared The heat energy that is given out by objects.

Magnetic field The area in which a magnet is able to attract anything made of iron.

Mantle The part of a planet between the crust and the core.

Methane A colourless gas that can be found in marshes and swamps on Earth.

Microscopic Something that is too small to see with the naked eye.

Nucleus, nuclei The centre or centres of atoms or objects.

Nutrient Nourishing food.

Orbit The path a planetary object follows as it revolves round another.

Organic Any substance made up largely of carbon.

Panoramic A complete view of the landscape.

Primeval soup Organic substances dissolved in oceans from which early life may have sprung.

Solar System The Sun and the planets, asteroids and comets that move round it.

Tenuous A thin consistency.

INDEX *(Entries in **bold** refer to illustrations)*